THE ROAD
OF DREAMS

THE ROAD OF DREAMS

*A Two-Year Hiking and Biking Adventure
Around the World*

Bruce B. Junek

Photographs by

Tass Thacker

An

Images Of The World

Book

Images of the World was created by the husband and wife team of Bruce Junek and Tass Thacker to promote awareness of the world's cultures, respect for the Earth's environment and to encourage personal fulfillment in all people.

To order additional copies of The Road of Dreams, see page 288.

To book an **Images of the World** slide program, see page 287.

Images of the World
PO Box 2103
Rapid City, SD 57709-2103

Printed in Boulder, Colorado on recycled paper

All photographs © by Tass Thacker, except pages 43, 52, 71, 84, 103, 106, 182, 186, 207, 210, 235, 264, 272 by Bruce B. Junek, page 17 by Bill Harlan, page 208 by Don Looney, and page 275 by John Knecht.

Library of Congress 91-073331

ISBN 0-9630448-1-8

This book is dedicated to the people
who greeted us with smiles,
opened their homes to us,
and allowed us to be a part of their lives.

CONTENTS

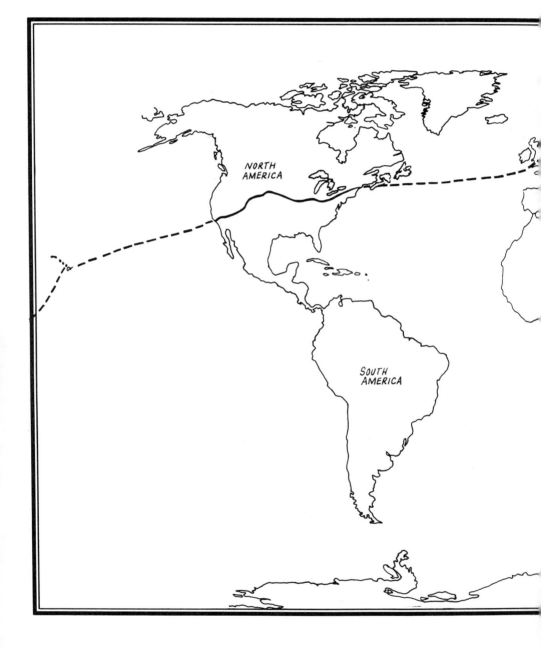

NORTH
AMERICA

SOUTH
AMERICA

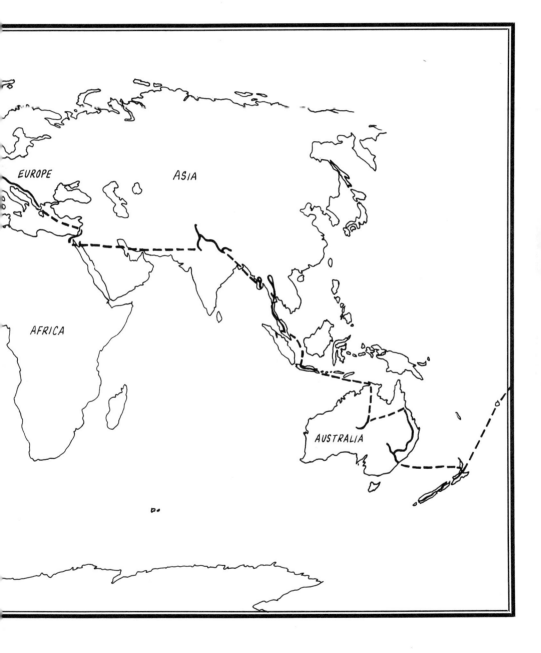

EUROPE

ASIA

AFRICA

AUSTRALIA

9

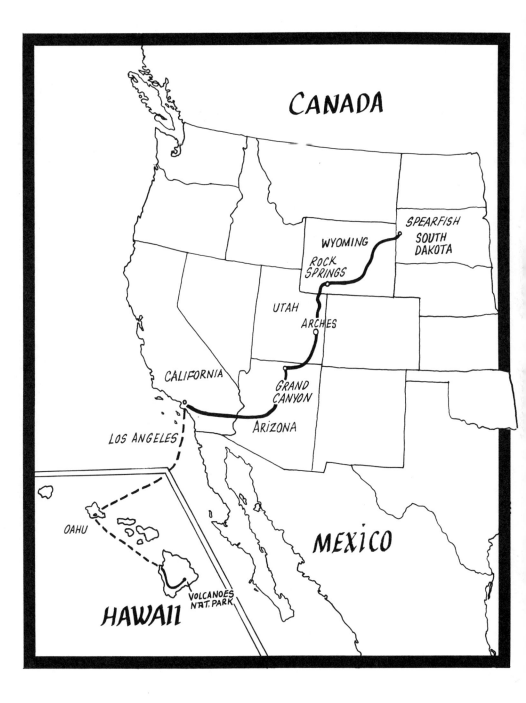

Yes, it all fits on the bikes!

1

The Trial Run

At 6:00 a.m. on Friday, October 5, 1984, we rise out of bed. It is raining. Not the weather we wanted, but we are so excited to start our trip that nothing--rain, sleet, nor even common sense--will keep us from departing today.

Although we have been planning our trip for years, the last week has been a bit hectic. We quit our jobs just four days ago and have since moved out of our house, liquidated our larger possessions, stored everything else, and worked day and night running last minute errands, packing bags and organizing equipment.

Finally, at 7:45 a.m., just fifteen minutes prior to our proposed departure time, the bikes are loaded. Actually, they are overloaded. The zippers on our panniers look ready to burst. Since neither of us has ever ridden fully-loaded touring bikes, we take a quick spin around the block to make sure we can ride the monsters. We don't want to crash in front of the small crowd of friends and relatives gathering to see us off.

At 8:00 a.m. the crowd is ready. We are not. We run frantically through my parents' home packing up the remaining boxes for storage. After the fifth final-check we think we have everything either packed away or on the bikes.

Due to the rain everyone who has come to see us off is crowded into my parents' garage. Our bicycles, which are poorly packed for a storm, are balanced against a wall. Our luggage needs to be reorganized, but we don't have time to do that now. Most of our audience has to go to work soon. It feels too anticlimatic to ask everyone to wait while we rearrange our gear for the hundredth time.

Instead, we begin the hugs and farewells. This is it. We carefully push off, ride down the driveway and turn to wave good-bye one last time. Yaahoo! Our trip has started! We are on the road!

The moment we are out of sight we begin discussing our situation. The bikes feel unstable, the rain covers are not on properly, nothing inside the panniers is wrapped in plastic. Just down the street live Steve and Myia Hauff, our good friends who are always late and who were not even at my folks' house to see us off. We pull into their garage to get out of the rain.

Steve and Myia come out to greet us. They can't believe we are leaving--that we are actually doing it. Neither can we! We stand in their garage wearing our dripping rain gear and laugh as we tell of our "official" departure moments ago. We seem so unorganized. Do we really think we can ride to Asia? The idea suddenly seems absurd.

We use up all their plastic bags to double wrap the contents of our panniers. We also shift the weight to balance our bikes and reduce the shimmies. Steve tries to convince us to wait for a better day.

"Be realistic," he says.

"If we were realistic we wouldn't be going at all," we reply as we put on our wet rain coats. We climb onto the bikes and leave Spearfish--this time for real--in a cold drizzle.

Although we grew up in the Black Hills of South Dakota, Tass in Deadwood and I only sixteen miles away in Spearfish, we met in Jackson, Wyoming. Tass had been living in Jackson for two years when I came out with her brother on a ski trip. She was living in a little log garage that had been converted into a one-room cabin. I was invited over for lasagna. We met again seven months later when I moved to Jackson. But at that time Tass was just leaving for the winter to bird in South America with a woman friend. When Tass returned the following spring we talked of spending time together, but we were both busy with other commitments. Finally, near the end of the summer, we did a two-day climb of the South Teton. Upon our return we moved in together, rotating between her cabin in town and my double-walled, winterized tipi on the Snake River. We have been inseparable ever since.

I had caught the travel bug two years out of high school, after a six-month trip across Africa with my older sister. And Tass, fresh from her journey through South America, was also eager to see more of the world.

We had both dreamed of hiking in the Himalaya, yet Asia remained a

14

far-away goal. Instead, we spent two winters in Mexico and Guatemala studying Mayan ruins, birds, and beach life on the Caribbean. After our second trip we knew we were excellent traveling companions -- and soul-mates as well. We moved back to the Black Hills, got married, started managing a retreat center owned by the United Methodist Church, and began saving our money.

Our initial plan was to fly to India and travel around by bus and train before going trekking in Nepal. Two years before our departure Tass began competing in local triathlons. She bought a bike and soon convinced me to get one too. After a summer of riding we began discussing changing our Nepal journey to a bicycle trip. Why not bicycle to Asia? By 1984, five years after starting our jobs at the retreat center, we have our money saved and are ready to go.

Our first destination is southern California. We want to cross Wyoming, drop south into Utah to backpack in Arches and Canyonlands National Parks, ride to the Grand Canyon for more backpacking, and then pedal to Los Angeles. Since neither of us has previously toured by bicycle, we consider this part of the journey our trial run, a chance to make sure we have the proper gear and equipment before we head overseas. Then we plan to travel through Hawaii, Fiji, New Zealand, Australia, and enter southeast Asia via Indonesia, Malaysia, and Thailand. Our ultimate goal is still the mountain kingdom of Nepal, where we want to trek to the base of Mount Everest. We hope to be there in 18 months.

The first day is spent riding in rain and cold mist. Our rain gear, much of which was sewn by Tass, works great. The day passes like a dream; the light is soft, the fog swirls around us hushing all sounds. The moist smell of prairie grass fills the air. We feel vibrant and alive--free. The world is before us! We can do anything we want, go at any speed, stop whenever something interests us, and move on any time the urge to ride pulls us down the road. The pressures of work, of maintaining a household, of juggling schedules and commitments is gone. The fact that it is raining is of little concern. It is a glorious day to ride.

During the sunny afternoon of our third day riding, we hear a car honking behind us. Figuring it is someone who wants to pass, I wave my arm to encourage them around. The car keeps honking. I finally take a good look in my mirror to see my parents grinning inside the car. We stop to stand beside the road, drink tea from their thermos, and laugh about how our view of time and distance has changed. After three days of riding we were feeling we had made a good start on our trip. Yet in a quick morning drive my folks easily zipped across that distance. We really haven't gone far at all.

But the days tick by. In the evenings we log the amount ridden each day in a notebook. 58 miles. 66 miles. 78 miles. The Wyoming prairie, which can be a monotonous landscape when viewed from a speeding car, is alive with sights and smells at a slower pace. Between Alcoa and Muddy Gap we stop on a lonely stretch of highway, take a swim in Sweetwater Creek and pitch our tent at the base of Independence Rock, a solid piece of granite a quarter-mile long and 100 feet high. After supper we climb the rock in the soft light of a full moon. We are surrounded by the Seminoe Mountains. The Oregon Trail ran directly up the valley below us, past Independence Rock, and off to the western horizon. Early settlers often stopped to carve their names on the rock. In the moonlight we search for names from long ago etched in stone, and talk of the hardships the settlers faced. We feel an affinity for the pioneers. This is big country. Traveling on our own power has given us a different perspective of the mountains, valleys and plains.

One of our biggest surprises on the road is our incredible increase in appetite. We are always hungry. We cook a huge pot of oatmeal each morning, yet within hours we are famished. We eat two lunches each day, one at ten o'clock and another at two o'clock. Despite double lunches we often stop for late afternoon snacks and always eat an early supper. Dessert is a must.

Our biggest difficulty is trying to find where we packed things. We both carry two rear panniers, each with a large main compartment and four side pockets, two front panniers and a handlebar bag with three pockets. That means between the two of us there are ten large compartments and twenty-two smaller pockets where something can get lost. Often we can't remember which of us is carrying what. Then we both have to search for the missing item.

After seven days we arrive at my brother's house in Rock Springs, Wyoming. We lay siege to Mark's kitchen, still eating four meals daily. We also completely unpack our panniers in an effort to reduce weight by sending unused items back home. After three days of having his living room knee deep in bicycling and camping equipment, Mark generously offers to give us a lift out of town. But after eating all his food we feel energized and ride out on our own power.

We battle headwinds again, cold headwinds. On a ridge I break a spoke and nearly freeze as I replace it. Traces of snow begin to fall. In the afternoon Mark drives out to meet us with sandwiches and a thermos of tea. We planned on a picnic, but the icy wind forces us inside the truck. Again Mark offers to give us a lift over the pass ahead. We sit with the heater running, watch the windshield wipers clear snow off the window, and think about his offer.

In planning our trip we discussed whether it should be a "bike only" journey. But we decided we didn't want the emphasis of the trip to rest solely on the bikes, like **We Always Have To Bike**. We prefer to bicycle, but under some circumstances we will consider other options. The choice before us now is to travel in a car or wait for the weather to clear. Since we just had a three-day break we feel like moving on. We accept his offer.

The snow continues to fall. It seems as though the three of us are traveling together on a ski trip. The top of the pass is covered with three inches of snow so Mark drives us into the next valley, below the snow line. In one hour we travel as far as we would pedal in a day. We spot a stand of cottonwood trees near a lake and find a sheltered spot to camp.

I get teary-eyed as we say good-bye. When Mark drives away I completely break down. Suddenly I feel bad for not spending more time with him over the years, for not telling him enough that I love him, for not being as good a friend and brother as I could.

I said good-bye to many people in the last few weeks, but due to the excitement of preparing for our trip the emotional reality of leaving slipped by unnoticed. Now it all begins to soak in. We plan to be gone for two years; much can happen in that time. It is possible that we may never again see some of the people we have left behind. And deep inside I

Cold weather greets us during much of our ride across the United States.

17

know there is even a chance that we may not make it back home ourselves. I lay in the tent and cry while Tass gives me hugs. After a while I don't even know what I am sobbing about, it just continues to come out. When all the emotions of our departure are finally released, I fall asleep.

Due to work commitments we started our trip in the first week of October. We hoped for a pleasant fall with warm sunny days and cool nights. Instead we get an early winter. The next few days we slip through the small, localized blizzards without hitting a storm head-on. Cars drive by with mounds of snow on the roof but the roads remain mostly dry. Our pile coats and mountain parkas keep us toasty while our rain pants, boot covers and overmitts seal out the sleet.

In Utah's Uinta Mountains we hear rumors of a big storm. We pick up our pace to cross Indian Head Pass before the weather changes. The road climbs for 45 miles up a series of valleys to the base of the pass, an eight percent grade for eight miles. The cold headwind turns icy and increases its buffeting. We struggle up the hill with our faces tucked down out of the wind. The only thing keeping us from freezing is the work of bicycling uphill into the gale.

The top of the pass, at 9,200 feet, is bitter cold. It is 5:30 p.m. and will be dark soon. We don't want to get caught at high altitude during a blizzard so we only take a second to look at the view before heading down the mountain. We instantly freeze. We rode up the hill with jackets, pile mittens, and wool hats. Now we stop and dig through our panniers to get more clothing. Tass even wraps her bikini around her neck as an extra scarf. We try to hurry off the pass, but each time we allow the bikes to pick up speed on the downhill the wind chill freezes us to the bone. We stop every few miles to get off the bikes, put our hands under our armpits, and jump around to get the blood flowing to our extremities. My fingers are numb; Tass's look nearly frostbitten.

Just as daylight fades we spot a place to camp out of the wind. We set up our tent and crawl inside to huddle under our sleeping bags and make supper. The tent shakes as the wind howls. At 2:00 a.m. Tass wakes me up. The side of the tent is six inches from my face. Only one thing can make a tent droop so low--heavy, wet snow! We pound on the nylon walls until the snow is knocked off and go back to sleep. At 4:00 a.m. we wake and knock off more snow. At 6:00 a.m. we do the same.

When the call of nature finally forces us up, Tass unzips the door to find the world covered in eight inches of snow. We make a leisurely breakfast in the tent and discuss our options. Should we stay put for a day or two and wait for the weather to clear, or ride through the snow and get off the pass before another storm blows in and burys us until spring? We decide to move.

Outside, a single set of vehicle tracks winds through the snow down the mountain. One person, at least, made it off the pass this morning. We dig out the bikes, break camp and, with freezing fingers and toes, load everything up. Just as we get set to push off, a snowplow roars past. Now we have a definite path!

The bikes track surprisingly well on snow and ice. The worst part is when we get down into lower elevations. Deep snow turns to deep slush, which is sprayed all over us by every passing truck. We get soaked. We stop in Price where the town librarian, Marge Pierce, invites us to spend the night in her house. The next day the road south is already dry.

Three days later we arrive in Moab, Utah, to meet Bob Miller, an artist friend from South Dakota. Bob is coming in on a bus, and will ride with us for three weeks. We find him at the edge of town, sitting on the sidewalk, packing the panniers on his bicycle. Bob is ecstatic to see us. I think he doubted we would meet him on time. Actually we are half an hour early!

We ride to Arches National Park. The weather clears as we pedal up the highway sharing news and stories. Although we have only been on the road three weeks, we now feel like old pros compared to Bob, who spends half of every rest break searching for lost items in his panniers. In the evening we camp behind a massive group of rock formations and then climb up the rock to sit quietly beneath two high arches. No one talks. We listen to the silence.

The temperature drops; another storm blows in. The next morning we wake to eight more inches of heavy, wet snow. We crowd into Bob's tent and huddle around the stove, eat one batch of pancakes after another, melt snow for tea, and talk about the weather--where did we get the idea October would be warm and sunny in the Utah desert?

It stops snowing in the afternoon. We emerge from the tent, bloated with food, and resume exploring. The next morning we ride on plowed roads further into the park. At Devil's Garden campground the snow is a foot deep. We borrow a shovel from a retired couple in a camper and dig out two spots for our tents. Again we hike in the snow until dark. We return to camp and head for the men's restroom, where we sit on our sleeping pads on the cement floor and cook supper. After two snowy nights crowded three-in-a-tent to eat, these are luxurious accommodations. We even have lights and heat!

A couple who saw our bikes stops in to talk. When they leave we laugh about how we are not only eating in the restroom but entertaining guests as well! It is not the last episode of such behavior. The next day we ride out of the park and camp in a stand of trees behind a rest area. The women's restroom has hot water and a floor drain where we can shower by pouring water over ourselves. During my shower a woman interrupts the process to use the bathroom. I stand outside with only a towel wrapped around my waist and shiver in the wind until she leaves, and then finish my bath. Bob and Tass tell me I should carry a "Restroom Closed for Cleaning" sign. Then I could post it on the door while I shower, and be assured of no interruptions.

Most days on the bicycle are enjoyable. But some are hard. A few are torturous and never seem to end. We joke about the harder days being like "all-day-Nautilus." Imagine going to the gym, being strapped into the leg machine, and told you can not leave until you do 10,000 leg presses.

Our ride through Monument Valley is all-day-Nautilus. We climb a long series of endless plateaus into a strong headwind. We pass beautiful scenery in the morning but by noon it is all work. We don't speak, except for shared sentiments on the soreness of our legs, arms, backs, and seats. We each withdraw into our own inner world.

I lead the three of us into the wind, staring at my reflection on the polished metal of the handlebar stem. Keep pedaling. My head drops and I watch my spinning feet. My knees bob up and down...up and down...up and down. Keep pedaling. Don't let up the pace. Keep it up. Keep it up. Sometimes, for a few minutes, the aches and pains disappear in the rhythm--the burning turns to a warm glow. What was pain becomes an almost euphoric state of awareness. I watch my body work from a detached viewpoint, like it is someone else's legs pedaling below.

In the dusty town of Kayenta, Arizona, we stop at a grocery store and collapse, exhausted, on the front bench. We don't even have enough energy to go inside. In fact, for a few minutes we are too tired to even get any of our remaining food out of our panniers. Finally Tass takes the initiative and starts making sandwiches from the last of our supplies, while Bob and I stare off into space.

We are on the Navajo reservation. A group of old Indian women sits and watches us; one asks about bike riding. I, in turn, ask about the weather, and if it gets cold at night. She thinks a moment and replies, "Sometimes it's warm, sometimes it's cold," and then laughs. After eating we revive enough to go inside to buy food. We come out, make another batch of sandwiches, and eat again before pedaling on down the road.

In Tuba City, Arizona, we set up camp in a grassless park where the ground is covered with broken bottles of Thunderbird wine. Early the next morning a young Supai Indian from another reservation appears at camp. The sun comes up as we talk. Occasionally Navajos walk by and try to speak with him. He does not understand their language, and each time a Navajo realizes he is not of their tribe they look at him as they do us--as an outsider. He tells us the tribes don't get along very well, especially the Navajo and the Hopi, who are having land disputes. This saddens him.

As the sun climbs higher the warmth wakes up a few winos, who are curious to find us camping in their park. Being basically friendly, and in need of spending money, they come over to visit and ask for goodwill donations. We soon tire of repeatedly answering their hungover questions and fending off requests for money. We say good-bye to our Supai friend and break camp to eat breakfast elsewhere.

Across town we cook oatmeal beside a supermarket. It is not long before a very drunk Hopi staggers over to tell us his story. After brushing off the inebriated characters at our campsite, I make another effort to communicate. It doesn't work. Finally I tell him he is too drunk to talk and I would like to eat in peace. He stumbles a few steps away and begins yelling oaths and threats in every direction, claiming he is going to kill all white people in 1985. Luckily 1985 is still two months away; we have plenty of time to ride out of his territory before the carnage begins.

Minutes later he comes back. This time we have better luck, and I piece together what he is saying. His father was killed in WWII. His brother died in Vietnam. He shows me gruesome scars on his chest, arms, and neck--his own mementoes of fighting in southeast Asia. He has a bad leg, and one hand has three crippled fingers. His relentless question: how come he risked his life for the U.S., and now no one cares about him?

He screams into the air in outrage and yells about his people not being cowards, and never being afraid to fight. Yet he has been abandoned, and says he could die from grief. He asks me what I can do for him, but before I can answer he replies for me.

"Nothing, there is nothing you can do for me." I acknowledge what he says is true, which only adds a frustrated sadness to his voice.

"Nothing. There is nothing you can do for me. Nothing."

He is a victim, a product of his environment as surely as I am a product of mine. I wish I could say something that would ease his pain, but his troubles are too deep. Instead, I simply hear him out. Finally he calms down enough to shake my hand and stagger away.

A trace of snow covers the ground as we ride by the soft light of a rising moon the last few miles to the Grand Canyon. The next morning the sun comes out. We take a rest day to read and relax before packing up for a three-day hike into the canyon. We store our bikes at a nearby Catholic Church and pull out our frameless backpacks which we carry rolled up on the rear of our bikes. The next morning we get up before sunrise and head for the South Kaibab trail, which drops nearly 5,000 feet straight into the Grand Canyon. Hiking down through the various layers of rock is like walking through time. Each layer has its own history. We descend to the age of dinosaurs, into the age of reptiles, through times of great oceans and seas, times of immense jungles, until we reach the level of the trilobites. At the bottom, the Colorado River cuts through the Brahma schist, igneous rock two billion years old, the oldest exposed rock on the continent.

The next day Tass and I go for a hike up a narrow side canyon. After a few miles we stop in a sunny spot and talk of our journey.

Bruce sharing a sandwich with two nuthatches, Grand Canyon, Arizona.

Our method of travel leaves us exposed. On the bikes we are at the mercy of not only the weather, but of every driver on the highway. At each stop we interact with the mainstream and also the fringe of society. We are in a constant state of vulnerability. We have no roof over our heads. No walls to hide behind. No doors to lock.

Bicycle touring gives a close-up view of life in all its variety. Rather than being nervous about our vulnerability, we want to embrace it, and view our new intimacy with the world as a pilgrimage.

Our destination may have little to do with the ultimate purpose of the journey, which might be revealed somewhere along the route, or even somewhere inside ourselves. Pedaling to Asia will require us to lay ourselves bare before the world. We must trust the world will treat us gently.

To maintain our trust we have to keep a strong faith within ourselves. Already our vulnerability has encouraged us to examine our own deepest beliefs about the meaning of life. Being cut off from the normal anchors of security--home, job, family and friends--further drives us to search within ourselves for something beyond the transience of day to day existence.

We talk of the need to take time to meditate every morning, no matter what our schedule or what the weather, to focus on the inner aspects of our journey. We also plan to visit areas along our route that are held sacred by people of all faiths. Our hope is that by learning about others we will learn more about ourselves.

South of the Grand Canyon we rendezvous with friends from Tucson in Wupatki National Park and pedal together to Sunset Crater. As our friends pack up to leave on Sunday, Bob loads his bike into their truck to catch a lift to the nearest bus station. After riding together for three weeks it is hard to believe he is leaving. We stand alone in the campground, waving good-bye as the darkness and chill of another cold night close in.

In Sedona, Arizona, we are tracked down by a couple who saw us riding through town. Once off work, Paul and Rose drove around town until they spotted our bikes at a cafe, where we are having a cup of coffee.

"We didn't want you to slip out of town before we had a chance to get to know you," Paul tells us as he reaches out to shake our hands. He explains that he has missed opportunities to know people because he didn't make an effort to meet them. "When I saw you ride past I promised myself I would find you and invite you in."

We spend the evening chatting and eating enormous quantities of Rose's chocolate chip cookies. The next morning as we pack up to leave, Paul tells us to take our time, leave when we want, and lock the door behind us. It is sad when Paul goes to work. He dislikes his job yet doesn't see any way he can financially make a change. After he leaves we talk of the many people who are unhappy with their work. Many stay with boring, unfulfilling jobs because they don't want to lose their security. Yet if work creates ulcers, job security is a curse, not a blessing!

The cold weather of Utah and Arizona turns to wind and rain in California. When the weather is nasty we keep an eye out for laundromats where we can stop for lunch. At home laundromats always seemed rather grim. Now we view them as oases of comfort in bad weather. They are always warm, generally quiet and usually have a pile of magazines to read. Still, Tass is quick to point out the irony--scrimping and saving for five years to hang out in laundromats. We dream of Hawaii.

As we near Los Angeles we stay with friends and relatives and slow to 35 miles per day, working our way from suburb to suburb. On December 3rd, we complete the first leg of our journey. It has taken us 60 days to travel 1,800 miles from South Dakota to the Los Angeles Airport.

We strip down the bikes, remove the pedals, turn the handlebars sideways and wrap the chains in paper. In an effort to keep our check-in luggage under the weight limit, we put on three layers of clothing and stuff all our pockets with camera gear, books, bicycle tools, and other heavy items. The plan works; our bicycles are shipped at no charge.

We waddle with our heavy loads to the terminal gate. The trial run is over. It's time for a vacation.

23

2

Beach Break

We get off the plane at midnight wearing hiking boots, sweaters and rain coats. Our friend Shena Sandler meets us in shorts, a T-shirt and rubber thongs. We throw our gear in the back of her truck and ride into Honolulu talking of old times.

Shena is a friend from our Jackson Hole days. I met her on a climb of Buck Mountain in the Teton Range. Later, she worked with Tass at Bru's Buns and Breads, a local health-food bakery. Shena now owns Wilderness Hawaii and takes groups camping into remote regions of the islands.

We spend much of our first week on the island in the South Pacific section of the Honolulu public library, where we read in the sun on the second floor balcony overlooking the trees and plants in the library courtyard below. Using Shena's address, we get a library card and daily carry home stacks of books.

The following week we pedal across the island to the town of Kailus and work a few days cleaning up storm damage at the Methodist-owned Camp Kailani. In exchange we get free use of a bungalow on the beach. When Shena goes out on trips with Wilderness Hawaii we stay at her house, water the plants, and feed the goldfish.

During our first few weeks on the island the trade winds blow fiercely and we get five to ten-minute downpours that roll in once or twice per hour. After each storm the sun comes out, dries everything off, then, wham!, another cloudburst. Yet we leave our rain gear at the house; the weather is too warm for nylon coats. When the clouds appear we scramble for shelter. Sometimes we find it, sometimes not. During the smaller storms we just keep pedaling.

Hawaiian drivers are fickle. Just when we think they are going one way, they turn the other direction. All the cars make erratic lane-to-lane changes, abrupt stops and instantaneous take-offs. We hear stories of hit-and-run accidents and wild crashes. Yet it is great to ride without the weight of our gear. The traffic simply adds to the excitement. Riding a bicycle in a large city is a dance--we waltz with the buses, jitterbug with the compacts, and sometimes, when large trucks refuse us room, we wallflower it out on the shoulder.

On Christmas Eve we pedal to a mall for some last minute shopping. Just as we finish it starts raining. We watch a troupe of Samoan dancers while waiting for a break in the weather. More rain. We wait another half hour. The storm turns into a torrential downpour. Finally, when it is almost dark and we can't wait any longer, we head out into the storm.

The shortest route back to where we are staying is straight through downtown Waikiki. Luckily, because of the lack of visibility, the traffic creeps along and we have little fear of being hit. Stop lights, street lights, building signs and all the vehicle lights reflect off the wet cars, the water running over the sidewalks, the water filling the streets. My glasses are covered with water droplets, adding to the dazzling reflections. I constantly wipe the lenses but still everything has a prismatic perspective. The road is six inches under water. Our feet are immersed on each downstroke of the pedal. We begin tailgating vehicles to ride in the wake created by their tires. Buses work the best; behind their wheels the water is only a few inches deep. Our only fear is of riding into one of the giant submerged water drains and being sucked into the ocean!

We arrive "home," take a hot shower, and during a break in the storm, bicycle to a Christmas Eve candlelight service. Just as we get to the church the storm returns with increased fury. We sit in the pew and try not to listen to the rain pounding on the roof. Afterwards we dally at a social gathering while waiting for the rain to let up, and eat taste delights prepared by the elderly women of the congregation, who stand by each plate encouraging everyone to eat more and more and more. We need little encouragement. After an hour we are stuffed, but it is still raining. The last of the women pack up and go home. We stand outside under a porch and watch the storm. Finally we ride back out into the rain. Where did we get the idea it would be warm and sunny in Hawaii?

After Christmas Shena leaves for Wyoming, so we move back into her

25

house for the month of January. The weather finally clears, and we quickly establish an enjoyable daily routine. When the waves are calm and the water clarity is high, we load up our snorkeling gear and ride fourteen miles to Hanauma Bay, an underwater state park with beautiful coral and a variety of fish.

When we spot something exciting we use snorkeling lingo, language spoken underwater into a plastic tube, to communicate. One day Tass spots a Black-speckled moray eel deep in a coral crevice. She yells "Ruceruceitsamoray!!" ("Bruce, Bruce, it's a moray!")

I swim over and exclaim, "Weisit--Weisit?" (Where is it? Where is it?)

"Downner! Urrygoowook!" (Down there! Hurry! Go Look!) The Moray is exquisite. It is two and a half feet long, one and a half inches in diameter, and looks like a snake doing ballet as it slithers through the coral and out across a sandy spot on the bottom of the ocean floor.

"Ooaahitseeuniful" (Oooh, it's beautiful!) We make repeated dives and follow it until it arrives at a little hole in the sand and disappears.

After an hour in the water we head for the warmth of the beach and check off the sightings in our Hawaiian fish book: brightly colored Hawaiian Cleaner wrasse, Red Lip parrotfish, Fourspot butterfly fish, Yellow tangs, Flame anglefish and Reef triggerfish. When the heat of the sun begins to make us drowsy, we swim back out to the reef. The days slip by.

Bruce snorkeling off the island of Hawaii.

26

The end of January is family reunion time. Tass's mom, Jeanette, arrives for two weeks. A week later my parents, Betty and Jerry, fly in for two weeks. So we have a week alone with Jeanette, a week with the entire crew, and a week with just my folks.

Since Shena is still in Wyoming, we all stay at her tiny apartment, which doesn't even have a bedroom. Bet and Jer sleep on the futon couch while Jeanette sleeps on a rented rollaway bed that fills up the remainder of the living room. Tass and I sleep on the kitchen floor with our heads against the fridge and our feet under the table. It is a bit crowded but since none of us is very modest, and some of us aren't modest at all, we have a great time.

The day after Jeanette leaves my folks treat us to a flight to the island of Hawaii. Our third day on the Big Island a morning news bulletin announces that Pu'u O'o in Volcanoes National Park has started to erupt. The four of us pile into a rental car and head for the park.

We first see the volcano from a lookout on the Hilo highway. A steady fountain of lava 700 to 1200 feet high roars out of the volcano. Even in the sunlight the eruption is bright orange.

A van pulls up with "Volcano Photographs" lettered on the door. We interrogate the driver. He shows us close-up pictures of previous eruptions shot from a cliff face near the eruption. He tells us it is a seven mile hike one-way to the cliff, and there is no guarantee of a clear view. The volcano is often covered in mist.

If we hike in we will never be out before dark. Since we foolishly left our camping equipment and rain gear at the hotel, we stop and buy two flashlights and a box of garbage bags--rather primitive coats, but after years of leading kids on nature hikes Tass and I know garbage bags can keep people warm even in mild snowstorms.

At first the trail is well marked. At a lookout on a volcanic cone we get another view of the eruption, still six miles away. It is 3:00 p.m. If we want to arrive at the cliff before dark we need to pick up our pace.

We head out onto a huge lava bed. The trail deteriorates on the rough surface of solidified lava. Sometimes the lava bed is hard, other times it is fragile and crunchy, and sometimes we hear hollow thuds below our feet. Before long mom decides to go back to the car. She recently hurt her ankle skiing and the reality of a 14-mile forced march sounds unappealing. But she encourages the three of us to keep going. We tell her we will try to be back at the car by midnight.

Crossing the lava beds is like walking over the surface of a black and barren planet. There is no vegetation, only the cracked and splintered surface of rock--solidified rivers turned to stone. There is no path, no sign of footprints. Even now, in daylight, we have to occasionally stop to search for the trail markers, piles of rock every forty or fifty feet. It will be tricky hiking out in the dark. The trail winds and zig-zags around lava mounds, deep volcanic pits and large craters. Dad, who is sixty-five, hikes like a trooper. Not only does he keep up, he enjoys the hike.

At last we climb onto a forested ridge. On a small rise we get our third glimpse of Pu'u O'o. A low cloud covers most of the lava fountain. Sunset is half an hour away and the colors of the sky are subdued. We press on through the forest.

At the lookout we sit on the edge of a 150-foot drop-off and watch the show. Although clouds still cover most of the lava fountain we have a good view of the mountain. The cone of Pu'u O'o formed over the last two years. It started as a simple crack in the ground, erupted 29 times in 24 months, and grew to 700 feet in the process. The initial eruptions lasted longer but had less volume of lava. Now the eruptions are brief with more flow--up to half a million cubic meters per hour.

Just before dark the clouds lift. At last we see the entire lava fountain. A swirling cloud of ash billows into an immense pillar of smoke towering above us into the upper atmosphere. Like a beautiful sunset, the sky around the volcano is bright orange. The roar of the eruption fills the air, the vibration shakes the ground and us as well.

We have a clear view for fifteen minutes, then the clouds return. We

A 13-mile hike brings us close to the dramatic eruption of Pu'u O'o in Volcanoes National Park, Hawaii.

watch and wait, occasionally getting glimpses of lava through holes in the mist. Four hours later we catch sight of a lava river flowing down a ridge away from us. We decide to hike back to the car and drive to the southeast coast to better see the running lava. We will have to hurry. The eruption has been going for 13 hours. The average length of the eruptions is about 15 hours. The spectacle could end any minute.

The trail back through the forest is easy to follow. The reddish light of the eruption lights the sky. At the barren lava field, however, it is hard to see the first marker. But soon our eyes adjust to the black void and we begin to pick out the rock cairns with our flashlights. We split into two groups. I stay fifty feet ahead, and whenever I lose the trail I yell for Tass and dad to stop before they lose sight of the last marker. That way one of us is always on the trail.

Half-way across the lava bed we find two people wandering about totally lost without a flashlight. We get them back on the trail, though none of us expect them to go 100 feet without getting lost again. Next we meet six high school boys, also without flashlights. They have no idea where they are, where the trail goes, or how far it is to the lookout. We give them directions and they disappear into the void behind us. If there were ever two groups likely to spend the night walking in circles, we just met them.

We arrive back at the car and wake mom, who has been sleeping in the back seat, and drive off toward the southern road. It begins to rain. Visibility drops to 200 feet. We keep going anyway. We drive up and down the road until the clouds lift and we can see two four-mile-long rivers of lava.

As the lava flows through the forest, nearby trees ignite from the heat. The rain continues to fall. Finally a thick cloud bank moves in. We call it a night and drive back across the island and crawl into bed just before sunrise. The next morning we find the eruption stopped less than forty-five minutes after we left the park. It was perfect timing; we were in the area for 14 hours of a 20 hour eruption.

We fly back to Oahu. Bet and Jer catch a flight home, and we pack up to leave. After more than two months of easy living, our beach break is over. We are tan, well rested and ready to resume traveling.

PAPUA NEW GUINEA

DARWIN

AUSTRALIA

OLGAS
ULURU
(AYERS ROCK)

ALICE SPRINGS

CAIRNS
MAGNETIC ISLAND
HENNING ISLAND

GREEN CREEK STATION

SYDNEY

TASMANIA

FIJI

AUCKLAND

N. ISLAND

S. ISLAND

NEW ZEALAND

MT. COOK

QUEENSTOWN

STEWART ISLAND

3
Bula! Bula!

We arrive on Viti Levu, the largest of the Fijian islands, at 3:00 a.m. on February 17th. Tass's bike arrives with a bent luggage rack and rear wheel, despite being shipped in a box with a backpack, rain gear, foam pad and sleeping bag for padding. My wheel had been bent flying from Los Angeles to Hawaii and had to be replaced. Apparently airplanes don't like bicycles. Luckily, I am able to re-true Tass's wheel.

We leave the airport in the pre-dawn light. Fiji is our first experience riding on the left side of the road. Every time cars approach we hesitate against the urge to steer to the righthand side. Our plan is to ride counter clockwise around the island to Suva, the capital, and return in a month to fly to New Zealand.

As we ride into the city of Nadi we are surprised to find most of the store signs written in Hindi, the rest in English. Forty-five percent of the people on the island are of Asian Indian descent, and they own nearly all the shops in town. Another 45% of the population are native Fijians, and the last 10% are a mixture of everyone else. Since Fiji was a British Colony until 1970, almost everyone speaks English.

At the market, a large concrete building with a tin roof, we don't find much fresh food. Most of the local crops were destroyed in a hurricane

31

last month. So we stop a sidewalk vendor for *bare*, an Asian Fijian dish made of peas, taro and curry. Our meal costs less than twenty cents.

Next we search for *kava*, the powdered plant we'll use for gifts while on the island. We meet a friendly vendor and ask how much powder to use in each drink. When he learns we have never had *kava* he insists we sample his product before we buy. He sets out two wooden stools in the bustling market aisle and chats with us while we spend the afternoon slowly drinking bowl after bowl of the milky liquid from the shell of half a coconut. *Kava* is made from the root of a local pepper plant. In the past, the green root was prepared by chewing the fiber and then spitting the juice into a bowl. The chewers were hired by the well-to-do or by village chiefs. Mastication of the green root altered the chemical properties of the *kava*. The resulting mixture if drunk in sufficient quantities produced hallucinations and sometimes religious experiences.

Since the early 1900's *kava* has been prepared differently. Now the root is dried and pounded in a large pestle. Water is added to the powder and the fibers are strained out. This method does not result in such a strong drink. Instead of a powerful drug it is a mild intoxicant.

This less potent form of *kava* is now the national drink of Fiji, and the local doctors claim it is an excellent health tonic. It tastes chalky. By the third bowl my teeth feel numb. By the fifth bowl my whole body feels numb. Convinced that this is a high-quality product, we buy a few bags for gifts, a few more for ourselves, and saunter off in a state of euphoria.

The next afternoon we have tea with a superintendent of the Methodist Church, the predominant religion of native Fijians. Methodism, founded by two English brothers, came to the island along with the British. The superintendent tells us of a Fijian village where we can spend the night. Traditional Fijian villages are close knit, like huge extended families, and not always easy to get into. Our contact is the village minister.

At the village entrance we are stopped and asked who we came to see. A small group of people escorts us to Paul, the minister, who invites us to stay in a *bera*, a thatched-roof house kept for village guests. Inside the *bera* we are joined by more elders and the village chief for *suva-suva*, an ancient Fijian tradition. We sit in a circle on the floor. I pull out a bag of *kava*. Even though the gift is for the village chief, protocol requires that it be given to an elder who will then give it to the chief. I give the *kava* to Paul.

Paul speaks a few words in Fijian and then, along with another elder and the chief, claps his hands together three times. The *kava* is passed to the second elder. He likewise speaks for a time in Fijian, with his words punctuated by hand clapping. Finally the *kava* is placed in front of the village chief. His speech is a blessing upon all of us. At appropriate times all three men rhythmically clap and shout. At last the chief touches the *kava* on the floor, a sign our gift is accepted. We are now members-at-large of the village.

We are fed rice and vegetables and are constantly given tea. After supper we sit in on a meeting of the local Methodist Youth Fellowship in a room with no screens on the windows. We are told that normally few biting flies or mosquitoes are found on the island, but the recent hurricane brought a horde of the pests. Now everyone repeatedly slaps at mosquitoes on themselves and also on the backs and arms of those next to them in a communal effort to avoid being bitten. The mosquitoes are so bad it takes all of our will power to keep from bolting from the building.

After the meeting everyone sings traditional songs for us. We reciprocate with a few animated camp songs which are received with gales of laughter. Just before midnight more food is brought in. We eat and retire, itchy and exhausted.

Our house is also full of mosquitoes. We put up our tent inside the house so we can sleep under its mosquito netting. Once inside the tent we spend two minutes killing the mosquitoes who came in with us and then lay down to sleep. But there is little air movement inside the house and even less in our tent. Even with a net door, two net windows, and a ceiling vent, the temperature in the tent skyrockets from the heat of our bodies. It would be much more comfortable to pitch the tent outside in the breeze, but we don't want to offend our hosts by refusing their hospitality and the house they have cleaned for us. So we stay inside the house, in the tent, laying in a pool of sweat, listening to the hordes of mosquitoes buzzing on the other side of the netting.

In the morning we visit an incense factory in the village. The incense is sold to Asian Fijians, who use quantities of it in their religious devotions. The building smells wonderful. After our tour we have tea with the old woman who runs the place. When she finds out we have no children, she assumes we have no sex life.

"You two are wasting your lives," she exclaims. "Sex is the greatest thing in the world." She wags her finger at us and further admonishes us.

"Get off those bicycles and get into bed!" It is a line that we will jokingly repeat to each other throughout the remainder of the trip.

By the time we leave the village it is the hottest part of the day, a fact Tass repeatedly points out to me. She is an early bird and hates late starts. I also get up early but am not as eager to jump right on the bike. I prefer to dally around camp, explore the area, and leave mid-morning. So far it is our one minor conflict.

The heat mounts as we ride through steep, rolling hills covered with sugar cane. When the afternoon rains begin we take a break to eat under a thatched roadside shelter. An hour later the skies clear. As we remount our bikes a car pulls up. The driver, an Indian named Singh, invites us to his house for some refreshments. His home is just up the road through a sugar cane field.

Singh parks his car at the turnoff to a dirt road leading to a hut on a hill. Since we don't want to leave our bikes on the highway, we begin pushing them to the house. After the first corner the road turns into a quagmire of soft mud. Moments later it begins to rain. Against all common sense we continue pushing our bikes. The path turns into gooey red clay which clogs the tires with mud. The wheels stop turning. Just as we contemplate giving up a group of kids come and help push the bikes. We arrive soaked and covered with mud.

A bucket of water is brought to wash the mud off everyone's legs. We are ushered under a thatched awning, a focal point for family activity. Everyone is paraded under the shelter and introduced to us. It turns out Singh is not even a member of the family yet. He is engaged to one of the daughters. Fourteen people live in the small tin building beside us. It has two rooms: a bedroom for the mother and father and a room that is the dining room in the daytime and a bedroom for everyone else at night. Nearby is a smaller building, the family's kitchen, where two more people sleep. In back is an even smaller hut where an older uncle lives.

The father, Ram, and one of the sons speak English well, the other sons less fluently, the mother and daughters not at all. Everywhere we go one of the boys carries a chair for us. We can't stand for thirty seconds without everyone getting excited that we are not sitting in the seat of honor. We are served tea and repeatedly asked if we are hungry, to which we reply we have just eaten. Later we are again asked if we are hungry. We say we will eat when they do. Finally, after another hour, we realize no one is going to eat supper until we ask to be fed. We announce we are hungry and seconds later a large supper, which was obviously being kept warm in the kitchen, is served. By bedtime we are on excellent terms with our hosts. Ram and his wife insist that we sleep in their bedroom.

The next morning while everyone else does chores, Ram, Tass and I are served a breakfast of rice, curried potatoes, *dahl*, a spicy lentil sauce, and *roti*, a light, flaky tortilla. We eat without silverware, using only the fingers of the right hand. Tass and I watch Ram squish his food into little balls and pop them into his mouth. We try to imitate his style but have a hard time getting the food to ball up. Instead we end up with a mass of squished food between the fingers that always falls apart half way to our mouths. It is great fun nonetheless. After we are through four of the boys take our place at the small table. The process of feeding three or four people at a time is repeated until the entire clan has eaten.

One of the girls asks Tass how old she is, and I tell everyone that today is her birthday. The family insists we stay for a birthday celebration that evening. The fact that Tass is 33 causes much discussion. Everyone

Prem Kishore gets up every morning before sunrise to cook fresh roti chani *over a charcoal fire, Fiji.*

repeatedly asks Tass if she is 23. They are convinced there is a mistake. Ram and his wife are just five years older than Tass and already have two grandchildren.

We spend the morning doing chores. I take the wheels off our bikes, clean up the mud and do bike maintenance, including moving our mirrors. For the next year, the traffic in every country we pedal through will travel on the left-hand side of the road. As Tass cleans the panniers she jokes with the kids and shows them a few items of gear. Our snorkels and goggles are a big hit. So are the bicycle helmets, which two of the boys wear while rounding up cows.

In the afternoon Ram and I walk to a creek to bathe. The water is muddy red from the runoff of all the rain but that does not daunt our bathing. It is cool and refreshing. As we hike back to the house we stop on a hillside overlooking the rolling hills of sugar cane. All the land we see is owned by native Fijian landlords and leased out to Asian Fijian farmers. Ram shows me the land he would like to own, yet he is prohibited by law from buying it.

In the late 1800's the English governors of the islands fought against hiring villagers to work the large foreign-owned plantations, believing it would disrupt the lifestyle of the native Fijians. So the plantation owners

35

turned to India for labor.

Large groups of poor peasants were hired in India and shipped to Fiji. The wages were low, the work exhausting and the housing, for which the workers were forced to pay exorbitant rent, was wretched. The Indians were basically hired slaves. At the end of the first five-year contract, few had enough money to go home and most signed another contract, this time with the freedom to live where they chose. By the time the second contract expired many had become accustomed to life in Fiji and decided not to go back to India.

When the immigration of foreign workers stopped in the early 1900's approximately 35,000 Asian Indians lived in Fiji. Today there are 370,000. In the last thirty years many large plantations were divided into smaller plots. Asian Fijians, whose ancestors were virtual slaves on those plantations, now manage most of the farms.

But there are problems. To keep native lands intact, the English governors long ago decided native Fijians should not be allowed to sell their property to non-natives. The well-meaning but paternalistic law was enacted to keep one man from selling his land, blowing the money, and leaving his family with no money and no land. Today only 30 percent of the land is freehold, land that can be owned by people who are not of native Fijian ancestry. Like all of his neighbors, Ram rents his land and has no hope of buying the farm even if the Fijian who owns it wished to sell.

In the evening a beautiful table is set with flowers, sweets and a cake with candles. To prepare the meal the women have cooked over the fire most of the afternoon. Tass is very touched. We are no longer referred to as Bruce and Tass. We are "Uncle" and "Auntie."

The women insist on dressing Tass in their traditional clothing. Her long, blond hair is brushed with coconut oil and braided with a red ribbon. Then she is whisked into the mother's bedroom. She puts on a long cotton slip with a draw string waist and then a tight midriff blouse, which makes it hard to breath deeply. Tass, ever the jokester, breaths in small chipmunk breaths to let the women know how tight it is. Giggles and laughter flow from the bedroom.

Next comes the sari. The material, six yards of red silk embroidered with gold thread, is wrapped around several times before being folded into pleats and tucked in the front. The leftover length is thrown over her shoulder and pinned. Later Tass tells me the best part is having all the hands dressing and fussing over her. It is a nurturing feeling that she wants to last forever, but all too soon she is pronounced dressed. She is brought out of the bedroom and seated in the family room. The final touch is a red dot on her forehead. She looks stunning.

Everyone gathers around the table. We light the candles on the cake and then, to much applause, Tass blows them out. Tass and I are instructed to feed each other cake, and then we all eat. After the meal two of the teenagers, Roshni and Mukesh, perform Indian dances. They try to teach us but we can't get the rhythm. Our attempts create hysterics. We share folk songs and teach each other the simpler choruses. Tass tells the family it is the best birthday party she has ever had. We leave the next morning, and promise to stop back on our return to Nadi.

Compared to the moderate temperature of Hawaii, Fiji is sweltering. On the southern side of the island mudslides from erosion due to excessive lumbering and hurricane damage cover portions of the road. We carry the bikes over the short sections of mud, but on the long stretches we have no choice but to try and ride, or push. After each crossing we stop for half an hour to scrape the mud out of the fenders and off the brakes. Sweat runs into our eyes and drips off our chins. Obnoxious flies land on our faces and lips. Tass vows to bite the head off the next one that lands on her mouth, but she is too slow to carry out the threat.

We pass through countless villages where everyone rushes to the side of the road to shout *Bula! Bula!* "Hello! Hello!" We often hear this greeting when riding through farm land and have to search the fields and surrounding hills to finally spot, off in the distance, a waving native Fijian. If they are within shouting distance, they always yell hello.

We camp behind budget hotels and cabannas on the beach so we can

Bruce ferrying loads across mudslides on the island of Vitu Levu, Fiji.

get drinking water and take showers, a nice treat for our sweating, insect-bitten bodies. As we approach Suva many locals warn us about being robbed. We arrive in the capital expecting a town with hustlers and shady characters on every corner. Luckily it turns out to be an interesting city. We stay at the Coconut Inn, a normally crowded haven for budget travelers that has been deserted since the big hurricane.

"Businessman Bashed in Suva" is the headline of the morning paper. A gory close-up photo shows an unlucky man with a battered head. Luckily he survived. Bashings, derived from the days when everyone on the island used war clubs, are a problem in the capital. It seems there are gangs of native Fijian thugs roving the city who are not ready to abandon ancestral habits to the history books.

At the Fijian Museum we see a fascinating collection of war clubs, some with heavy bulbous ends, others with inlaid sharks teeth and razor sharp chunks of jade. We also examine an assortment of cannibal forks, used for eating *long pig*, as human flesh was called. In the past, cannibalism was universally practiced on Fiji. Most shipwrecked people were eaten because it was believed they were cursed and abandoned by the gods. Prisoners of war and lowly workers were also eaten. Cannibalism was not only a ritual used in ceremonies but was practiced on a frequent basis because it was enjoyed. Everyone liked the taste of *long pig*. How quickly societies can change! Today, with the exception of a few gangs in the capital, this feels like the friendliest island in the world.

Our main reason for coming to Suva is to get New Zealand visas. But the New Zealand High Commission won't give us visas until we have ongoing visas to Australia. At the Australian embassy we are told the visas won't be ready until the following Monday, five days away.

We ride to Colo-i-Suva, a nearby national park, to camp and hike while we wait for bureaucracy to do its work. When we return on Monday we get our visas but then we can't leave because of the weather. Hurricane Gavin arrives and dumps thirteen inches of rain in twenty-four hours. Eight hundred people lose their homes. All the roads out of town are closed. We spend another three days at the Coconut Inn with a group of eight other stranded travelers, reading, writing, and telling travelers' tales.

Stifling, muggy weather follows the hurricane. We ride back across the island, battling heat and the "black whirlies," the dizziness that comes from riding up hills in sauna-like weather. Ten miles from Sigatoka we camp behind a restaurant. The cook we met when staying here before has taken time off to prepare for his sister's wedding. His replacement, an older fellow named Mac, has been told to expect us.

Mac treats us like royalty. The next morning he serves us coffee at our tent and invites us inside for an unusual but delicious breakfast: hard boiled eggs with passion fruit ice cream. In the evening he cooks us a huge pot of curried vegetables and rice. Later, Johnny Abdul, the Indian owner of the restaurant arrives and we have a party.

Johnny also owns a sawmill in the mountains. Since he has helped construct some of the largest meeting halls on the island, he is a good friend with many of the native Fijian elders. He offers to take us on a tour of the interior, but due to the hurricane the roads won't be passable for another week. Unfortunately, we have to catch our plane to New Zealand in six days. Undaunted, Johnny invites us to the wedding of the sister of the cook we met on our previous stay. We happily accept his offer.

The next morning, during a repeat breakfast of boiled eggs and passion fruit ice cream, Mac asks us to come and stay at his village. He promises he will have a big feast and cook us many different traditional foods. We tell him we must leave for the wedding and then ride back to Nadi. He offers to give me his shirt if we come with him. We again explain we must leave to catch our flight. For a while I am afraid we have hurt his feelings, but as we finish packing up he comes out and smiles at us once again.

We ride for a few hours and then take a bumpy side road that ends at a cane field. Following Johnny's instructions we push our bikes through the field and cross two narrow footbridges before spotting the banners and ribbons on a house on a hillside. Under a pavilion of brightly colored awnings 75 people congregate around a shrine covered with tinsel, woven fronds and ribbons.

Johnny and Rakesh, the cook, greet us and in a whirlwind tour through the crowd introduce us to at least two dozen people. A group of women take Tass into the house to see the bride being dressed for the ceremony. I sit with Johnny and the men on one side of the altar. The women sit across from us. Between us designs of colored rice cover the carpeted floor in front of the shrine. Incense sticks, vessels of holy water and other religious items dot the pavilion. Unlike the native Fijians, who are mainly Christian, most Asian Fijians are Hindu, the predominate religion of India. The three-day Hindu wedding celebration culminates today in a lengthy ceremony and a big feast. Tonight the groom will take the bride home, but they will not sleep together. Tomorrow she will return to her parents' home to stay for one to four weeks before finally moving in with her husband to consummate the marriage.

The band plays a few songs and the ceremony begins. The groom is brought out first. He wears a yellow turban and white silk jacket and pants. He is shoeless, his toenails painted red; colorful patterns are painted on his feet. Piles of tinsel and flower garlands hang from his neck. He looks about 17 years old. Despite the merrymaking he holds his face down, his eyes on the floor.

Next a group of women escort the bride, who wears a bright red sari. She is also covered with tinsel and flower garlands. The women direct her to kneel next to the groom. Neither the bride nor the groom acknowledges one another, or even glances at the other. They stare at the ground. Our hosts tell us the bride and groom are too embarrassed to look at each other or at the audience. Like most of the Indian weddings in Fiji, their marriage was arranged in traditional Hindu fashion by the parents. The bride and groom met just a week ago and have spoken only once, during a brief introduction in the company of their parents.

To our surprise, we are told fixed marriages generally last longer than "love" marriages, which became popular in the 70's but are now on the decline because so many ended in divorce. Perhaps there is less divorce in fixed marriages because neither partner expects to find a passionate, fairy tale love. A fixed marriage is like a business contract, an agreement to work together to raise a family. Couples rarely interact publicly with each other. Men and women are segregated in seating, eating and nearly all social activities. Like the other guests, Tass and I sit separately, yet throughout the afternoon we catch each other's eye. How lucky we are to be married, lovers **and** best friends!

After the priests finish their rituals the band resumes playing and the guests, men first, are fed. Huge amounts of delicious vegetarian food are brought out and everyone eats until they are stuffed. Men stop to talk with me, and women flock around Tass to make sure we understand all aspects of the ceremony. After the feast we reluctantly leave the wedding and push our bikes back to the road.

The daily afternoon rains begin and we are soon soaking wet. We ride on to the home of the Kashore family, where Tass had been given such a memorable birthday party. A few days before, in the town of Sigatoka, we went to a variety of Indian shops to buy gifts for the family: kava and tobacco for the men; bracelets, hair clips and make-up for the mother and daughters; and Phantom comic books, an island favorite, for the boys. At the house, everyone is shocked we would buy something for them. We explain our custom of guests bringing gifts for the hosts. They in turn ask us how much we paid for each item. Everyone smiles and nods approvingly when they think we struck a good bargain.

The next day ten-year-old Johnny takes me on a hike over the farm. We sit on a hill and eat a huge stalk of sugar cane he has cut with his machete. It is very sweet but doesn't hurt my teeth like processed sugars or candies. We chew big wads, swallow all the juice and spit the pulp onto the ground. He tells me about each stage of the sugar canes development and of the hard work during the six-month harvest. Finally, the afternoon rains drive us back to the house. We spend one more night with the family and then say farewell.

Back in Nadi we scour a number of discount electronic stores in town. Tass buys supplies for her camera while I get a cheap radio for news and weather broadcasts. The next day, as we are tearing apart our bikes to ship to New Zealand, we hear the first weather report over our radio. Another hurricane is bearing down on Fiji. It will arrive tonight. The hotel manager advises us to take our tent down and move into the building. It is going to be a big storm.

Since our hotel is near the airport, many die-hard travelers--the last to abandon hopes of flying out tonight--end up at the front door when the airport closes. We all sit in the lobby and have a calm-before-the-storm hurricane party as we listen to weather broadcasts.

The situation grows ominous. The storm is thought to be more powerful than hurricane Eric, which destroyed 8,000 homes a month before we arrived. Workers board up the windows on the north side of the hotel, while everyone inside moves to the south side of the building. When we go to bed at 11:00 p.m. the electricity across the island has been turned off to prevent accidents if lines are broken in the storm. We fall asleep to the sound of the wind rattling the doors and windows.

The big winds begin at dawn. It is a violent, deafening roar that makes us nervous about standing near the windows--even on the downwind side of the building. We brave our way out to a spot on a porch that is sheltered from the wind. Occasionally large sheets of tin torn from nearby roofs sail past. Guillotine frisbees.

By late morning the brunt of the storm has passed. The neighborhood store opens at noon and does a thriving business selling candles and food. Although the wind still bangs loose doors and shutters, everything now seems more relaxed.

Luckily, after last month's devastating hurricane, everyone was more serious about boarding up buildings. Because of this, the storm causes less damage than expected. The airport opens the next morning. We catch the first flight to New Zealand.

4

Kiwis

Our friend Sue Elliot greets us at the New Zealand airport. We met Sue and her boyfriend, Mark Blazey, three years ago on a small island off the coast of Mexico's Yucatan peninsula. Although Sue and Mark have traveled the world together, when home they live in separate houses. Sue shares a house in Auckland with three other people. Since one of her "flatmates" is on the South Island, we stay at her house and sleep in the extra room.

Each morning we eat a traditional New Zealand breakfast: toasted Vogels bread with Maramite spread, a black yeasty paste with a foul smell but an appealing taste. We spend our days exploring Auckland and each evening prepare huge feasts with Mark and Sue and discuss route options through the country.

We ride out of Auckland on March 27, at the end of the New Zealand summer. It is raining lightly. We wonder if we are going to repeat our ride across the States--leaving late to miss the hot weather and tourist crunch, hoping for pleasant fall weather and never finding it. We have a three month visa. Hopefully winter is at least three months away.

We ride toward the Coromandel Peninsula on the east coast. Unfortunately, two storms beat us to the region. When we take side-

Tass fording a flooded road on New Zealand's North Island.

roads into the mountains, we end up pushing our bikes through knee-deep streams overrunning the *metal* roads, New Zealand slang for gravel. However the roads are more mud than anything else. We change course and head toward the center of the North Island. The sky clears as we ride through steep, rolling hills covered with dairy cows. I practice my cow imitations and manage to convince a herd of twenty cows to trot beside us until the road veers from their pasture.

We stop in Rotorua for four days, visiting Maori villages and craft centers and soaking in the local thermal pools, and then ride southeast to meet Mark and Sue for a backpack trip in the Kaweka National Forest. At the park ranger station Tass and I store our bikes in a maintenance shop, pull out our frameless backpacks and load up our gear.

The ranger tells us the first part of the trail has a few missing sections. Still, he thinks we can reach the first hut in four hours. New Zealand is famous for its hut system. All the national parks and most of the state parks have cabins with bunk beds, fireplaces and/or stoves. Each cabin is spaced three or four hiking hours apart. So hikers, or *trampers* as they are called in New Zealand, can backpack, or *tramp*, through the parks without a tent. Due to the rain Tass and I are a bit cautious and decide to bring our tent along, just in case.

Our route follows the Ngaruroro River up a narrow canyon. In less than a mile the trail deadends where the river runs up against the bottom of a cliff. Since there is no trail up the steep, brush-covered hillside around the cliff, the only alternative is to ford the river. It is a cold morning. We take off our long pants and put on shorts to cross the icy river, three feet deep and 50 feet wide. The rocks on the bottom are too slippery and sharp to cross with bare feet so we wear our boots and hold hands for balance in the swift current.

On the other side we change again, wring out our socks and stick our feet into our now cold and wet boots. A chilling mist rolls down the canyon. It begins to drizzle. Half a mile later the trail disappears again where the river meets another cliff. Again we change into our shorts and wade into the icy water. On the other side we find the trail again so we must be on the right route. Strange way to hike. Was this path made for ducks?

Fifteen minutes later we arrive at another dead end crossing. This time the water is deeper and even faster moving. We find a spot that looks the least dangerous and "give it a go," as New Zealanders say. By the time we make it to the far shore, Tass, the shortest of our group, is soaked to the waist.

At the next river crossing we stop for a group meeting. The ranger at the trailhead said we **may** have to cross the creek at first and we **might** occasionally lose the trail. We pull out our map and peer at the small dots showing the trail between the squiggly contour lines of the canyon. The map does not show enough detail to tell if the trail crosses the river or not. We decide to keep going. To go back means three river crossings. Hopefully the trail will get better up the canyon.

It doesn't. At the seventh river crossing we pull the map back out. To go back now means six crossings. We don't even want to cross the river **once** more! We try an alternate route on a faint trail leading up the steep bank next to the cliff. We struggle through tall grass with razor sharp edges and encounter a dozen types of shrubs, all with scratching branches, barbs and thorns. When the going is especially tight we shove our way backwards through the thick growth using our backpacks as battering rams. After forty-five minutes of pushing and grunting up the hillside we cross the cliff and then spend another fifteen minutes forcing our way back down to the trail along the creek.

The further we hike up the canyon the more we are convinced we can't go back, and yet the worse things become. We battle the bush until we can no longer cope, then hike in the river until freezing feet force us back into the bush. We have a few discussions about the ranger who sent us this way. Apparently no one has hiked the canyon since the last few storms, and the trail, which must normally follow the side of the river, is now underwater.

The sun drops below the canyon and the light begins to fade. Group morale also fades. Just as darkness descends we find a trail in the direction of the hoped-for cabin. After six hours and fourteen river crossings we finally reach Cameron Hut!

"Our" hut has three bunk beds, a fireplace, pots and pans for cooking, and a pantry of staples hikers have left behind: peanut butter, honey, dried milk, sugar, salt and spices. In the corner are washbasins and buckets to carry drinking water from the creek, and axes and saws to cut firewood. During the summer tramping season, December through February, the huts are often full each night. But now, in April, there are few trampers. The hut logbook doesn't list anyone being here for two weeks.

The next day dawns clear and warm. After a pancake breakfast we retire to a meadow to relax, lay in the sun, and take turns reading aloud from the entries in the hut's huge logbook: stories of rainy weather, good and bad fishing, and complaints about the trails. Ian and Ted write multiple entries of being lost; Bunky slips and gashes his leg; Mary falls off a cliff and has to be rescued by a helicopter.

Since it is Good Friday we bake hot cross buns, a New Zealand tradition, over the coals of the evening fire. The next morning we climb out of the canyon on a well-marked path into a moist tropical forest of beech trees covered with lichen and moss. But in the afternoon our trail once again disappears. Moments later it begins to rain. We spend the rest of the day bushwacking through the wet, heavy undergrowth, stopping only to pull out the map and stare at more squiggly markings. At dusk we are exhausted and soaking wet. We have no choice but to abandon the idea of finding the hut.

It continues to rain as we put up our tent. Then we take turns standing in the rain, stripping off wet clothes and diving inside, trying to bring in as little water as possible. One by one we dry off and jump into our sleeping bags, to lay squished, side by side, shivering. Since we planned on cooking on the hut stoves, we didn't bring our backpack stove, so our supper food, which requires cooking, is useless. Instead we eat tomorrow's lunch and two huge chocolate Easter eggs Sue brought for an Easter treat.

Mark and Sue are grand companions! They both have a great sense of humor and are always enthusiastic. Even in trying circumstances, like right now, they can objectively remove themselves from their discomforts to enjoy the comical aspects of the ordeal. But just because we laugh about our circumstance doesn't mean we aren't ready to put an end to this misadventure. We decide tomorrow is time to make a major retreat. We abandon the idea of a loop through the mountains and decide to hike out on the one trail we know, back down the Ngaruroro River.

Easter Sunday morning we climb out of our cozy sleeping bags to put on our wet clothes, socks and boots. Within three hours we have hiked back to our old cabin. We cook a pot of oatmeal and then head for the river. It is a clear, sunny morning. This time we don't make any effort to avoid the water, and take the fastest route down the canyon. Three hours, and twenty-four river crossings later, we arrive at the trailhead.

Tass and I decide not to take any more chances with the weather. Since winter comes first to the mountains of the South Island, we are not going to waste any more time in getting there. We catch a ride south with Mark and Sue and board the first ferry across Cook Strait to New Zealand's South Island. From the ferry we take a train to Dunedin, three-quarters of the way down the South Island's eastern coast. We'll explore the mountains of the Southern Alps first and then bicycle northward.

The next day we ride the length of the Otago peninsula on a scenic highway hugging the shoreline. The sky is clear blue, there is little wind, and the bay is calm. We feel frisky and ride at a fast pace. Tass pulls in to draft behind me as we zip past an older man on a ten-speed bicycle. Moments later I glimpse the man in my mirror, tucked in behind Tass, his front tire inches from her rear wheel. He must have made an impressive sprint to catch our draft. We race along the coast. In my mirror I repeatedly catch glimpses of the man behind Tass's silhouette. I increase the pace, curious to see how fast our shadow can go.

After twenty minutes we slow down and the man pulls up beside us. We are stunned to find he is 75 years old! He was a bicycle racer in the 1932 Olympics in Los Angeles and still rides 10 miles every morning to keep in shape. When he learns of our travel plans he gives us a big smile and then says farewell and turns up a steep hill toward the center of the peninsula.

We head for Tairaroa Head, a controlled breeding sanctuary for the Royal Albatross. We spend our one-hour pass in a blind, peering into a thick mist, trying to make out the few chicks left in the nests this time of year. Once they get their feathers, the chicks wait for a strong wind to pick them up for their maiden flight. Albatross are famous for their lack of take-off and landing skills. It's no wonder; they hardly ever do it. From the moment the juvenile bird takes to the air its feet may not touch the earth again for three to five years. The first flight is literally a world tour, a circumnavigation of the globe following the 40th parallel, jokingly referred to as the "roaring forties" in birding lingo. During this time some birds will occasionally land on the ocean to feed, but only if there is a strong enough wind to lift them back into the air.

We leave the reserve via a bumpy gravel road that twists up the steep, windswept hillside overlooking the ocean. After a thrilling descent on a rutted track we stop on a hill overlooking a small colony of Yellow-eyed penguins, the rarest penguin in the world. As we set up our tent the fog rolls in again and visibility drops. We sight some Southern Fur seals on a rock ledge. Just before dark we catch a glimpse of a few penguins strolling out of the ocean. They waddle across the beach and trudge up a steep, sandy hillside to their sleeping area. Moments later darkness and mist end the show and we head back to our tent.

We get up before dawn and sit on the hillside waiting for the penguins to head out to the ocean to feed. Again mist shrouds our vision. We glimpse a few birds shuffling and sliding down the sandy hillside, dragging their feet in the steep, soft sand. As they waddle across the beach their gait makes us chuckle. But the mist continues to plague us so we decide to move down the coast. Following a tip from a local birder, we get permission from a farmer to camp on a private beach where there is a larger colony of penguins. After riding over rough sheep trails across miles of pasture, we arrive at the beach. As I put up the tent Tass scours the area with binoculars and notices three dots on a hillside across the beach. Penguins! We load our daypacks with enough food and clothing to last until nightfall and take off across the half-mile beach.

Giant bird footprints cover the sand. Even though the Yellow-eyed penguin is small by penguin standards, it is still thirty inches tall, with large webbed feet for swimming. As we near the penguins we pause occasionally to watch their behavior. They preen themselves and don't seem bothered by our approach. At 100 feet they stop preening. We stand still until they resume grooming and then slowly move closer. At fifty

Yellow-eyed penguins, Otago Peninsula, New Zealand.

47

feet I stay out on the beach as a decoy while Tass takes the camera and does a flawless stalk using the rolling sand dunes and bushes for cover. At fifteen feet she stops, shoots some pictures, and waves for me to join her.

We move in even closer for an eye to eye staredown with two penguins. We can see every tuft of each little feather. We take a few more photos and then retreat to a more respectful distance for long-term viewing. They preen themselves and occasionally each other, stopping every two or three minutes to glance our way before returning to their own business. Every ten minutes they stretch, flop their wings a few times, and shake their heads. Penguin yoga.

In the late afternoon after a day of feeding in the ocean, groups of three to six penguins begin coming out of the water, crossing the beach, and marching into the dunes to spend the night. By evening 150 birds have waddled past. When it is dark and we are sure all the penguins are out of the ocean, we walk back along the beach to our tent.

We ride inland toward Queenstown over steep rolling hills covered with golden grass. The area reminds us of Wyoming. But unlike Wyoming, which is cattle country, the livestock here are sheep. We chuckle at the differences between the New Zealand sheep farmers and the Wyoming cowboys. The sheep farmers wear shorts and use "Japanese quarter horses" (motorcycles) and dogs to round up their flocks. When on a real horse most New Zealanders wear a helmet, a carry-over from the British school of horseback riding. We chuckle as we imagine the reaction if a Wyoming ranch hand arrived at round-up dressed in loose, baggy shorts and a crash helmet!

Queenstown is a small resort community on the shore of Lake Wakatipu. Across the lake the mountains of the Remarkable Range rise from the lake at 1,200 feet in a single unbroken ascent to 7,700 feet. We set up our tent in a caravan park and then head to town to buy supplies for an 11-day *tramp* into Mt. Aspiring and Fiordlands National Park.

In the evening we begin packing. When preparing for a short backpack trip at home, we commonly spread gear across the entire living room floor. Now we pack for an 11-day hike inside our tent. We sit waist deep surrounded by clothes we have just washed, piles of food sorted into various colored stuff sacks, backpacking equipment, cold weather gear, 10 bicycle panniers, shoes, boots, helmets, reading books, notebooks, guidebooks, maps, sleeping bags, ground pads, more food, cooking pots, stove, camera gear, and binoculars--trying to decide what to bring and what to leave behind.

In the morning we get up before dawn to glimpse snow-covered peaks poking through the clouds and mist. It is the season's first snowstorm and the mountains look majestic. We don't like bicycling in the snow but hiking in it is a different story, especially since we will be staying in a hut each night. Since the Routeburn track is a well-traveled route it should be easy to find the cabins; we leave our tent behind.

The trail winds up a valley full of beech trees covered in lichens and moss. The forest floor is covered with ferns. Above us, through the tree branches, glimpses of snow-capped peaks fill the skyline. As we gain altitude it begins to snow again. We hike under the protection of the tropical forest watching the snow swirl out in the valley until finally the storm pierces the upper canopy of beech trees. We put on coats and rain pants. Soon a layer of snow covers the ground, a beautiful contrast to the lush, green vegetation.

We dally through the afternoon enjoying the storm, the scenery, and the hike, and don't arrive at the hut until nearly dark. It is a small cabin. The main room has a stove and two sets of bunk beds while each of two side cubicles has four bunks, making a total of 20 beds. Normally there are few people in the huts this time of year, but the snowstorm yesterday and today has caused a backlog of hikers waiting to cross the pass ahead. Ten of us spend the evening sitting around the coal stove swapping stories and tidbits of information about the trail.

The next morning we are the first ones out of the hut and break trail through six inches of snow as we work our way up the pass. The weather warms and we are soon hiking in shorts, but we continue to wear gaiters to keep the snow out of our boots. The air is still, the sky deep blue. At the summit we sit in the sun and eat lunch surrounded by rugged, snow-covered mountains. Even though we descend the pass into a deep valley we stay above the snow line all day.

The second hut we stay at is often referred to as the Routeburn Hilton. It has 40 beds, and we hear stories of the hut being so crowded during the summer that people have to sleep on the floor! Tonight six of us stay in the hut, a personable group. This time of year most of the hikers are Europeans, Canadians and Americans.

The next day we drop below the snow line. Ferns and mosses reappear from under the snow. Everything is lush and dripping wet. We take a seldom used trail off the main route and drop rapidly down into the Hollyford Valley. Much of the trail is underwater. Perhaps the path was built during a dry spell, and now the stream simply follows the trail down the mountain. Or, more likely, the stream was here first. New Zealanders consider water no obstacle to hiking; they view creeks as excellent hiking paths--which saves time in building trails! We slosh through the water in giant descending leaps, following the creek down the steep gully, splashing all over ourselves with each landing.

By afternoon we are at the bottom of the valley, only 400 feet above sea level. Around us tower 5,000-9,000-foot, snowcapped peaks. Even though it is late in the day we begin hiking the Hollyford track. Three hours later we arrive, exhausted, at Hidden Falls, the first hut on the new trail. We had been hoping to meet a friend from the U.S. along the hike. But the logbook shows he has not yet been here, nor has anyone else during the last week. We decide to take a rest day to see if he catches up.

The next morning I meditate on the porch and watch the sunrise illuminate the upper snowfields of Mt. Tutoko, nearly 9,000 feet above me. The soft glow of the early morning light on the mountains touches something within me. What is it in the human psyche that makes us awed by a big pile of rock covered with snow? My emotions surge with a deep contentment, a knowledge that I am somehow connected to the earth, that I am a part of nature, a part of something larger than myself.

After breakfast we go birding and spot four new species, which leaves us with only three birds found in this area that we have not yet seen. In the afternoon we lay in the sun and read. Life is wonderful.

The next morning there is still no sign of our friend Chuck, so we leave him a message at the hut detailing our route. We are hiking to Martins Bay on the coast where we hope to find a seal colony and, if we are not too late in the year, Fiordlands Crested penguins.

We hike in dense rainforest while the exotic songs of the Bellbird and Tui reverberate through the valley. Although it has not rained for four days, all of the plants and trees are soaking wet. Giant tree ferns grow everywhere. The forest floor is thick with moss. The path is tricky walking. Slick, moss-covered rocks and rotten logs, scattered through puddles and bogs, provide the only footing. We never know when we will leap onto what looks like solid ground only to have it give way beneath us.

At the next cabin, located on Lake Alabaster, we sit down to read the cabin's logbook, a favorite pastime. In the last three huts there has been a debate concerning which trail in the area is in the worst condition--the Lake Olvine track which leads through the Black Swamp or the route to Martins Bay called the Demon Trail. Nearly all the entries lament the weather. This part of the South Island gets almost 200 inches of rain per year. Reading each entry reminds us how lucky we have been--we are on our fifth day without rain.

The next day we have a minor tragedy. The sole on the rear half of my left hiking boot delaminates. Using our clothesline, I tie a series of loops around my ankles and under the boot to hold the heel in place. The ropework seems to work but I am now nervous about each step. If the boot comes apart I will have to hike all the way out in rubber thongs.

On our eighth day of hiking we are ready to face the Demon Trail. We head out at morning's first light. Again, sections of the trail are like small streams; much of the hiking is over smooth river rocks covered with slick green moss. Snot rocks. Tass leads a fast pace while I lag behind, carefully searching for good footing for my loose-soled left boot. But after our madcap hike with Mark and Sue in the Kaweka Range, the Demon Trail seems relatively easy. We cross the worse section in less than four hours, take a lunch break and then head back out. By late afternoon we arrive at the ocean.

The coast is packed with enormous boulders that have been smoothed and rounded by the waves. The rocks are a variety of colors; many look like giant eggs laid by dinosaurs or prehistoric birds. There is no trail so we jump from rock to rock to make our way down the coast. There is no sign of penguins. They must have already migrated from the area, but we do find a colony of Southern Fur seals.

Throughout our time hiking on the Hollyford trail we have been pestered by sandflies. On the coast they are absolutely fierce. Even with our bodies covered in insect repellent the little buggers fly into our hair, ears, and up our noses. They constantly get trapped, flying Kamakazee style, between my glasses and my eyes. Since it is low tide we hop as far as possible across the giant rocks to catch an ocean breeze and get away from the shoreline--and hopefully the sandflies. The seals abandon their rocky perches as we work our way toward them over the rocks. When we can't go any further we settle down on a large boulder and begin a quiet wait.

Soon the inquisitive seals start to swim close to our rock to investigate us. The water is crystal clear. We watch the seals swimming deep in the ocean. Their movements are fluid and graceful, their fur sleek. They look at us with large brown eyes. The pups swim in playful arcs with looping, backward somersaults. Others bodysurf on the small waves between the rocks. Just before dark the incoming tide forces us to abandon our ocean outpost. We boulder hop back to the beach.

We spend a night at Martins Bay and then begin the hike back. On the first day the sole on my other hiking boot comes off. I have to constantly stop to retie the soles as the rocks keep cutting the cord. By the end of the hike our clothesline has disappeared.

We never saw our friend Chuck on the tramp, and when we get back to Queenstown we find we missed him there as well. A letter for us at the post office says he left the previous day for Mt. Cook, the highest peak in New Zealand. We call his hotel at Mt. Cook, but miss him yet again. He has left for three days of skiing on the Tasman Glacier. He has to return to the U.S. the following day. It seems crazy to be so close and miss seeing Chuck, my skiing, kayaking and mountaineering partner when I lived in Jackson, Wyoming. We had a similar mix-up and missed him by just an hour in Mexico City a few years ago. This time we want to make the extra effort to find him. We decide to postpone our next hike and try to rendezvous. Mt. Cook is 175 miles to the north over mountainous terrain, and is in the opposite direction we planned to leave Queenstown. Rather than attempting a stressful, high-speed bike ride to catch Chuck, we decide

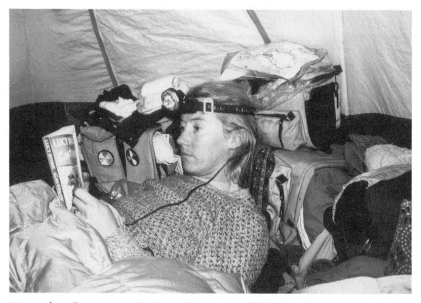

Using a headlamp to read, Tass relaxes in our Walrus Tent, New Zealand.

to spend tomorrow organizing food and gear for our next hike. Then we will hitchhike up to see Chuck on the following day.

The hitchhiking goes well, and by evening we are at Mt. Cook. At the Ranger Station we are told a large storm is moving in. Chuck and his friend have radioed from their hut that they are coming out a day early. We greet Chuck as he steps off a shuttle bus from the trailhead. Chuck and Chris, his climbing partner, are both wound up after the thrills of extreme skiing. That evening we get the full story of their adventures. Listening to their tales we find ourselves wishing we had our telemark ski gear as well. The only problem with bicycle touring is we can't carry all our sports equipment.

We sleep on the floor of their chalet, and the next day stretch breakfast into a whole morning affair. In the afternoon we make a weak attempt to do some ice climbing but can't find any good ice on the lower section of the Tasman glacier so we head back to the room and resume eating.

The following morning we reluctantly pack up to leave. We catch a ride with Chuck and Chris for 40 miles to a small town where the road divides. Moments later we stand on the side of the road and watch their rental car drive on northward. Tass and I are heading south, and the traffic is sparse. A cold wind blows out of the mountains, which are again covered with storm clouds. We sit by the side of the road. An average of six cars per hour drive by. The first 19 don't give us a ride.

Being left out in the cold on the roadside seems especially hard after spending the last two nights in a comfortable chalet and riding with Chuck and Chris in a warm car. We are suddenly struck by the poverty of our traveling lifestyle. Here we are, sitting on a road with little traffic, freezing, trying to catch a ride so we can save a $12 bus ticket.

Finally a car pulls over. Terry, the woman driving, offers us both a lift and a place to spend the night. Even though it is early in the afternoon we take her up on the offer. The hitchhiking is terrible and the chance to stay with a local farm family sounds great.

Dalranchney Sheep Station turns out to be 25,000 acres of golden tussock grassland located in the high country near Lindis Pass. When we arrive, Edward, age three, and Hanna, age two, give us a tour of the wool sheds and dog kennels while Terry and her husband, Rick, do chores. After supper Rick asks if we would be willing to help the next morning "out in the paddock" with some rabbit control work.

Before the arrival of Europeans there were no rabbits in New Zealand. A few bored settlers, who thought it would be nice to have something to shoot, decided to bring down a few hundred rabbits from England to use for target practice. The rabbits, having no natural predator in New Zealand, quickly multiplied into an ecological disaster. Today they threaten both the sheep ranches and the native grasses, many of which have been destroyed due to overgrazing. Deer, which were also introduced to New Zealand, have eaten much of the native bush into extinction.

Only a few outlying islands in New Zealand have managed to remain clean of introduced pests. Both environmentalists and sheep ranchers want to see all the rabbits removed. To do so groups of farmers join together to form rabbit boards and share the costs of extermination campaigns. Rick tells us farmers in his area have to poison rabbits once every five years. To help in the project the rabbit board rents a helicopter. First they distribute two batches of yummy cooked oats covered with molasses throughout the fields, winning the rabbits' confidence. Then they distribute oats laced with poison.

Today they distribute the oats with molasses. Because of the cost of renting a helicopter, it is important that we load the oats quickly during each of the helicopter's forty scheduled stops. The helicopter flies in at a high speed and lands a foot away from where we stand. We have to be careful not to touch the metal casing on the chopper before it touches the ground or we can get a jolt of static electricity. The moment one of the runners hits the ground we pour 100 pound bags of oats into the fiberglass panniers on the sides of the helicopter. The instant we finish the pilot guns the motor and the chopper, with a gale force wind and a loud roar, takes off again. After just a few landings the four of us, working together like an Indianapolis pit crew, can load the helicopter in seconds.

Our work is finished by noon. We eat lunch with the family and head out onto the highway. Rather than hitching back to Queenstown, we save time by plotting a course due south. Our backpacks are loaded with food and gear for another *tramp*, and our next destination is Stewart Island off the southern coast of the South Island. By noon the following day we arrive at the coast. The price of the ferry to Stewart Island has skyrocketed. It is much cheaper to fly stand-by, if you don't mind waiting around to catch a plane. We hang out in the unheated airport for two days, reading and shivering. At last we are called for a flight.

Stewart Island is 40 miles long and 25 miles wide. The island has only nine miles of highway, if you include all the city streets on the island's only town. Nearly all the 400 residents earn their livelihood from fishing and are generally a gruff lot who don't have much time for tourists. There is no public electrical system. The homes with electricity have diesel generators. Telephones are hand-crank vintage and island phone numbers have just two digits.

New Zealanders are often called kiwis. Our objective in coming to the island is to see a real kiwi--the national bird of New Zealand. Because it is nocturnal it is difficult to spot. We have yet to meet a New Zealander who has seen a kiwi in the wild. Stewart Island is one of the few places where we have a chance of sighting one.

The kiwi is the oldest bird in New Zealand, all of its relatives are extinct. It is an evolutionary oddity. Its tiny wings are unsuited for flying; even its feathers are useless: they have no barbules, the tiny ridges that "zip" together feather hairs making the feather rigid enough to sustain flight. The kiwi lays the largest egg in relation to the female's body weight of any bird--sometimes the egg is one fourth the weight of the bird which laid it! Luckily the male kiwi is no chauvinist. After the female has done the work of laying such a large egg, the male takes over and sits on the egg until it hatches, about 75 days.

We have the best chance of spotting a kiwi near Masons Bay on the other side of the island, a three-day walk each way. Since Stewart Island has a reputation for the muddiest hiking trails in all of New Zealand, we have come prepared with gaiters to wear over our boots. Our first day hiking is a short, four-hour *tramp* to the North Arm hut. We hike through the rain forest, stopping occasionally to bird and enjoy the scenery. The trail is muddy but not as bad as we expected. In the larger bogs the Forest Service has made short boardwalks or placed stumps in the mud so we can hop from log to log.

The next morning we get up extra early. Since yesterday's hike was so easy, we want to hike the next two sections of trail, which normally takes two days, in one day. But the moment we leave the hut the trail degenerates into a slippery obstacle course. The mud is three to six inches deep. It is thick, gooey stuff that clings to our boots and threatens to hold our feet in its murky depths. The suction of the mud makes each step a major effort. Our footsteps sound like someone drinking the last bit of a thick milkshake through a straw. Thouck, tthhoouucckk, ttthhhhooouuuccckkk.

Tree roots also try to slow us down. Trail erosion is a serious problem; the soil has been washed away in the heavy rains leaving a thick web of gnarled roots hanging six to twelve inches over the trail. We try to balance and walk on the wet roots but they are like slick, uneven tightropes. When the roots are too precarious, we step over each root and drop our feet through the larger openings--splash--into the muddy path below. It reminds me of the old football drill where players run through a net suspended off the ground, yet here it is impossible to get a good walking rhythm. We stop, step, slip, catch ourselves, step, splash, whoops, look again, go around, step and slip all morning long.

We arrive at the next hut at noon, exhausted but on schedule. Lunch helps revive us and we take off again at a fast pace. By mid afternoon we enter the legendary Chocolate Swamp where the trail is always under a foot of water. We have been warned never to stray from the small trail markers, for an elaborate system of logs have been submerged to give a

Bruce wading through the Chocolate Swamp, Stewart Island, New Zealand.

firm ground to stand upon. Off the trail is thigh deep, waist deep and even chest deep muck, or so the stories in the hut logbooks report. After reading accounts of every tramper who missed a corner or veered off the trail in the last two years, we are a bit apprehensive. But the crossing turns out to be fun, at least more fun than mucking through the thick mud in the forest. Here we just slosh along from marker to marker.

By mid-afternoon the slogging through mud and water begins to take its toll. Wet boots make our feet soft and tender. Blisters form. By late afternoon our backs and necks ache from the weight of our backpacks, which we can't remove as we are surrounded by water and have no place to set them down for a break. Just as we come to the end of the swamp it begins to rain. We enter an open section of tussock grass and a cold headwind blowing across the ocean from Antarctica forces us to put on rain coats, wind pants, mitts and hats. The last two miles we hobble in, neither of us saying much. We are each in our own world, searching for the energy to continue onward.

We arrive at the Masons Bay hut to find a man from New Zealand and a woman from Australia finishing supper. A fire crackles in the cookstove. We change out of our wet clothes in the unheated bunk area and scamper back into the room with the stove. Ah, how quickly the day's hardship becomes a story to share and laugh about. Later, I head back out into the rain on the odd chance of seeing a kiwi. Tass stays in the hut; she doesn't think any sensible kiwi would be out on such a stormy night. After an hour of hiking by flashlight in the drizzle, I decide she is right and give up the search.

The next day we explore the beach, which is seven miles long and two hundred yards wide. We run and walk on the hard-packed sand and then scavenge along the high tide line. Huge piles of Bull kelp lay scattered among driftwood, old buoys of all colors, skeletons of dead shags (a seabird), old nylon ropes, crates, mussel shells and more. The major find is the skull of a Right whale.

At dusk we begin the kiwi hunt in earnest. We search fruitlessly in an area close to the bay, then try another spot further away. No kiwis, not even a call. We walk around and then stand around until we are freezing. Finally we return to the hut to drink hot cocoa and warm up. Tass has two large blisters from the Chocolate Swamp and decides to call it a night. I head back out alone.

After a twenty minute hike I arrive at an area that is a known kiwi hangout. The weather alternates between starry skies and light drizzle. I snoop around with my flashlight, looking in the tall grass and bushes when the sky is clear and standing stoically under the branches of large trees when it rains.

Then it happens. At midnight I hear the loud, hoarse call of a female kiwi. My heart pounds as I race toward the sound as fast as I can, trying not to let my rain pants swish and make too much noise. I stop and listen again for what seems like an eternity until I hear the puffing, wheezing noise of the kiwi. Kiwis find grubs and worms by poking their long beaks under dead leaves and into rotting logs. Since the bird's nostrils are at the end of its beak, dirt and leaves often get caught in its nose as it sniffs for food. When its nostrils become plugged the Kiwi simply snorts and sneezes to clear the passage. At the sound of the next snort I aim my flashlight and turn it on. All I see is a small mound before me. The kiwi must be just on the other side of the rise. I take six quick steps and suddenly stop. Directly in front of me is an 18-inch tall, female Stewart Island Brown kiwi.

The kiwi is totally uninterested in me and seems unoffended by my flashlight. She goes about her business, probing the soil with her long beak, searching for worms. She moves at a steady pace, and I have to move quickly through the grass to keep up. It walks unlike any bird I have seen, with no trace of the bobbing neck syndrome common to other birds. I follow her for a minute and then suddenly she steps into a small patch of grass and disappears. I search the entire area, but the kiwi has given me the slip.

Half stunned, I don't know what to do. Should I wait around in hopes of seeing another one? Should I go get Tass and come back with her to try to spot another kiwi? Or should I just get out of the cold rain and go to bed? I walk across the field and suddenly right in front of me is another kiwi! Again I follow it for a minute until it disappears into thick bush. Now I know what to do. I have seen two birds so there must be more.

I run back to the cabin, wake Tass, and we both scurry back to the field. We stand and listen till 2 a.m., hear a few calls, make a couple of wild chases toward the sounds, which lead us splashing into bogs, but we see nothing. Finally, exhausted, we call it quits and head to bed.

We spend the next morning walking on the beach and the afternoon scouting out new areas for kiwi watching. As it grows dark we break out the flashlights and begin our evening search. Again we hear calls and frantically run from one area to another to get a sighting. We hike through swamp, bush and forest to no avail. After four hours we return to the hut for a late supper. By the time we start a fire, cook our meal, eat and clean-up, we are exhausted. It is late, and we can't seem to make ourselves put on our cold, wet boots. Tass is sad she didn't see a kiwi but not sad enough to go back out into the night rain.

On the hike back across the island we finally become one with the mud. After constantly trying to find routes around big, mucky bogs on the hike in, we now slog straight through even the swampiest sections. On the part of the trail where the tree roots hang over the path Tass tells me she is having difficulties walking, that she can't get to the **root** of her problem. In a follow-up pun she christens the path the Alex Hailey Memorial Trail. Two days later we emerge from the bush looking like a couple of kids who have been wallowing in the mud for a week. We have.

We would like to stay longer on Stewart Island but it is time for another rendezvous. My brother, Mark, and a good friend, John Moritz, are flying into Christchurch for a ten-day vacation. We show up at the airport just in time to meet Mark and John as they get off the plane. They rent a car, which we christen the Red Rocket, and we all pile in for a whirlwind tour of the South Island.

Our first stop is Mt. Cook. When Tass and I were here with Chuck, storm clouds kept us from seeing any of the mountain. This time the weather is perfect. The next day is Mark's birthday. Mark and John announce they are going to treat themselves, and us, to a plane ride over the mountains. We take off from the narrow valley floor and gain altitude by circling an immense bed of scree and boulders left by retreating glaciers. We fly up the Tasman Glacier, a snow-covered river of ice up to 2,000 feet thick with 11 miles of skiable terrain. Further up the mountain ravines of twisted and fractured ice give way to steep snowfields and rock faces jutting into the air. We buzz around the summit of 12,346-foot Mt. Cook and then fly to the western side of the range to land on the Franz Joseph Glacier.

Fox glacier, South Island, New Zealand.

The Franz Joseph Glacier was named by an overtly patriotic geologist who happened to be the first European through the area. Because of his lack of imagination this timeless creation of nature is stuck with a dated name of a king from another continent. Nearby Mt. Cook is named after a ship captain who never laid eyes on the summit. The Maori name for the peak is *Aurangi*, which means "Cloud Piercer." It is a descriptive name, full of dignity. The name Mt. Cook conjures up an image of a sea captain, or a frying pan.

The ten days with Mark and John pass quickly. Before we know it we are back at the airport gate, only this time we are waving good-bye. Tass and I get an empty feeling as we watch Mark and John board the plane but nothing as traumatic as the last time we said good-bye to Mark at the lonely campsite in northern Utah.

We pedal west out of Christchurch toward Arthur's Pass, but on the second day we run into a big storm. The road ahead goes into the mountains well above snowline, so we decide to play it safe and ride up the east coast. The same day we talk to a traveler who tells us that a large *sing-sing*, a dance festival which we hope to see in Papua New Guinea, will be in September, not October as we had originally thought. Panic sets in. Suddenly our schedule is too full. If we go to the *sing-sing* that will only leave us two months in Australia, which hardly sounds like enough time. We spend a rainy morning in our tent pouring over maps and plotting routes. We decide to abandon the idea of one more hike on the South Island and make plans for a hasty exit of New Zealand.

Another storm brings a cold wind and rain showers. We ride in freezing rain and arrive at the North Island ferry on June 8th, the first day of winter. As we ride across the North Island we encounter more nasty weather. Suddenly it seems crazy to be wasting valuable time fighting New Zealand storms when Australia and warmer weather are calling. We hop on a bus to Auckland, spend a weekend exploring the northern coast with our friends Mark and Sue, and catch a flight to Australia.

5

G'Day Mate

We arrive in Sydney, Australia on June 19th. After assembling the bikes we ride into the city in search of a cheap hotel. It will take some time to get our visas for Papua New Guinea and Indonesia, so we pay for a week's rent at the Young Travelers Hostel. The first two nights we share a room with a woman from England; when she moves out, a couple from Italy moves in. They sleep all day, party all night, and between the two of them smoke six packs of cigarettes per day. Under heavy pressure from us they agree not to smoke in the room when we are around, except for their last cigarette of the day, which is smoked at 4:00 a.m. as they noisily climb into bed.

By the end of the week we have seen most of the museums and much of the city. We retrieve our passports and pack up the bikes. Our plan is to ride west over the Great Dividing Range through the Blue Mountains and out onto the rolling plains that lead to the outback. We plot a route through a variety of National Parks and also plan to visit an old friend of mine from a trip I made through Africa ten years ago. Then we will return to the eastern coast and ride north to Cairns and the Great Barrier Reef.

It takes most of the first day just to get through Sydney. By late afternoon we finally leave the last suburb and begin our climb over the Great

Dividing Range. We ride on the Great West Highway, the main link between Sydney and all of western New South Wales. It is a busy road with little room for us. Cars and trucks roar by only inches away.

At Blue Mountains National Park we take a side road into an oasis of eucalyptus trees and small, rocky canyons. A friendly ranger fills us in on the whereabouts of a small mob of Grey kangaroos that have recently been reintroduced into the area.

There are 59 species in the kangaroo family. This includes the familiar Red and Grey kangaroos and also the lesser known wallabies, Tree kangaroos, Rat kangaroos, the Pademelon and the Potoroo. Our recently purchased marsupial book has all sorts of hints on discerning various species, like whether the tip of the nose is hairy, partially hairy, or hairless, or whether the color of the fur is red, reddish brown, or brownish red. From the looks of things it may take some time to become "roo" experts.

We spot our first kangaroos at dusk feeding on a nearby hillside. It is too dark to use binoculars so we are unsure about the amount of hair on their noses, but we guess they are Grey kangaroos. We watch in excitement until they slowly hop out of sight.

We spend the next few days bicycling, hiking and birding as we cross the Blue Mountains, rugged country with towering limestone cliffs and deep canyons. It is winter in Australia. Some mornings the frost on our tent is so thick we knock it off in big sheets. But each day we are in shorts by noon. It is perfect riding weather.

Between stopping to observe birds--there are 53 species of parrots and lorrikets alone in Australia--and visiting with friendly locals, we slowly move westward. The hills become less pronounced, forests give way to cultivated farmland. I love biking across such open country. We crest small rolling hills and look out at broad valleys with the next ridge, miles away, shrouded in a blue haze. Then, maybe hours or even days later, we arrive at the ridge and gaze at the next goal in the distance. It is exhilarating to look back over our shoulders and see mountains, crossed days ago, receding on the horizon. The land is immense, the sky vast, and we are two tiny dots slowly but inevitably crossing the landscape under our own power.

After a week of riding we arrive in Dubbo, and I dig out a notebook with directions to Barbara Rogers house. I met Barbara 11 years ago, in 1974, when I was traveling with my sister on an overland trip through Africa. Barbara was the oldest member of our group and gained everyone's respect as a hard worker who never complained when the trip got rough, which was quite often. Now Barbara meets us at the front gate of her 40-acre farm with a loud cry and a big hug. We get a tour and are introduced to her cat, two dogs, two birds, six cows, and seven horses.

The first night Barbara digs out slides of Africa and we laugh and tell stories of old times. Barbara caught malaria during the trip but didn't find out till nearly a year later when she suddenly became deathly ill. She was sick for another year before she recovered. Luckily she has not had another attack.

Barbara asks about our plans. We tell her we would like to go further into the outback but we are unsure how much time we should spend riding west. If we are going to be in Papua New Guinea for the September *sing-sing* we only have two months to visit a growing list of National Parks and ride up the east coast. Barbara suggests we save time by catching a lift into the outback, and promptly calls some friends to find us not only a ride, but also a family to stay with "back of Bourke."

"Back of Bourke" is Australian slang for "out in the sticks." The family we are going to visit lives west of, or "back of" (if you live on the heavily populated eastern coast), the town of Bourke--which itself is a long way from anything else. The road from Dubbo to Bourke is famous as a lonely and desolate highway with long stretches of straight road, in some places over 75 miles without a single bend.

Green Creek Station, the home of John and Betty Holmes and their family, is 50 miles west of Bourke. We arrive after sunset to find a neighborhood party. The Holmes's "next door" neighbors, one family who lives 12 miles away, the other 20 miles away, are in for supper and a few beers. Things go smoothly for the first ten minutes, until Betty asks us what we want to eat. We are both vegetarians, yet we don't want her to go to any special effort to feed us. We say we will make do with whatever they are eating, thinking we would pass on the meat and fill our plates with whatever else is on the table. But supper is huge quantities of steak, a platter of white bread, a few sauteed onions and one tiny bowl of sliced potatoes.

As we sit down, John, who has a rather boisterous way, asks, "Why don't you eat meat?"

"Oh John, let them eat in peace," Betty quickly comes to our rescue.

"No! I want to know why they don't eat meat," John replies with a roar. The volume of his voice instantly silences all conversation in the room. Everyone's eyes turn to us. Now, in a room full of three-meal-a-day meat eaters who butcher all their own food, we attempt to explain, without sounding judgmental, that we, personally, don't wish to kill animals.

"Well, um," I begin, "we believe people who eat meat should be willing to kill animals themselves. Since we are not comfortable butchering animals, it seems hypocritical to eat meat someone else has killed."

"We simply eat lower on the food chain," Tass tries to help me out, "and get our protein from plants." From the shocked look on many faces we stop any further explanations.

"Well, I've heard of a vegetarian," speaks up a fellow on the far side of the table, "but I've never met one." Another crusty character nods in agreement. But Warden, John's son-in-law, is absolutely dumbfounded. He has never heard of such a thing. Since we just bicycled from Sydney to Dubbo no one can argue that a person will die without eating meat, even though that is what they are all thinking. The rest of the night we try to blend into the conversation, but the topic of vegetarianism repeatedly comes up, prompting jokes about our eating grass and weeds with the sheep.

The next morning I skip my daily meditation just to make sure I am sitting at the kitchen table when John gets up. Whatever else he believes, I am determined that he won't think I am a lazy sleepy-head. As the sky slowly turns bright orange, the roosters crow in the yard, parrots squawk in the trees, and the bandsaw whines in the butcher shed while Betty grinds through bones as she cuts up a sheep. Breakfast is lambchops, white bread and coffee. We pull out our box of museli, an untoasted granola, and listen to comments about our meal looking like bird seed, which it does. After a few jokes John relents and somewhat apologizes.

"I guess I was a little hard on you two last night" he mumbles.

"Thats O.K.," we joke back, "now it is our turn to give you a bad time." Despite the comments it is mostly we who continue to get ribbed, but now

John Holmes with his two dogs, Pepsi and Cola, ready to muster sheep, New South Wales, Australia.

63

there is a lack of malice in the jokes.

After breakfast John and Lance, the farmhand, go out to mark calves. We head to the corral to watch. Each calf gets a tag in one ear and a big square chunk cut out of the opposite ear if it is a heifer, or two chunks if it is going to become a steer. John sharpens his pocket knife on a stone before castrating the males, and, last of all, a hot branding iron is pressed onto the animal's flanks. Although both Tass and I grew up in ranch country this is the first time either of us has watched the marking process. It is a rough and violent affair.

Fifty cattle must be sorted and loaded onto a truck to be driven to another paddock 170 miles away. I help run groups of cattle from one pen to another to cull out specific cows. The other hands use plastic hoses to whack the cows along the chutes while the truck driver uses an electric prod. The cows scramble down the wooden chutes, sometimes panicking in wide-eyed confusion and getting stuck sideways in the narrow rampways. They are poked, kicked, swatted, and cursed until they are all in the trailer. There is room for one person in the cab so I climb aboard for a ride further into the outback. Meanwhile, Tass joins Betty and one of the daughters on a trip to town. It will be an all day ride for both of us.

Outback roads are unpaved and twice the width of a normal highway. The center of the road is built to sustain the weight of loaded trucks. Since many roads are only graded every three years, they are terribly corrugated, especially in the center. Cars and empty trucks drive on the sides. The truck I am in blasts down the road at high speed trailing an enormous cloud of billowing dust. At times the cab shakes so violently I expect the windows to crack. The driver and I yell at each other trying to carry on a conversation. The noise of the truck, combined with his outback accent and Aussie slang, makes me continually ask him to repeat what he says.

We pass groups of emus, the second largest bird in the world. It is great to watch them race next to the truck before bolting into the bush. Their three-foot-long legs look like they are moving in slow motion, a deceiving appearance as emus can run over 30 miles per hour. Like the ostrich and the kiwi, emu feathers have no barbules, the tiny velcro-like hairs that zip feathers together. The loose feathers sway like great floppy mops while the emu gallops. The emu is another bird that breaks the male-female stereotype. The male alone broods the eggs and then spends up to eighteen months escorting and protecting his new family. Sometimes the female remains in the nest vicinity, occasionally accompanying the male and the young; sometimes she wanders off to find a different mate.

On the drive back to Green Creek Station we drop the truck off at the neighbors, and I ride with John the last 20 miles to the house. John asks me a few more questions about why I don't like to kill animals. I try not to sound judgmental of his lifestyle without compromising the things I feel.

Suddenly, John spots a Grey kangaroo. He pulls off the road with the headlights shining toward the roo, grabs his rifle, and with one bullet shoots the animal through the heart. He throws the roo in the pick-up and says, "Got to feed my dogs." We drive home in silence. I get the feeling that while this is a normal occurrence, it is also John's way of reaffirming in front of me his own life choices.

Back at the house we joke around the table as John tells tales of the outback. He is actually quite a charismatic fellow. He is also very interested in America and constantly asks us what we think about things. We have some great laughs.

The next morning Tass and I go birding. Trees and shrubs dot the landscape but little else grows in the bright red soil. The earth is dry and dusty. Rainfall is sporadic, but when it does rain it can rain very hard. A light rainfall will sprout grass in one or two days. A good storm with two or three inches will enable the sheep to graze for four months. Despite its desert-like appearance the outback is full of wildlife. In three hours we spot 43 species of birds, 14 of which are first-time sightings. We also find plenty of trash and animal bones.

Back at the house, Sandy, one of the daughters pulls the dead kangaroo out of the truck. The farmyard comes alive as she quarters it. The dogs, chained at various places around the property, yelp loudly. The cats, chickens and pigs all crowd in close to the action. Sandy cuts chunks of meat off the roo and throws them toward the hungry audience. Each animal grabs a chunk of meat and drags it to a corner. Within minutes the kangaroo has disappeared.

As I watch the activity I wonder how many people would have pets if it meant shooting an animal, carving it up, and throwing it, half covered with fur and the other half covered with flies, into the dirt for the dog or cat to eat? Most people want their animals to refrain from such carnal banquets. People often rush to stop pets from eating the mouse cornered in the basement, the bird caught in the yard. Even if the mouse or bird is already dead people don't want their pet to eat it. Families prefer to feed the pet in a nice, yellow doggy dish on a well-mopped linoleum floor. Like all ranchers, the Holmes family simply sees firsthand the reality of being a carnivore--something has to die for them to eat.

After three days at Green Creek Station we reluctantly pack up to catch the truck back to Dubbo. John tells us of an old saying: Once a person travels into the outback past the Darling River, they will always come back. We believe that will be true for us.

Back in Dubbo we pick up our bicycles and say good-bye to Barbara before heading out for Warrumbungle National Park. Like many of our sidetrips, there is no available food at our destination so we have to carry four days of food and kerosene. I load my panniers with two pounds of oatmeal, a pound of museli, two pounds of powdered milk and a pound of brown sugar--and that is just for breakfast. I also carry peanut butter, honey, margarine, raisins, peanuts, three oranges, two apples, three pears, some broccoli, an onion, carrots, macaroni and cheese, lentils, two blocks of cheese, and a stove with enough fuel to cook eight meals. Since Tass carries the camera gear she gets off easy: one lunch bag full of dried fruit and nuts, two loaves of bread, a jar of mayonnaise, a pound of rice, a few apples, our plates, utensils, fry pan and five different spices in little canisters.

The road is covered with poorly laid patches. Mounds of tar and gravel, which were never flattened when laid down, stick up everywhere like mini speed bumps. We climb into the mountains, and come to a side road leading up a peak to a group of telescopes. We take the detour, and quickly shift into "granola gear," our non-sexist name for our little chainring (often called a granny gear). The road is so steep that even in "deep granola," the lowest of the climbing gears, we must zigzag from side to side to work our way up the road. We sprint the last quarter mile just for fun and arrive on top with burning lungs and wobbly legs.

The Warrumbungle range is a steep group of mountains with exposed rock pinnacles from ancient volcanic activity. The hills are covered with White Box trees, but the valleys are clear and have good grazing resulting in a large kangaroo population. Back down off the mountain we ride through fields full of Grey kangaroos before stopping at an isolated campground. We search a nearby field and find the spot with the most kangaroo droppings to pitch our tent. We feel like having neighbors. The sun sinks behind the mountains as we eat under the open sky. It is a wonderful night to be alive.

We spend the next day hiking the ridgetops to get a closer look at the rock formations. Time and erosion have removed all but the hardest rock. Lava plugs from volcanic extrusions stand in forests of eucalyptus and gum. Returning to camp we have a remarkable encounter with a female Red-necked wallaby. When we meet on the trail the four-foot high kangaroo makes no move to hop away. Tass digs for the camera as the wallaby bounds over and starts sniffing my shoulderbag.

"Wait until I have the camera ready before you lure the roo next to you!" Tass admonishes me.

"Who's luring?" I reply. The wallaby is nearly in my lap, trying to get its nose into my bag--it smells our gorp. I grab a peanut and throw it to the ground, creating a diversion. Even though the wallaby seems gentle I want to be careful. Kangaroos have very strong legs and lethal claws.

When attacked by dogs, larger kangaroos can grab the attacker with their forearms, rear back on their tails, and with one powerful kick from their hind leg, use their claw-like toenail to rip open the dog's stomach.

Kangaroos have also been known to hop into waist deep water, grab a pursuing dog, and drown it.

So we cautiously warm up to the wallaby. I feed it peanuts and we let it lick our hands clean of salt. The wallaby gently nibbles at Tass's rings, delicately holding Tass's hands in its front paws, careful not to claw her. The roo has big brown eyes and thick black eyelashes. It looks much like a deer, except for its split front lips, which resemble a camel or a rabbit.

The next day we set off on a Koala expedition. The name Koala comes from an Aborigine word meaning "non-drinking." The Koala gets all the water it needs from its weird diet of gum leaves, which often contain poisonous oils including cyanide.

We find a Koala thirty feet up a gum tree. Although they are called "bears," the slow moving animals are actually marsupials with a pouch that opens upside-down toward the mother's rear. This means baby Koalas, which are born in a semi-embryonic state, must always hold onto their mother's fur, even when sleeping, or they could fall out of the pouch. The reason the pouch is upside down may be due to the Koala's diet. The pouch gives the baby access to its first solid food--the mother's feces. Some scientists believe this introduces microbes into the baby's stomach which will later help it digest the toxic gum leaves.

We leave Warrumbungle and head east, back through the Great

"Skippy," a tame wallaby who frequents campgrounds in search of hand-outs and a scratch behind the ear, Gibraltor Range National Park, Australia.

Dividing Range. After stopping in two more national parks we drop back to the coast. Despite growing up in landlocked South Dakota (or maybe because we grew up there!), we both love being at the ocean and living on the beach. The weather is perfect, warm but not too hot. We take an entire week to travel up the 15-mile Gold Coast, a series of small towns that have grown together into Australia's most commercialized resort area. After nine days camping alone in three different national parks in the mountains, it's exciting to be a part of the gregarious beach scene. The crowds are fun and everyone is friendly.

We dally further north on the Sunshine Coast. This time it is the appeal of empty beaches and privacy that lures us into spending four days at Noosa Heads National Park.

Our next major stop is nearly 600 miles further north at the town of Arlie Beach, a step-off point for the Whitsunday Islands. We store our bicycles, buy a stockpile of food, and head for a local boat taxi service. After a day studying charts and scheduled runs, we catch a ride on a boat going by uninhabited Henning Island. For $60 U.S. the boat makes a detour to drop us, our gear, and 20 gallons of fresh water on the island's sandy beach.

As the boat leaves we carry our belongings just far enough to get past the high tide line and set up camp near the shade of a tree. "Our" island is three miles long and a quarter of a mile wide. We have a week of romance all alone camping on the beach. It is valuable time, giving us a chance to totally relax, have long talks, and stare dreamily at each other. Even soul-mates need to take time to make sure their relationship is running smoothly.

We wake before sunrise each morning to the sound of the Kookaburra revving up its howling chuckle. By 7 a.m. we have finished our morning meditations and the breakfast fire is crackling. Since we normally cook over a stove, it is fun to have a fire, not only for cooking, but also to sit around while reading, or simply to stare into.

We snorkel four times a day. The water quality is not as clear as we had hoped, visibility is 30-40 feet, but we still see a variety of fish and coral. One of my favorite coral growths is a huge ball the size of two cars growing off the ocean floor. Its surface is a network of fat, four-inch-long spikes that look like a collection of cow teats on a huge udder. Most of the spikes have small, fuzzy tenacles poking out of the end, each looking like a little toilet bowl scrubber. They come in every color: blue, green, orange, and yellow. This is the living part of the coral that spreads its tenacles to grab all the microscopic taste treats floating past. When we get too close to the bristly creatures, they fold up like inverted umbrellas and disappear into the hard casing faster than we can blink.

Just as we are about to run out of fresh water our week is up and the

68

boat comes to take us back to Arlie Beach.

We resume pedaling northward through sugar cane country. The sun beats down without mercy. We ride past a number of dead animals lying on the side of the road. With the heat, the smell of putrefying flesh hangs in the air around each carcass. We try not to breathe as we ride past but that only works on a limited basis.

Death on the road has no dignity. The bodies on the pavement have been run over so many times that the remains look like a gruesome collage adhering like patchwork to the road: hides squished paper thin, bones crushed into the tar, teeth pummeled into the pavement until they look as if they are growing out of the road itself. The bodies of once beautiful animals are laid to waste. Food for flies.

Why does death make me so sad? The alternative would be to live forever, which would be fun for the first 500 years but then things would get rather redundant. As much as I enjoy life I'd go bonkers if it never ended. There has to be more to existence than life on planet Earth, no matter what its quality or length.

Sometimes the thought of death makes a mockery of my life. All the stuff I have collected, all my projects and hobbies, all the sports equipment I have acquired, all of it will mean nothing when I am dead. The things that I have worked on, the filing system in my study, my collection of books, it will all end up in garage sales or garbage cans, or, if I have nostalgic relatives, stored in someone's attic. After they die someone else will throw it away.

The writer of Ecclesiastes says everything we do is vain, everything we create turns to dust. Sometimes I feel that way, yet what other choice do we have--to do nothing? That would also be rather boring! I want to do something with my time on earth. I want to have meaning in what I do with my life. I want an awareness, a positive quality in each day. The smashed bodies on the highway remind me of the importance of living right, because death is real.

We don't go far up the coast before we stop again, this time on Magnetic Island. It is a small island, five miles in diameter with 1800 people living on a third of the land and the rest reserved as a national park. We camp in the yard of a small hostel on the grounds of a Uniting Church Camp.

A group of Aborigine kids staying at the camp want to know if we, being Americans, have met Michael Jackson or Mr. T. I teach them to play hacky sack, which is a big hit, and they give us a *didgeridoo* concert and perform some traditional ceremonies.

One evening three Aborigine group leaders come over to socialize. We talk about Australian national parks and some of the animals we have seen. Esther, a woman from Switzerland, asks Tass and me if we have ever seen Drop bears. Obviously, someone has duped Esther into believing in the mythical animal that attacks by dropping out of the trees onto victims' backs. Immediately, the three Aborigines pick up on the spoof.

"Aye, you 'ave to be careful 'round Drop bears. They can smell yer clothes miles away. That's what brings em in." Henry, a stocky Aborigine with a wide grin and a cowboy hat, leans forward to make his point. "To be safe in Drop bear country, just walk naked through the bush."

Wade, a tall, thin fellow with wild hair, adds his advice. "Git rid a Drop bears by whistlin like a fish."

"Not just any fish!" Lenny is quick to add. "Best is a Black perch."

We chuckle at his choice of color, while he follows up with more advice. "Whistle like a fish by puttin yer 'ead under water. All folks in Drop bear country carry a bucket a water with 'em into the paddock."

Poor Esther. Just as she finally wonders if everything is *fair dinkum*, Aussie slang for the honest truth, the topic changes to Aborigine culture. I ask Lenny about the technique used when playing a *didgeridoo*, the long

Bruce with Aborigine friends, Australia.

tube that makes an earthy, vibrating noise. It is played by continually blowing out the mouth, even while breathing in through the nose.

Suddenly, Henry sits up and tells Esther that Lenny is pulling her leg. Now everything Lenny says that is factual, Henry contradicts, saying it is not true. Henry sits in the corner and shakes his head like a protector who would not think of letting anyone dupe a confused foreigner. By the time we go to bed my jaws ache from laughing.

We planned on spending two days on the island but the diving is so good we stay five. The best snorkeling is in a small bay a ten-minute bike ride away. Most of the larger fish hang out below deep coral ledges. We find two two-foot-long blue and yellow Spotted angelfish under a 30-foot-deep coral head. We dive down and hold our breath as long as possible, then quickly surface, gasp for air, and redive for another look. This is repeated until we get dizzy and nearly hyperventilate. Finally, we get out of the water and lie in the sun on huge boulders until the goosebumps fade away and our equilibrium returns. Then it's back to the briny deep.

Some of the coral ledges are only inches from the sandy ocean floor. This is where we see most of the rays and stingarees. The rays stir up the sand by flapping their "wings" and then lay concealed under a dusting of sand with only their bulbous eyes poking up like two round periscopes. When we dive down to look under the ledges we hold on to the coral, pull our bodies down next to the sea floor and poke our noses under the shelves before we can see.

It is under this type of ledge that we see our first shark, a Banded Wobbegon, who is sleeping peacefully. It is four feet long with a wide head, a rounded nose, and a series of stubby feeler whiskers which make it look like a giant catfish. It is surprising a fish of its size can wiggle into such a tight place to sleep. The next day we find a Spotted Wobbegon in a similar hide-a-way. Our fish book says it is "probably dangerous." We don't wake it up to find out.

The only reason we leave Magnetic Island is the quest for even better snorkeling up the coast. We catch the ferry back to the mainland and resume riding north. We pass through Tully, the wettest spot in all of Australia with an average rainfall of 173 inches per year, over 14 feet, and yes, it rains when we ride through.

At Mission Beach we hike into the rain forests in search of the Australian cassowary. At a height of five feet, the cassowary is the second largest bird on the Australian continent, after the Emu. The flightless cassowary is famous for the large, blunt, horn-like growth protruding from its forehead, which it uses like a battering ram to part the thick jungle as it runs head down through the forest.

We spot a cassowary, but it is skittish and doesn't give us much time to view it before vanishing into the rainforest. We try to follow it into the thick undergrowth but are quickly stopped by woody tendrils and barbed vines. Shorts and T-shirts are not the clothes for chasing cassowaries. If we had crash helmets and shoulder pads we might have a sporting chance. However, the cassowary does leave us a memento of its passing, a glob of fresh scat. We use sticks to inspect the feces, a huge lavender pile, the consistency of mashed potatoes, containing eight golf-ball-sized pits from some type of wild fruit. Cassowaries have a big mouth and throat and can eat large fruits in one gulp. Perhaps we have found an animal that eats as much as we do.

Although our destination is Cairns and the Great Barrier Reef, we turn inland for a five-day loop onto the Atherton Table Lands, a plateau off the coast that is a few thousand feet above sea level. As we climb we leave the sugar cane fields and enter vegetable garden and dairy country. Fruit stands appear along the highway, and we stop often for fresh produce. I have an insatiable craving for tomatoes and papaya, we buy huge bags daily. We camp in various national parks along the route, meet a few

Tass covered with wild Rainbow lorikeets, Currumbin Bird Sanctuary, Queensland, Australia.

groups of bicyclists touring the Table Lands, visit the famous town of Kuranda on market day, and then make an exhilarating downhill ride into the town of Cairns.

September 6th is our sixth wedding anniversary. We celebrate by treating ourselves to a snorkeling trip on the Great Barrier Reef. We join twenty other people, most of whom will be SCUBA diving, for a two-day trip to the outer reefs on a 112-foot ship. Our budget keeps us from renting tanks and regulators for diving. But since most of the reef life is in the first thirty feet of water just below the surface, which we can easily reach while snorkeling, we think we'll have just as much fun as everyone else.

At noon we arrive at Michaelmas Cay, a seabird sanctuary that is a small sand spit surrounded by coral reefs. We make repeated dives all afternoon and spend the evening studying our fish guidebook to confirm the day's sightings. The most exciting find is a huge, white-tipped shark resting beneath a coral head. Unlike the Wobbegons on Magnetic Island, this fellow looks ferocious.

That evening about half the SCUBA divers decide to take a night dive. Only one other snorkeler is interested in trying it, so we go together to share the rental cost of a light ($5 U.S.). He goes out first and comes back soon saying the dive was kind of weird and black. He looks slightly spooked and heads for his cabin. Tass is now uncertain about going out, so I go next.

Since what little there is to see at night is mostly deeper in the water, I decide to use a small weight belt to help hold me down.

By the time I enter the water the divers are long gone, off somewhere far below. I am completely alone. The ocean is fifty feet deep where we are anchored. Since my light only penetrates 30 feet I find myself swimming in a great black void, unable to see the bottom. I have the hardest time making my way to the reef. It is impossible to tell if I am swimming in a straight line or going in circles. I constantly stop to take a bearing off the lights on the boat. Finally, I backstroke, but the weightbelt lowers me just enough that the ocean waves keep breaking over my face.

During the day the reef is bright and alive with fish. Now it is vacant and void of color. The few fish I see are half asleep. I swim up and touch them. A turtle appears and I pet it briefly before it wakes up to what is happening and bolts away.

Unfortunately, the weight belt throws off my balance. I now realize this is a poor time to have my buoyancy change. I don't automatically float to the surface--I have to swim to get there. The problem is that in the dark it is hard to tell when I am at the surface. I often think I am there and take a breath, only to find my snorkel is still a few inches below the water. My stomach is soon full of saltwater.

Suddenly, I catch a glimpse of something shiny out of the corner of my eye. When I shine the flashlight in that direction I see nothing. Again, something catches my eye. Finally it occurs to me to turn off my light. I float in total and utter blackness. At first I see nothing. After a moment I begin to see glowing shapes in my peripheral vision. A little shrimp-like creature, a quarter of an inch long, swims past inches from my face. It has a clear, see-through body with a small light like a fire-fly coming from its thorax.

Abruptly, a shining array of color appears in front of my mask. Startled, I flick on my light, but I can't see anything. Half afraid, I reach to feel if I can touch anything.

Nothing.

I timidly switch the light back off and instantly glowing colors appear before me. It looks like a phosphorescent jellyfish two inches from my face. I quickly turn the light back on and swim the opposite direction.

After a few more spooky episodes I return to the ship. Back on board I listen to the divers, who were in a group lead by an instructor, confess that their dive was unnerving. After hearing about all of us getting the willies, Tass decides to pass on the night dive.

The next day, after an early morning snorkel, our ship heads for Hastings Reef. When we drop anchor Tass and I are the first ones into the water. From the moment we hit the ocean we realize this is going to surpass any snorkeling experience we have ever had. The water is indescribably clear. Tass floats next to me, 60 feet above the ocean floor, as if she is suspended in space. The water's surface is a bright silver, like florescent mercury. We swim toward a large bommie, an immense coral growth rising up from the ocean floor. It is like snorkeling up to a six-story building covered with coral and surrounded by fish swimming up and down the sides of the wall. The colors leap at us: fish with electric blue stripes, neon red dots, and bright orange and fluorescent yellow bodies swim beside huge lavender staghorn coral, bright lime-green brain coral, yellow flowerets, and softly undulating pink and red coral fans.

The Great Barrier Reef is the largest living organism on the planet. It is an awesome experience to interact with such an abundance of life. We feel a communion with nature, with our own roots. We snorkel until we are frozen then return to the ship, warm up, and dive again and again. It is a day we will never forget.

On the boat we become better acquainted with three Canadians we met a week ago while bicycling the Atherton Table Lands. On returning to Cairns we camp together in the city caravan park. Russ, Kevin, and Tom are traveling around Australia in a van, carrying bicycles which they ride in scenic areas. When they leave for a week-long loop northward to Cape Tribulation, they offer us a lift. We accept, happy for the chance to see the

Bruce relaxing on the beach, Australia.

northern rainforests during our last week on the coast.

We head out with their bikes strapped on top and our bikes crammed inside along with the five of us, everyone's gear, and bags of food. We arrive at Mossman Gorge and set up camp in a drizzle. The next day the serious rains begin. We huddle in our tent and read the mail we picked up in Cairns--twenty-three letters!--and write return postcards.

It rains through the following morning, but in the afternoon the sun pops through the clouds. After two days in the tent we need a bath and some excitement, so we go for a quick dip in a creek reputed to be full of crocodiles. We don't go far into the water, however, and help each other keep an eye out for anything that looks like a fast moving log with big teeth.

The next day the dirt road has dried enough for us to get on our bikes and ride up the coast. We navigate around most of the mud until we come to a two-foot deep, forty-foot wide creek. Kevin, Russ and Tom all have mountain bikes and begin, one by one, to attempt the ride across. Kevin is the only one to make it without falling in and is so excited that he tries a repeat performance and fails miserably. Half-way across he flies head first over his handlebars into the creek. A perfect face plant.

Tass and I "give it a go" on our Trek road bikes and get a respectable half way across before we lose traction on the slick, moss-covered river

75

rocks. Further up the coast we ride onto the hard packed sand of an isolated beach and cruise up and down the coastline. It is exhilarating to ride on the beach with the wind blowing off the ocean, the smell of the sea, and the laughter of new friends.

On the ride back to Cairns we discuss our travel plans. Tass and I have been vacillating about our route and now make a major itinerary change. We wanted to go to Papua New Guinea and spend a few months hiking in the highlands. However the nightmare logistics of bringing our bikes to a country with few roads, finding places to store them, and always having to backtrack to pick them up after each hike makes us decide the idea is not practical.

The change of plans means the next country on our route is Indonesia. Since the Canadians are also going to Indonesia, we plan a rendezvous in Bali in ten days. With our new schedule we can now squeeze in one more adventure before leaving Australia. A month ago we purchased open airline tickets from Cairns, Australia, to Cairo, Egypt, that enable us to go any route we choose and stop as often as we want at no extra fee. Instead of flying to Papua New Guinea, we fly into the center of Australia to Alice Springs. We want to spend a week riding to Ayers Rock.

Our plane lands an hour before sunset. We reassemble our bikes on the sidewalk as the sky turns pink and then orange, and then ride a few miles from the airport and pull off the road to camp. The area is full of clumps of spinefex grass that leaves stinging needles in our legs if we brush against them. Everywhere else the ground is covered with goathead thorns. Once out of sight of the road we sweep the ground clean of burrs before pitching our tent. The soil is baked so hard we can't use tent stakes. Our bed feels like a slab of cement.

The next morning we ride into town. With a population of 15,000 people, Alice Springs is the second largest city in the Northern Territory. The Alice, as it is known locally, is surrounded by buttes of the MacDonnell range and lays along the dried-up creek bed of the Todd River. Groups of Aborigines sit in the hot sun in the dusty river bed. They look like displaced squatters, nothing to do but wile away the hours in scorched monotony.

The Aborigines came to Australia about 40,000 years ago. They are considered by many anthropologists to be the oldest culture on earth. Since most of Australia is either arid or semi-desert, the Aborigines developed a lifestyle adapted to living in a waterless environment. Scarce and valuable water was seldom used for bathing. Today a number of the Aborigines around the Alice still follow old traditions--they are surrounded by dust and dirt, and their bodies are similarly covered. Feet, arms, and faces go for days without being washed, clothing weeks and even months. Despite the heat, many wear heavy coats, sweaters and wool hats. All wear black or dark colors.

After a day exploring town we head into the outback. The weather is hot, the air incredibly dry. We go through quantities of ointment trying to keep our lips from chapping and cracking. The landscape is covered with mulga shrubs, acacia trees and a few desert oaks. The pointed clumps of spinifex grass are the only ground cover. The first night out we take a bumpy, dusty, eight-mile side road to the Henbury Meteorite Crater and camp next to a family in a four-wheel drive camper who refill our water containers.

The next day we see a few mirages. The desert landscape is harsh but has a desolate beauty that can be better appreciated at slow speeds. The scenery varies every 10 or 20 miles. Flat mulga-covered valleys turn into red sand dunes covered with spinifex grass. Rolling expanses of sparse vegetation give way to areas where recent bush fires have revitalized a delicate carpet of fresh green shoots.

In areas of rolling hills we keep a watch for billowing clouds of dust, the sign of an approaching road train, a huge truck pulling three oversized trailers. The tendency of the last trailer to weave makes road trains the undisputed king of the outback highways. Because of the narrow tarred roads in the outback, the outside wheels of road trains kick up huge amounts of dust and gravel. As the metallic monsters draw near, all other traffic slows and pulls to the opposite shoulder to let the trucks roar by, followed by an accompanying shower of gravel. Road trains are merciless to anything which opposes them. The weight of three long trailers combined with high speed means the drivers can't stop even if they want to--which they don't. The front of the truck is covered with reinforced bars and bumpers designed to remove, without the slightest damage to the truck, any cow, kangaroo--or bicyclist--that wanders in its path.

On the third day we crest a small rise and get our first view of Ayer's Rock, 20 miles away. The largest rock in the world rises abruptly out of a flat desert landscape to tower 1,140 feet above the sand and gnarled mulga bushes surrounding it. The rock is one solid piece of arkosic sand-stone--two and a half miles long, six miles around the base. Yet, like a giant red iceberg, only the top of the immense rock is exposed to the heat of the Australian sun. The majority of the rock lies hidden below the desert sands.

The Aborigines call it Uluru. Today none of them knows what the word means, or, if they do, they are not telling. The first white person to see the rock re-named it after George Ayers, a local politician. But the days of Ayer's Rock are over because the politicians have given it back. In 1985 the Australian government returned the land title to the Aborigines. The National Park Service, which will continue to manage the area, now leases the land from the old/new owners. Ayers Rock is Uluru once again.

We ride until we are within 12 miles of the rock and pitch our tent. We want to stay on the eastern side to see tomorrow's sunrise illuminate the rock. Early the next morning the soft pastel shades of orange and pink on the rock look unreal, like a painting propped on the horizon. After breakfast we ride to the national park village and campground. In the evening we ride to a lookout to watch the sunset colors from the western side.

The next morning we walk around the rock. As we hike we keep a constant lookout for small caves where we can escape the hot desert sun. They are surprisingly cool. Air conditioning, Uluru style. Inside some of the caves' Aboriginal artists have covered the walls with figures and patterns out of the Dreamtime. On the orange sandstone we see the marks of the Marsupial Mole Men and Hare Wallaby Women.

In the Dreamtime, mythical beings, the predecessors to the Aborigine race, walked the vast outback of Australia. It was an era before time existed, when legends were born. The Aborigines believe the earth's landscape, animals, and people were all created in the Dreamtime. The Dreamtime is both the background and the fabric of Aboriginal philosophy. The activities of the mythical beings of the Dreamtime represent an era long past. The Dreaming, however, is an ongoing state of mind that gives the Aborigines a link between the world of today and the actions and lessons of the world of the past.

Outside in the sunlight the landscape stretches to the horizon in a sea of desolate beauty. Our six-hour walk around Uluru gives us a chance to see the desert from yet another perspective. We walk through the desert shrubs and prickly spinifex grass in the cool season, which is a misnomer as it is never really cool here, and think of the nomadic Aborigines waltzing through the same landscape on a broiling summer day. They had no clothing for protection from the sun's rays or to help retain valuable body moisture. Neither did they have shoes to protect their feet from the spiny thorns or blistering sand.

Today, the owners of Uluru live in a reserve within the park boundary in an area surrounded by barbed wire with signs saying "Aboriginal Living Area--Do Not Enter" to keep the hordes of tourists, people like us, from invading their space. We stop at the one spot visitors are allowed, a general store, but it is closed. A group of girls play listlessly with a small ball on the porch. Their skin is caked with red-brown dirt, bites, and open sores. Their clothing looks like it has never been washed and has an intense odor. We smile at them and they shyly come next to us. Their faces have several days' accumulation of snot, which the flies consider a banquet. We stand surrounded by houses made of scrap corrugated tin and plastic tarps. The nearest town is 300 miles away. Like my own country's attempts to deal with an anachronistic indigenous culture, the

Australian government's present reaction is to give the people a chunk of land, an allowance of money, and hope they will somehow turn into middle-class consumers.

The desert gets an average of 14 inches of rain each year, usually in short, heavy rainstorms. Surprisingly, much of the plant life has evolved out of a tropical past, when rainfall was abundant. To adapt to the drier climate many bushes have modified leaf stalks which lose little moisture in the heat. Animals have also learned to survive in a dry climate with only sporadic cloudbursts. On one hike we find a Thorny Devil, a lizard with pointed armor plating. The lizard's skin is so porous that if it walks through any water the moisture is absorbed into small channels and travels up its feet and across its body to saturate the skin near the mouth. It then laps up the water with its tongue.

Other outback animals will mate only if there is an ample water supply. Some of the rodents have a gestation period of only a few weeks. After raising their young in lightning speed, they hastily repeat the process if there is still water around. But the animal that responds quickest to a rainfall is the Black-faced woodswallow. It builds its nest at the sight of a rain cloud developing on the horizon, and begins mating before the first drop of water hits the ground! It breeds as long as the moisture lasts.

The next day we climb Uluru with the family who gave us water at the Henbury Meteorite Crater. Tony and Margo Wood have been traveling in their four-wheel drive camper through the Northern Territory national parks for six weeks. Their son Tim, who is our age, has been traveling with them for much of the time, as was a daughter, who just left to go back to work.

We arrive at the base of the climb to find a chain railing along the lower exposed section of rock. A howling wind threatens to blow us off. The gale subsides once we are on top and we are rewarded with a view of the desert stretching out below us. In the distance we see the Olga formation, our next destination, 30 miles away.

The Olgas are a group of nearly 20 rocks, each large enough to be a complete mountain in itself, grouped together and sticking a thousand feet into the air. We arrive the next morning and hike into a mile-long canyon between two of the giant rocks, eight feet wide at the closest point, with walls 500 feet high. On the other side is a gigantic ampitheater, a region the Aborigines call *Katatjuta*, Many Heads. Our map shows we are south of the camp of the Opossum Men and north of the camp of the Mice Women.

In the evening we meet Tim Wood at the sunset viewing area. The Olgas turn bright, surreal red as the sun drops below the horizon. As it grows dark the three of us make camp in the desert, build a small fire, and sit beneath the stars. Tim works for the Australian conservation commission as a freelance environmentalist. He has helped live trap, examine, and release large groups of kangaroos. He has also worked on rhino programs in Africa. His "top story" is catching fresh water crocodile hatchlings in a four-foot-deep *billabong* swamp one night. Armed with small flashlights held between their teeth, he and a few other workers waded into the murky water, chin deep, and grabbed the eight-inch baby crocs as they swam by the light. Each croc was held between two fingers until there were four struggling and kicking hatchlings in each hand. Then the whole lot was thrown into a big bag and the process repeated.

"What about mom and dad?" I ask.

"We catch them too!" Tim replies with a grin. He helped live trap a crocodile four feet wide and over 17 feet long--a foot longer than the monster in the Darwin Museum. Tim tells us the big fellow is still alive, living up north on a croc farm.

Although he won't be there, Tim offers to let us stay at his house in Darwin when we pass through in a few days, and gives us the name of a "top birder" whom he suggests we contact. The next day we rendezvous with Tony and Margo, do more hiking, and then head bact to Uluru. Out of time, we get the first bus back to Alice Springs and a plane on to Darwin.

In Darwin we run last minute errands before flying into southeast Asia.

Tony, Margo and Tim Wood in the Olgas formation, Northwest Territory, Australia.

80

We need zippers repaired on our panniers and tent, more bike parts, and new walking shoes. We still don't have bird books for Indonesia and southeast Asia, and we need another Indonesian-English dictionary.

To make matters worse, Tass began developing boils at the Olgas. She has never had a boil in her life--now she has four: one on her back, her stomach, her thigh, and a small one on her cheek. They are the ugliest things imaginable and it is painful for her to sit, walk, or lie down. She bathes three times each day. Afterward I help replace the dressings over each wound.

Despite Tass's illness we phone John McKeon, the "top birder" Tim told us about, and make plans to get together on our last morning in Australia. John takes us on a whirlwind tour of the local rivers, marshes, mangrove swamps, sea shores, and even the city sewer ponds. We spot 34 **new** species in three hours! John knows the area and where to find birds. And no wonder, he has seen more Australian birds than anyone in the world! Of the 758 birds that live in Australia, or even occasionally migrate through, John has seen 719. Although we are not in the same league as John, after today our own bird count has soared. Tass has seen 235 species in Australia, and I am close behind with 233.

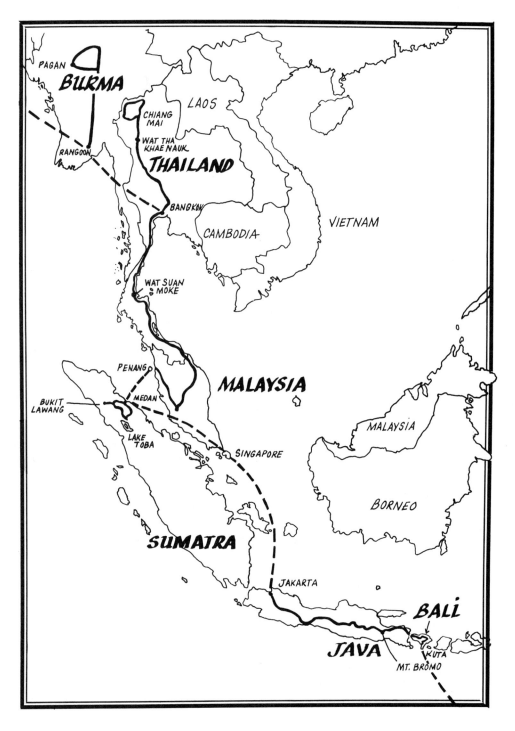

PAGAN
BURMA
RANGOON
LAOS
CHIANG MAI
WAT THA KHAE NAUK
THAILAND
BANGKOK
CAMBODIA
VIETNAM
WAT SUAN MOKE
PENANG
MALAYSIA
BUKIT LAWANG
MEDAN
LAKE TOBA
SINGAPORE
MALAYSIA
BORNEO
SUMATRA
JAKARTA
BALI
JAVA
KUTA
MT. BROMO

6

A Tour Of Heaven On Earth

We have heard horror stories about Indonesian drivers, yet the traffic isn't too suicidal from the airport to the town of Kuta, on the Indonesian island of Bali. The major difficulty is adjusting to the honking horns--the noise level on the crowded road is deafening. Every truck, bus, car and motorcycle honks when passing every other truck, bus, car, motorcycle, bicycle or even pedestrian. We join the cacophony and chuckle as we ring the bells I mounted on our bikes in Darwin, ding-a-linging everyone we pass.

Kuta is a bustling tourist center famous for its beaches and souvenir shops. The town is a maze of small streets and alleys called *gangs*, which are like wide sidewalks winding through stores bursting with crafts, clothes and art work. We ride up and down the *gangs* dodging traffic and gawking at all the sights trying to absorb everything at once.

We check into a *losmen*, a small inexpensive hotel designed like an upper class Balinese home. The property is surrounded by a six-foot wall which keeps out noise and creates a peaceful atmosphere. Inside, the buildings are snuggled against the wall creating a large courtyard in the center full of plants, flowering trees, religious statues and altars.

Our room is only a place to store luggage and sleep. A bare 40-watt bulb hangs from the ceiling next to a dilapidated fan; two single beds are the only furniture. All relaxing is done outside in the cool breeze with a bucolic view of the gardens. Our private porch has two comfortable bamboo chairs, a small writing table and a thermos of tea kept perpetually full.

We spend our first evening on the porch. Tass takes notes from a guidebook while I study Indonesian. I started learning the language during our last few weeks in Australia. Each day I put a list of 30 words in my handlebar map case and memorized the list while riding. Now I practice stringing phrases together. Two boys stop their work in the courtyard to tutor me. In return I help them with their English.

The next morning after a breakfast of black rice pudding and fruit salad we head to Kuta beach. The beach is full of topless sunbathers--mostly from Australia and Europe. The women of Bali, who were the original topless sunbathers, now wear blouses in concession to a western modesty that apparently no longer exists. A small troupe of native women flocks around us to offer a massage. We each get a wonderful 45-minute massage, complete with scented oils, for 1,000 *rupiahs* ($.90 U.S.). Each masseuse has a conical straw hat with a number so foreigners can find their favorite masseuse for a repeat. We like number 38.

Between catnaps on the beach we explore town. One evening as we

Tass, wearing a sarong and a temple sash, next to our favorite temple carving on the island of Bali, Indonesia.

84

are out for a walk, sidestepping pedestrians and food stalls and trying not to get run over when the crowded sidewalks force us into the street, we hear the sound of chanting and singing in a nearby temple. We pull out our temple scarves, which we bought our first day on the island and now always carry with us, and enter the courtyard.

Inside the compound 40 men sit on the floor singing the *Kecak* dance. It is a fast paced, frantic chant with frequent and abrupt changes in tempo and volume. When the pace quickens the group sits up at attention. Shoulders vibrate with the staccato rhythm, knees bounce in time on the floor. Even the facial expressions change--the eyes appear hypnotically intense. The pace of the chant reaches a crescendo. Everyone throws their arms into the air, shaking their hands wildly. Suddenly, half the group falls back into the laps of the men behind them. The song ends in gales of laughter. Many of the men lay comfortably in the arms of the people who caught them. It is a diverse group--old men in *sarongs*, businessmen in dress clothes, young men wearing T-shirts with foreign logos. Chanting together they capture the spirit of the island, a blend of traditional and modern lifestyles.

The next day our *losman* proprietor tells us of a large funeral ceremony in the capital, Denpasar. We pack a few things on the bikes and set out for the cremation, about 20 miles away. Unlike the relatively calm ride from the airport, the traffic between Kuta and Denpasar is fierce. Motorcycles, cars and diesel trucks roar up and down the road with wild abandon. The worst part is still the honking horns. We rely heavily on our mirrors for reassurance that the blasting horns from behind are not a last second warning of impending death but a polite though nerve-wracking reminder that a vehicle is passing.

Yet the biggest danger is not from behind, but from the front. The boundary between the right and left side of the road seems hazy; on the corners it is especially nebulous. The Balinese have a compunction to fill any space or void in the road. If there is a moment without oncoming traffic, all vehicles immediately fan out and use up the entire highway. When oncoming traffic appears the drivers on the wrong side of the road wait until the last moment to swerve back to their half of the tarmac.

At a stoplight in Denpasar both lanes on the intersection across from us fill with cars and motorcycles. By the time the light turns green a wall of vehicles is coming straight at us. Yet we are not alone. The cars and motorcycles on our side of the stoplight have similarly spread out to fill the highway. Like two charging armies, the mass of vehicles meet in the center of the intersection and are soon hopelessly jumbled together. Motorcycle riders rev the motors, slip the clutches, and inch their machines through the throng. We follow suit and work our way through the congestion. After the knot of vehicles clears, the road again becomes a two-way highway.

We arrive at the home of the deceased Brahmin to find a beehive of activity. Like so much of Indonesia, everything appears to be happening at once. The air is filled with music, crowds of people laugh and talk, women carry offerings in and out of the temple in the family's yard, and neighborhood children scurry about. While Tass shoots pictures, I join a throng of people sitting under an awning near a *gamelan* orchestra.

A *gamelan* looks and sounds like a small, rich-toned xylophone. The arms of the players swing rapidly in a blur of activity. Immediately after the musician strikes each note with a wooden hammer, he touches the resonating chime with his other hand to silence the vibration, making each note distinct and crisp. The orchestra is a collection of *gamelans* of various octave levels which are tuned slightly out of key to make the music shimmer. Accompanying music is supplied by guitars, drums, bells, chimes, cymbals and gongs. To the western ear Indonesian music can sound fast-paced, disjointed and chaotic. Yet the Balinese consider the *gamelan* music from the rest of Indonesia slow and boring; Balinese music has an even faster pace.

Four men work their way through the crowd giving out cigarettes and drinks. I accept a small drink and, like everyone else, gulp down the contents quickly. It is *arak*, a distilled rice brandy, which helps get me in the proper funeral mood--in Bali funerals are a time of music, dance, and hilarity. And why not? The Balinese believe when you die, between reincarnations, the spirit goes to a heaven that is just like Bali!

At mid-morning the crowd under the awning joins the throng on the street for the start of the procession. All traffic has long ago been halted by a group of structures sitting in the road. The most impressive is a three-tiered, thirty-foot-high golden tower covered with tinsel and an array of intricately painted designs, white scarves and small mirrored tiles. In front of the tower are two life-size wooden bulls covered with brightly colored paper. Both bulls have smiling painted faces. Large paper umbrellas shade their heads.

The body of the Brahmin, wrapped in white cloth, is carried out of the house by five men. It is unceremoniously hoisted into the air as the men clamber up the tower to place the body on the top tier. But the Brahmin is too heavy and unwieldly, and the men are unable to even get the body to the second level. Another group of men rushes forward and climbs over the tower, smashing tinsel and snapping decorations, trying to lend a hand. Finally the body is hoisted up to its resting place under a little awning on top.

The crowd is so noisy that even though I am standing next to a *gamelan* player I can't hear a single note. In front of the tower two men joke and laugh as they climb onto the backs of the wooden bulls. A group of 30 men suddenly congregates around the bamboo substructure of both the tower and the bulls, and, after a few strained and failed attempts and much shouting, picks up the burden, riders and all. The procession is underway!

First comes a long line of women carrying fruits, crafts and offerings on their heads. Next come a dozen priests dressed in black and white checkered robes with pointed black and white hats and red flowers tucked behind their ears. A full *gamelan* orchestra follows. A trio of *Legong* dancers, young girls who are allowed to perform Bali's most famous dance only until they have their first menstruation, are carried each on her own litter. The men carrying the bulls and their riders come next. Behind them a white cloth four feet wide and one hundred feet long precedes the tower. The cloth, held by a line of well dressed people, is a symbolic way in which friends and relatives help lift the tower. Everyone else follows behind. We join the mass of people swarming down the street, filling the road and spilling over to pack the sidewalks.

The *gamelan* orchestra plays with gusto, people shout and laugh, and tourists trip over each other taking photographs. The main comedy is the action of the men carrying the tower and the bulls. The Balinese believe in spirits, demons and ghosts. To ensure that the spirit of the dead man does not return to haunt anyone, both the bulls and the tower are jiggled, tilted, and spun in circles at each intersection to confuse the dead man's spirit so it can't find its way back from the cremation grounds. The tower sways precariously--it often seems the men will stumble over each other and fall with their heavy burden crashing on top of them.

Two men carrying long, forked poles rush ahead wherever low telephone and power lines cross the road and lift the lines so the tower won't catch the wires. Occasionally they struggle with one line while the group carrying the tower races at high speed toward another. Excited voices yell out warnings to the tower bearers who seem unable to stop or control their forward momentum. Just when it seems the inevitable crash will occur, the tower either stops, creating a backlash that sends the structure wobbling back into the crowd, or the men with the poles arrive just at the last second to prop up the lines as the tower lumbers through. Amazingly, after 30 minutes of winding through the streets of Denpasar, no one is electrocuted and not a wire is broken!

When the procession arrives at the cremation grounds the *gamelan* orchestra moves under the shade of an immense tree, playing continuously. The tower is left in a field while the two bulls are carried up a knoll and placed under a frail, thatched awning. The bamboo substructures are removed and a lid on the back of each bull is opened. The body of the Brahmin is carried from the tower and placed in the large bull. The small bull is filled with gifts. Moments later both are set on fire.

We sit for an hour and watch the bulls burn. A hose attached to a kerosene drum is occasionally thrust into the pyre to keep the flames roaring. It is the job of the eldest son to supervise the burning and, once the fire is out, examine the ashes to ensure all the remains burn completely. The orchestra continues playing as the crowd slowly disperses

Two young boys dressed as priests for a funeral celebration, Bali, Indonesia.

and another large funeral procession arrives. We walk over to a small pyre nearby built for a poor woman who lies dressed in her finest clothes between two kerosene-soaked trunks of a banana plant. I watch her son's face as he lights the fire. The act of cremation isn't viewed as being destructive. The Balinese believe it is a release, a gift, a freeing of the soul.

We stay in Kuta four days, long enough for the boils Tass picked up in Australia to heal, and then head out to explore the island. We plan to spend three weeks on Bali and use the remainder of our two-month Indonesian visa crossing Java before flying to Singapore. Since Bali is only 90 miles long and 35 miles wide, we should be able to ride nearly every road on the island and still have time to relax on a few sandy beaches.

Our first stop is the town of Ubud, 30 miles inland on the lower slopes of one of the island's four main volcanoes. It is a small town spread out through lush green fields of rice. Ubud is the cultural center of Bali and is famous for its art, music and dance. We arrive to find the main street lined with 40-foot high bamboo poles called *Penjors*, a symbol of the Great Serpent of Prosperity. Large woven bamboo designs, much like a God's Eye, hang from the top of the *Penjors* causing the thin end of each pole to droop toward the street like a giant fishing pole bending from the weight of a trophy catch. At the base of each pole is a bamboo shrine loaded with offerings of rice, flowers, incense and fruit.

The day of our arrival is also market day, which occurs every third day in Ubud. We slowly work our way through the maze of stalls, practicing our Indonesian by bargaining with the vendors and asking about the vegetables, fruits and cooked foods at each stall. We also follow the locals through the market and slyly listen to them bargaining to see what they pay for food. Bali is a land of fruit. More than 200 varieties grow on the island. Some of these can be found in other parts of Asia or Indonesia, some are found only on Bali. We find familiar fruits like bananas, pineapples, mangoes, and papayas, plus exotic fruits like guava, pomelo, mangosteen, starfruit, nangcur, rambutan, durian and zurzat. We try a new fruit each time we go to the markets. Today our favorite is the salak, which looks like a huge, brown strawberry with scaly, reptilian skin. The skin flakes off to reveal a fruit with the texture of an apple that tastes like a mixture of almonds and strawberries.

We flag down a vendor pushing a cart on bicycle wheels and buy a serving of *gado-gado*. The cook fills a bowl with crisp steamed vegetables, fresh peeled cucumber, bean sprouts and a handful of homemade sesame sticks. He smothers it all in a spicy peanut sauce and tops it off with an egg fried in coconut oil. Each serving costs 350 *rupiahs* ($.30 U.S.). This is a hungry bicyclist's paradise!

After trying half the food in the market we change into our temple clothes and head for the main temple. Two celebrations are now

Women carry offerings to the temple during the Pruscita Bhumi *celebration, Bali, Indonesia.*

occurring in Ubud. The first is an anniversary for the Great Hall Temple. This is normally held twice in the "Western" calendar year. The celebration must vary according to the positive and negative forces in the world; since the last celebration was simple, this ceremony will be large and festive.

The second ceremony taking place is a series of celebrations called *Pruscita Bhumi*, Purifying Mother Earth. All the festivals, dances and prayers of this celebration will come to a crescendo in a purification ritual on October 6th, five days away. *Pruscita Bhumi* last took place in the 1930's and is being held again because the Balinese feel the earth is out of harmony. The Balinese believe the world is created through two opposing forces which interact together to produce life. The role of humans is to help keep these two forces in balance. Supplications are made to encourage the actions of good spirits, and appease the anger of evil spirits. During *Pruscita Bhumi* offerings are also made to Mother Earth to appologize for the bloodshed of past wars, for excesses on the part of some Balinese in striving after tourist dollars, and for imbalances in various relationships and interactions: human and human; human and nature; human and spiritual.

The temple complex is a large courtyard surrounded by a four-foot high stone fence. Inside only three buildings have walls, the rest are simply awnings built for protection from the sun and rain. A *gamelan* orchestra plays in the outer compound while another orchestra plays a different tune in the inner courtyard 100 feet away. The entire complex is filled with people making offerings. Palm leaves are woven into various shapes with intricate designs cut into the fibers. Flowers and rattan sculptures are arranged with offerings of food and rice.

Elegant women bring three-foot-high offerings of fruit, beautifully arranged on large plates and balanced on their heads. Despite their heavy loads they move easily and gracefully. Each offering will be blessed and, at the end of the ceremony, taken back home and eaten.

I sit and watch two men create a ten-foot fruit sculpture. They work slowly, checking and rechecking each piece. Like workers all over the island, they don't appear to hurry. The emphasis is on making the sculpture perfect, not on finishing the task quickly. Nonetheless, much is accomplished. Temples overflow with offerings. Stores are full of carvings, paintings, and weavings. Yet in workshops people are always happy to stop to speak with us. The Balinese seem to have found a balance between action and rest, between accomplishment and relaxation.

During the next few days, between viewing ceremonies and visiting markets, we bike and hike throughout the area. Most of the rain forests were cut down long ago and the land was formed into rice terraces. One of the areas near Ubud that has escaped the ax and plow is the Monkey

Forest, a group of trees surrounding an old Temple of the Dead. On a path into the forest a young Indonesian entrepreneur sells peanuts to feed the monkeys, who have become spoiled from the daily feedings by villagers and tourists. The result of all this goodwill is the monkeys now expect, even demand, that people give them food. When the monkeys see someone with food they charge forward en masse to be the first to get a snack. If the food isn't promptly handed over, the bigger monkeys threaten with loud hisses and barred teeth. I have a heart-stopping, eye-to-eye standoff with a big male, and for a moment I wonder if he is going to lunge on top of me. But I hold firm to my banana. Meanwhile, his buddy sneaks up from behind and bites my leg.

After our first confrontation we are more careful during other visits, slyly sidestepping the big males to enjoy the smaller members of the troupe. They gently climb on us in search of treats, which we now wisely keep hidden. One afternoon while Tass is squatting down changing a lens on her camera, a monkey sneaks up behind her, jumps on her back and starts to groom her. Nimble little monkey fingers comb through her long, blonde hair, searching for bugs and mites. Not finding anything, the monkey decides she has already been groomed and gives up the search.

We also visit a variety of ancient temples, trying to get a better understanding of the Balinese religion, which has changed much from its original Hindu roots. The Balinese are not concerned with doctrinal

A family of monkeys, Bali, Indonesia.

issues: they have no sermons, no creeds, hardly even a defined idea of what is believed much less dogma concerning those beliefs. It could almost be called a doctrineless religion. Yet elaborate ceremonies and festivals abound. The main job of the priests, who are not teachers as much as technicians, is to figure out when each ceremony should begin. Because of the complexity of the Balinese calendar, figuring auspicious dates is a full time job.

The Balinese year has 210 days and four main types of concurrently running weeks. In each year there are 21 ten-day weeks, 35 six-day weeks, 42 five-day weeks and 70 three-day weeks. There are even a few one-day weeks thrown in just to keep things interesting. Sacred days are usually when the first or last day of various weeks coincide. All of this is woven together with the lunar cycle to form a calendar which looks like it was designed by an Einstein gone mad.

Figuring out the time of day for each ceremony is equally nebulous. The festival on our sixth day in town is to be the focal point for the entire celebration. Yet no one knows when the activities will begin, only that it will be sometime in the afternoon, or maybe early evening. We spend the afternoon in limbo, waiting. The entire village is milling about the temple compound or walking up and down the streets waiting for the start of the show. We stop a sidewalk vendor to eat supper and watch the villagers walk past.

Everyone is dressed in their nicest *sarongs* and clean white shirts. The villagers socialize and greet each other as they stroll up and down the streets. The sexes remain separate; groups of men walk together as do groups of women. The groups socialize among themselves. I watch the men. They are so at ease with each other; there is an absence of boisterous male energy. Many hold hands or walk arm-in-arm, while others have their arm around a friend's shoulder. A few have an arm around another's waist.

An hour or two goes by and the scene remains the same. We head back to the vendors to munch fried bananas and *ubes*, small deep-fried dough balls with a tasty chocolate sweet inside. Still no dance. We drink a few cups of coffee and eat *trambulans*, big, folded pancakes filled with nuts and jam.

Finally, at 9:00 p.m. the dances begin. The pavilion immediately fills to standing room only. The story, told through lively dance, drama and comedy, is an old Javanese classic that has been adapted from the Mahabharata of India--Asia's version of the epic mythologies of ancient Greece. And the performance on stage? Indonesia's answer to Shakespeare!

An hour later as I stand watching the ceremony in a squished and uncomfortable position, I am struck by the perseverance of the audience.

It is hot and crowded yet everyone is enraptured by the performance. Rice farmers, shopkeepers and toothless old women stare, enthralled with the dancers. Children crowd onto the corners of the stage for a better view. We stand, packed in the hot, stifling mass of bodies, until our feet ache and our throats are parched. Finally, after midnight, we work our way through the crowd and head back to our *losmen*.

The ten minute walk to our lodge is a complete contrast to the gaiety we left behind. We are attacked repeatedly by vicious dogs. Dogs have a strange role in Balinese society. People pay little heed to the dogs on the island. The dogs have a free pass to go anywhere, to do anything. They are ignored as if they were not there.

But with their freedom comes a curse. Most dogs are not groomed. Many are ignored even when sick or injured, resulting in plenty of mangy, vile-looking, fleabitten, sore-covered, nasty dogs that are unsafe to touch or even bump against, much less pet. Dogs with skin diseases have half of their body hair gone. Dogs who have been hit by vehicles crawl about with nasty swollen hips and crooked legs.

But the worst is how evil the dogs become at night. They howl like the end of the world has come. Worse still, they hate foreigners. It is risky to walk in many areas at night. We carry rocks in self defense, but we have poor night vision compared to our tormentors.

Why do the Balinese have an unusual attitude toward dogs? One reason is to keep a boundary between humans and animals, to keep "animal passions and tendencies" from affecting human behavior. Animals are never anthropomorphized and given human attributes. The practice of filing down the points on the incisor teeth of young adults likewise reflects the Balinese desire to distinguish between human and animal.

Yet all other Balinese animals are well cared for: cows are lovingly washed in creeks, ducks taken for strolls, songbirds kept in ornate cages. Why have the dogs been singled out? One Balinese theory is there has to be something on the island that is bad, for nothing in the world can be 100% perfect. Some say the mournful howling of the dogs keeps evil demons away. Others say the dogs **are** the evil demons. After our night on the road, we agree with the last theory.

After seven days of ceremonies we are festivaled out. We leave Ubud on a hot, humid day to descend to the coast for a counter-clockwise circle around the eastern part of the island. We pedal to the nearest beach and rent a little hut at Candi Dasa. The next few days are spent reading, writing, snorkeling, exploring the area, practicing Indonesian and simply lying on the beach.

Sitting on our *losmen* porch one morning I look up to see Kevin, Russ and Tom, our three friends from Canada whom we met in Australia, walking down the street. We had planned to meet in Ubud but missed each other by a day. Now we find they are staying in a *losmen* just down the beach. We take rides together to visit nearby villages and spend evenings sharing supper at local *warungs*.

Since arriving in Bali, we have been cooking less of our meals. Food is so cheap we save little by preparing it ourselves. Besides, it is fun to try local foods. After a year of making one-dish meals over our kerosene stove and eating inside our tent, it is wonderful to sit at restaurant tables and sip tea while someone else cooks and serves the food! Likewise, with the cheap cost of lodging, and lack of quiet out-of-the-way places to pitch our tent, we find we camp much less.

The next morning we make plans to meet the Canadians on the northern coast in two weeks or, if we miss each other, rendezvous at Mt. Bromo, Java, in three weeks. We pedal out of town for Gunung Agung, the highest and most sacred volcano in Bali.

After leaving the coast the road climbs up through the rice fields. In the lower elevations the rice is light golden, ready to harvest, and the air is full of finches flying in to eat the ripe grain. To stop the pirating birds many farmers move into small huts in the fields prior to harvest time and spend their days chasing away birds. Rows of bamboo poles with bundles of tin cans tied to the top are stuck into the ground. Each pole is connected to the others by a string. If one pole is shaken, the cans on every pole rattle. If the farmers can not scare away the birds with this system of clanging

Sculptured rice terraces cover the island of Bali, Indonesia.

95

cans, they walk through the fields with big wooden clappers.

The road over the mountains is steep and full of holes, but the view makes the effort worthwhile. The gorges and deep canyons are full of terraced fields that seem to hang in mid-air. As we gain elevation the rice turns deep green, making the landscape look like lush, carpeted steps. In some places the height of each dike is greater than the width of the terrace it forms. Five and six foot drop-offs hold back tons of waterlogged, mud-filled rice paddies. The binding agent that helps hold the dikes together is the same ingredient that makes this soil some of the most fertile in the world: ash deposits from frequent volcanic activity.

During the heat of the day we stop at roadside stalls and swig down numerous cups of hot tea. Indonesians love sweet tea, loaded with sugar. To get tea without sugar we order "teh tawar," which translates as tasteless tea. We have come to appreciate the value of hot liquids rather than ice cold drinks to help us cope with the suffocating heat. Hot drinks raise the body's internal temperature and make us sweat, which helps take away the dizzy, flushed feeling that comes from cycling up switch-backed roads in tropical climates.

As we pedal up the flank of 10,221-foot Gunung Agung, the skyline is filled by the symmetrical peak, lightly shrouded in billowing clouds. We circle the mountain and arrive at Besakih, the "Mother Temple" of Bali, 3,000-feet up the side of the volcano. We spend the evening packing our backpacks for a trip to the top of the volcano. Just as we finish Tass has an attack of diarrhea. She spends most of the night squatting over the toilet.

We planned on an early start the next morning, but it is long after sunrise before Tass decides she is strong enough to begin the 6,700-foot hike to the top. The trail winds through a maze of small farms and valleys. The sun is out full force. Tass--Ms. Always Start As Early As Possible--now feels healthy and chastises herself for delaying our departure. She wanted to hike the lower elevations in the cool temperatures before sunrise. But after a few hours we climb into the shade of a cool rain forest. Huge billowing clouds of mist roll up and down the hillside. We stop at small vantage points to peer through the mist, spot illusive tropical birds, and examine the Ti trees, which look like giant ferns.

Onward and upward. The trail becomes exceptionally steep. Whoever pioneered the route did not know the meaning of the word switchback. We meet a group of college students from Denpasar descending the volcano. They are in a nature club and spent the night at tree level further up the mountain. Each wears a coat, long pants, scarf, hat, and gloves; we wear shorts and tank-tops. They shiver and talk of the cold night on the volcano; we sweat and talk of the heat on the lower slopes of the mountain. They continue down, eager for hot weather; we climb up hoping for cooler temperatures.

As we hike out of a band of pine forest we meet two friends from the States, Larry Kaplan and Donna Zaino. We first met a few weeks ago on the flight to Bali, and then got to know each other better in Ubud. I next met Larry while snorkeling beyond the reefs at Candi Dasa. Before leaving Candi Dasa we made plans to meet on the volcano today. Because we got a late start we missed them at the base. Now Larry tells us he made it to the top, Donna most of the way. Since they climbed without backpacks they aren't spending the night on top, and are now on their way back down the mountain. Larry says there is not much room on top for a tent.

We climb above tree level, then the shrubs and grasses disappear. The upper cone is made of *lapilli*, small volcanic pebbles created from an explosive eruption. It is like climbing a hill of marbles: with each step forward we slide back half a step. Finally, the trail follows a narrow ridge with a large drop-off on first one, and then both sides. At the top we sit on the edge of the sheer rim and look into the immense crater, the throat of the volcano. In 1963 a violent eruption blew the top 1,000 feet of the mountain into oblivion creating the 2,000-foot deep, half mile crater.

After some scouting we find a place where our Walrus tent might fit. We gather rocks and build a platform on the rounded edge of the ridge and use larger rocks to anchor the tent in case of high winds. There is just enough room to shuffle around the tent to tie the guy lines, and a little

Bruce anchoring the tent on top of 10,211-foot Gunung Agung, Bali, Indonesia.

spot by the tent door provides enough space to set the cookpot. We brew up hot tang and eat fried tofu and rice pudding.

At 2 a.m. we wake to a gale-force wind tearing at the tent. Tass asks if the wind could blow us off the ridge. I confidently reply no. Reassured, she goes back to sleep leaving me awake to wonder--just how well **did I** anchor the corners? Visions of our falling down the mountain trapped inside a collapsed tent fill my mind. I sleep little the rest of the night.

But our tent holds securely, and at 4:15 a.m. we get up to view the pre-sunrise colors in the eastern sky. The wind has lessened, but the clouds look threatening. We eat breakfast and have the tent down by 6:00 a.m. The wind returns, punctuating the first hour of down climbing with nerve-wracking blasts that pull at our packs and nearly topple us off the mountain. Half way down the volcano the wind dies, but so do our legs. Climbing up the volcano we used the same muscles as bicycle riding. Climbing down we both get Gumby Leg Syndrome and wobble to the bottom where we collapse in a small tea house. After a second breakfast we hike back to our *losmen* for a nap.

The next day we are embarrassingly stiff. We mount our bikes to pedal up Gunung Batur, an immense volcanic crater with a three-mile-wide lake and another volcano inside. Also inside the crater are three towns, one named Air Panas, Indonesian for hot water. It is the ultimate incentive to get us riding. We want to soak our sore muscles in a thermal pool!

It takes most of the day to ride up the volcano but only an hour to make the high speed descent into the crater. The hot spring at Air Panas bubbles out of a bank and fills a pool twenty feet wide before flowing into the lake. A woman is doing laundry on a table in the center of the pool. We soak in a corner massaging our legs and letting the water soothe our tired muscles. Suddenly, a large group of people comes over the hill. Just off the evening bus, twenty men, women and children undress on the bank and enter the pool. Everyone heads for our corner, where the freshest water enters the pool. We are instantly surrounded by naked Balinese using copious amounts of soap and shampoo; everyone vigorously scrubbing their body, laughing and chatting all the while.

The next morning we ride back down the volcano to Ubud, and watch the last big night of the *Pruscita Bhumi* celebration. The following day we return to Kuta.

We planned on spending a day in the city running errands but end up staying a bit longer. I get a boil on my rear that makes bicycling impossible. Until a month ago Tass had never had a boil. Until a few weeks ago I hadn't had a boil since high school. Now we are infected with nasty, puss-filled, oozing craters. Gross.

When I am able to sit in the saddle, we tour another set of volcanoes. As we pedal up the first one I drop back, riding at a leisurely pace, studying a list of Indonesian words on my handlebar map case. At each village I watch the reaction as the locals spot Tass pedaling through town. Some wave and yell out greetings, but most stare dumbfounded. Since Balinese bicycles have only one speed, everyone is flabbergasted when Tass pedals up the steep roads. Many are so amazed by her they fail to see me riding 50 yards behind. When we stop men often comment on Tass's strength. Because she wears shorts they can see her leg muscles, which impress everyone. Those who speak English explain her strength by stating, "She is a sportsman." Others ask if we have been in the Olympics.

The next day we descend the north side of the volcano, an 8,000-foot drop on a newly tarred road. We race at high speeds, leaving our stomachs hanging in space as we rocket over steep drop-offs. We fly through small villages, ringing our bells and watching out for chickens running across the road. We zip through some villages so quickly the dogs don't have time to bark. At unexpected hairpin corners we strain at the brake levers to slow our speed, yelling out warnings to each other, along with whoops and cheers. At the bottom we vote the road as the most exciting downhill ride of the trip.

We spend three more days on the northern coast, snorkeling and exploring temples before reluctantly packing up to leave Bali. We could stay for months, maybe years. The only thing keeping us moving is the desire to see more of Indonesia.

Bruce riding with local traffic, Bali, Indonesia.

7

The Shadow Play

On October 25th our ferry docks, or I should say, runs aground, on a sandy, dust-blown beach on eastern Java. We push our bikes down a rickety ramp off the boat and up a rutted trail to a small town 200 yards away. The ornately carved temples and roadside statues that lined the roads in nearby Bali are nowhere in sight. Half the men wear the Muslim *pitji*, a little cap identifying those of the Islamic faith.

Our first stop is a village twenty miles up the coast. The instant we get off the bikes a small crowd gathers. I walk into a store to buy rice and come out to find 15 people surrounding Tass, staring at her every move. We need more food so we pedal, with the crowd following us, to a market two blocks away.

I leave Tass and our entourage with the bikes and head into a maze of stalls with a potpourri of smells. After a few minutes searching the dark alleyways I find tonight's supper. Between a table of dried fish and one with butchered chickens is a woman selling soft, homemade tofu in milky water. I bargain for four of the biggest pieces. Throughout the haggling process comments in Indonesian fan out around me. Since I am paying less than three cents for each piece, the excitement is not because I am paying too much. It is because a *turis* has stopped in the local market to buy food. Java has much less tourist traffic than Bali. Most foreigners spend their time in central and western Java and bus or fly over the less populated eastern part of the island where we are now.

I return to the bikes to find a large crowd. Since Tass is nowhere in sight, I guess she is in the middle of the throng. I work my way through the crowd to find her surrounded by a mob of wide-eyed Javanese. It is our first lesson about bicycling in eastern Java--if you don't want to be on center stage, don't stop for more than two minutes in one spot.

The next morning we arrive at the turn-off to Baluran National Park. As we look down the boulder-strewn track, trying to decide whether to pedal into the park, three familiar figures come into view riding toward us. Our Canadian friends, Russ, Kevin and Tom, left Bali ahead of us and have spent the last few days in the park. They say the reserve is hot and dry, there are few animals to see, and the road is so terrible that broken spokes are a major possibility. We decide to forget the park and join our friends for the two-day ride to Mt. Bromo, a volcano we all want to climb.

The westward highway has little traffic and is the smoothest road we have seen in months. Feeling in a racing mood, we ride in tight formation, drafting and working together to maintain our speed--which is five times faster than any other bicycle on the road. We even pass a few motorcycles!

At tea stops we are surrounded by crowds. While we are a novelty, it is our bikes that are the big hit. Even though they are road worn with scratched paint, old grease covering the hubs and crankset, and dust and dirt covering everything else, they still gleam when placed beside the local models: giant clunker bikes made in China. Everything on the bikes is of interest. The mirrors are a favorite. People constantly pinch the padded handlebars. The derailleurs and gears are unfathomable. Whenever we are away from the bikes, people play with the gear levers and always get the chain and derailleur bound up from the forced shifting. After eating in warungs, we often forget to check the derailleurs and jump on the bikes only to further jam the gears when we try to pedal.

After a long, hot day we ride into Besuki, where we are surprised to find no losmens. It is too dark to ride further and camping is out of the question--the entire area is covered with flooded rice fields. So the police let us camp in their backyard. We wheel our bikes into a courtyard and unload gear. As we work, the crowd that followed us to the police station builds until 100 people surround us as we set up the tents. We pull our bicycles and tents into a small huddle, like settlers in the old west circling the wagons. It doesn't hold back the crowd.

After two people crawl uninvited into a tent we decide to establish a boundary line. With a great deal of joking so no one will be offended by our request, we shoo the crowd back, making funny noises and waving our hands. Once we have breathing room, we draw an imaginary line on the ground. Each time the crowd presses in, we shoo them back to the line, creating general hysterics. Pretty funny stuff.

In the evening we sneak away to a carnival in town, but there is not much happening--everyone is at our campsite. We return exhausted and ready for bed. Tass walks through the crowd calling out *selmat malam*, good night. Most take the hint and head home. The rest stay huddled around camp. I get up to go to the bathroom in the middle of the night and find a small group sitting around a fire watching over us. In the early morning they are still there with big smiles. We pack up quickly before the rest of the crowd returns. After repeatedly shaking hands with half a dozen policemen and much of the crowd who stayed the night, we climb back on the bikes.

During the heat of the day we ride past a man on a bicycle wearing shorts, a T-shirt, and a heavy wool balaclava pulled down over his face. The first thing we wonder is where did he get the ski mask? The second, why is he wearing it? The temperature is stifling, it must be 180 degrees under the mask.

We stop in Probolinggo to buy medicine. Boils again. We come out of the pharmacy to find Kevin, who stayed with the bikes, surrounded by a large crowd. How unusual. By the time Russ and Tom return an irate policeman is demanding we move on. Our presence has created a large crowd that is blocking traffic.

As we near Mt. Bromo the Canadians decide to avoid the 30-mile climb ahead. They flag down a *colt*, a small shuttle bus, to take them to the town near the volcano's summit. Tass and I put our bikes in first gear and keep pedaling. We don't shift again the entire climb.

Half way up we ride into the clouds, a lifesaver from the sweltering heat of the lowlands. The clouds thicken. It begins to drizzle. When the rain intensifies we stop riding and push our bikes toward a tree to avoid the brunt of the storm. As Tass pushes her bike across a muddy ditch, her tire pump falls off and lands in a puddle of mud. Her pump has been loose for some time. She yells at me, the mechanic on the trip, for not fixing it. I snap back that fixing a pump bracket doesn't require much mechanical skill--she should take some initiative and fix it herself. She responds with a few choice words and throws the pump into the air in disgust. It lands clattering on the road. While we stand and argue in the rain, a *colt*, which we don't hear because we are yelling at each other, drives over the pump. Now we stare dumbfounded at the broken pump, too furious to talk. The rain continues to pour.

A little boy walks up. We are hardly in the mood for an audience. Just as I am about to tell him to take a hike, he shyly speaks the only English he knows, "I love you." How can we fight with him standing by saying he loves us?

Both of us have boils, and our frustration with the illness has made us short-tempered. We apologize to each other as the little boy looks on. The rain finally stops. As we get ready to ride, two trucks stop and offer us a lift. We decline the first offer, but after a bit of urging and a quote for a very low price from the second truck driver, we hop in for a ride to the summit. At the pace we were pedaling we would have never made it to the top by nightfall.

In the village of Ngadisari we join the Canadians in a cold, damp *losman*. We take a *mandi* bath, pouring buckets of icy water over ourselves while standing on a freezing concrete floor and then Tass and I doctor each other's boils. I have one on my hip and Tass has one on her stomach.

Being active with the boils is such a hassle. We would like to take a few days off and pamper ourselves, but our Indonesian visas expire in less than four weeks. We don't even have time to rest one day! Tomorrow night we want to be on top of Mt. Bromo for the full moon. We spend the evening loading our backpacks so we can head out with the Canadians at sunrise the next morning.

Mt. Bromo is an active volcano grouped with three semi-dormant volcanoes inside a larger, older, crater. We arrive at the immense outer

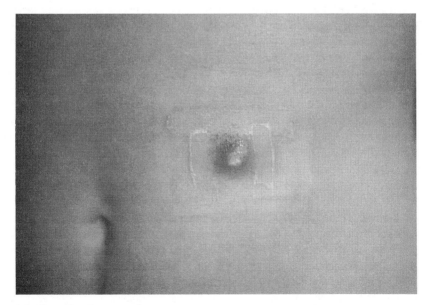

A boil on Tass's stomach.

crater to see Bromo sitting in slumber waiting for the next belch of lava to bring it to life. Surrounding the volcanoes is a vast sea of sandy pumice left from explosive eruptions.

We planned to camp on Bromo, but after looking at all the volcanoes it seems the highest one, Mt. Batok, would be a better place to view the moonrise. We descend into the large outer crater and trudge across the sand. The landscape is totally barren; everything is gray and devoid of color. Large black clouds hover over our heads. It seems we are on another planet.

We arrive on top of Mt. Batok, quickly set up the tents, and dive inside as a violent rainstorm hits full force. The rest of the afternoon we spend huddled in the safety of waterproof nylon, reading and listening to the rain beat against the tent. By evening the rain stops, but the sky is too overcast to see the full moon.

At 4:00 a.m. we climb out of our sleeping bags. The clouds have disappeared. We watch the full moon set in the west as the colors of the dawn appear in the east. A thousand feet below us lies the half-mile wide smoldering crater of Mt. Bromo. The air is filled with the smell of sulfur. After breakfast we break camp, descend Mt. Batok, and climb Bromo for a closer look. At the rim we gaze into an eerie pit of yellow sulfur stains and pools of vile, yellow-green water. It's a primordial landscape with only the dinosaurs missing. We decide to get off the volcano before it erupts, and head back to the bikes.

The Canadians join us in an exhilarating descent back to sea level. The road is rough, yet our speed carries us over many of the bumps. On the potholes too big to fly over, we bounce and rattle across careful not to bite our tongues. During high speed descents we stay alert for pedestrians suddenly stepping in front of us. The Javanese are so conditioned to mufflerless, honking cars and trucks that they use their ears rather than their eyes to check for vehicles. People always step onto the road without looking for traffic. And no one thinks to look out for cyclists. Since Javanese bicycles have such poor brakes, they must be ridden slowly down the hills.

But unlike the local bicyclists, we fly down the mountain highways at record speeds on deathly quiet machines. Even our bells do not always give fair warning. Many of the hills are so steep it is impossible to take one hand off the brake to ring the bells. So we call out to keep the roads clear. This keeps most people out of the way but does not work with livestock and pets. Nearing terminal velocity on a stretch of steep highway, Tass almost takes the death plunge when a panicked chicken reverses its terrified run across the road and nearly flies into her front wheel. I imagine the headlines: **Woman Dies When Bicycle Hits Chicken.**

When we reach the heat of the lowlands our health falls apart. The boils are raging, and we feel queezy. We are going to have to take a rest, so we plot a course for Malang, the nearest place of interest. The Canadians, who are always looking for an excuse to hold up somewhere for a few days, check into a room next to us. The next morning our *losman* proprietor takes Russ to a nearby bakery to buy breakfast supplies. Russ returns with bread and an invitation for us to stay at a house owned by the couple who own the bakery. When we ask Russ where the house is, and when we are invited to go there, he tells us he is not really certain.

I get nominated to return with Russ to find out what the invitation is all about. At the bakery we enter a side door into a shipping room where a woman escorts us to an ornate wooden door. We take off our shoes, step through the door, and find ourselves transported out of the suffocating city heat into a serene world. The sound of traffic is replaced by a chorus of melodic birds. The floors, which are cool and soothing to our bare feet, are made of marble. We are ushered into a living room with a beautiful overhanging balcony. A servant tells us that Ananton is in the middle of a business transaction and will be with us shortly.

An enormous stereo system is spread across a large sunken area in the living room floor. Behind the stereo is a two-story high aviary, 40 feet long and 20 feet wide. It is filled with an immaculate garden of plants, flowers, waterfalls and birds. The 40-foot set of sliding glass doors can be completely rolled into a wall leaving the aviary open to the living room.

Five minutes later Ananton bustles through the kitchen door. He arrives from his business dealings wearing a casual T-shirt, old brown shorts and floppy rubber thongs. It is a strong social statement in a land where the only people who don't wear long pants are bicycle taxi drivers, young school children and vacationing foreigners. He is a short, thin man with thick glasses and 10 hairs, each three inches long, growing under his chin making an interesting beard.

I tell Ananton of my interest in birds and we spend the next forty-five minutes standing in each of his **three** aviaries. Ananton feeds the birds by pulling huge cockroaches out of wire cages and throwing them in every direction. When he runs out of insects, we retire to a balcony over the last aviary, drink the best coffee in the world and eat hot treats from the bakery oven. Ananton repeats his offer to give us a tour of the vicinity and insists we stay in a home he owns in the town of Batu, 12 miles away on the side of a volcano. We accept his offer.

At the front gate we are greeted by a servant who helps us wheel our bikes to the house. Ananton actually has two homes here--the main house plus a guest house. We stay in a large bedroom with a giant window that lets in a wonderfully cool mountain breeze. Russ, Kevin, and Tom each have their own bedroom down the hall.

The next morning before sunrise Ananton comes up from Malang to

Ananton and our Canadian friends, Java, Indonesia. From the left: Russ, Tom, Ananton, Tass and Kevin.

take us sightseeing. We pile into his van and spend the day visiting tropical forests, waterfalls and temples. Throughout the day Ananton buys us mass quantities of any food we have not yet tried. He drives up to the food vendors, jumps out, and within seconds throws bags of assorted goods onto our laps. At small food stalls he sits with us on sidewalks and dirt floors while our food is being prepared. His wealth has certainly not made him pretentious. Ananton has mastered the art of spreading his money around without being condescending. He has a bottomless pocket of *rupiahs* which he constantly dips into for tips. Faces light up wherever he has been, but he doesn't stick around to revel in the thanks.

Three days later Ananton picks us up again, this time in a large landrover. We head toward Gunung Kelud, a semi-active volcano. Scientists monitoring the volcano recently built a 4-wheel drive road up a thin ridge to the summit. Sheer cliffs drop off both sides; moist clouds blow up and down the volcano obscuring our vision and shrouding the rainforest with an air of mystery and excitement. By the time we reach the summit the clouds have built to ominous size. If the storm should break, the road down would quickly become impassable. Ananton does a U-turn. We race down the mountain, and head for the coast to miss the storm.

It is well after dark by the time we arrive at the ocean. The small village we are in has no *losmen*, so we check into a guest house owned by the community. There are not enough beds for everyone, so Ananton pays for our lodging and then sleeps in the back of his landrover--while we get the rooms!

The next morning we finally get Ananton to talk about himself. He was a workaholic until a few years ago when he developed some health problems. Suddenly he realized his life was slipping by. He changed his priorities and reduced his work schedule. His tobacco business now runs without his constant supervision. His wife, Katarina, operates the bakery leaving Ananton to pursue his hobby of building houses. He personally designed and supervised the building of his home in Malang, which took his crew of 20 carpenters 16 months to complete. He is now building a home for a friend.

Despite Ananton's wonderful hospitality, Tass and I get itchy to hit the road. The boils have faded away and we are ready for a little exercise. Russ, Kevin, and Tom decide to stay with Ananton a few more days and then hop a train and catch us in central Java.

Indonesia has the greatest concentration of volcanoes of any country in the world. The island of Java alone has 121 volcanoes, 15 of which are above 9,000 feet. The bases of some of the larger volcanoes are immense--riding a bicycle around one can take most of a day. By late afternoon we have skirted Gunung Wilis and come face-to-face with

Gunung Lawu. Feeling frisky, we decide to ride over Lawu, a 9,000-foot climb, and check out the view.

Five miles from the top we sit in a *warung*, eat breakfast, and ask about the shape of the road ahead. Everyone tells us the road is too steep to ride, even motorscooters cannot make the climb. We shrug off their doubts. With bravado we tell them of other volcanoes we have ridden. We have yet to see a road we could not ride.

At the edge of town we come to the junction for our road. Without looking around the corner to see what lies ahead, we ride in circles shifting into our lowest gear for the ascent. A few people stop to watch what we will do next. We smile at each other. We'll be at the top in no time.

As we come around the building we face an almost sheer wall. Is this a mistake, can this really be the road? We strain every muscle trying to ride up the hill. I make it 300 feet before I stop, my heart ready to explode in my chest. Tass halts, flush-faced, behind me. Ahead the road continues straight up at an impossible gradient without a switchback in sight. The joke is on us. It is even too steep to push our loaded bikes, unless we both push one bike at a time. We opt for a lift in a truck, and lug up the road at a snail's pace. At the top we get out in a mist, check our brakes and push off.

Moments later we have a white-knuckled death grip on our brake levers as we strain to control our descent. A mile down the volcano we stop to check our brakes. A pile of rubber dust coats the pads and brake arms. The rims are too hot to touch.

Further down the volcano the mist clears and the road, although still steep, becomes more rideable. We enter a magical world of terraced vegetable fields. The patterns of the crops combined with the contoured terraces make beautiful designs on the steep hillsides. The volcanic soil and the heavy rainfall create exceptionally fertile fields. Corn can grow to maturity in seven weeks, a banana tree in ten weeks.

The people in the mountains are more subdued than the inquisitive and excitable lowlanders. Short men and women shuffle past at a fast trot toting vegetables hung in baskets on each end of a long bamboo pole. Their leg muscles bulge out enough to make a body builder jealous. Despite their heavy loads they stop to say hello, but only for a moment. No crowds hang around us, a refreshing break!

Back in the lowlands we ride past a road construction crew where we see a worker wearing a knit ski mask pulled over his face. It seems there is a group of people in Java who are compelled, despite the minor inconvenience of living in the wrong climate, to wear wool face masks. I coin the term *balaclavite*, from the famous European ski mask, to label this strange sect, of which we see three or four members daily. Sometimes *balaclavites* wear shorts and T-shirts but most opt for long sleeved shirts and pants. A few hardcore members wear gloves and neck scarves. In the tropical heat their brains must be close to boiling, yet they function normally in other respects. They often wave to us; through the doughnut hole mouth we glimpse smiles and pearly teeth.

No one is impressed by the weight we carry in our panniers, because the Javanese carry even more on their bicycles. This man is bringing baskets to market, Java, Indonesia.

One afternoon while we take a break outside a tea stall a *balaclavite* bicyclist pedals by bundled in a hat designed for winter exploration in Antarctica. It has a three inch pile lining complete with ear flaps and a neck guard to keep out blowing snow.

In Surakarta we check into a small *losmen*. As we wheel our bikes into the courtyard, Donna Zaino, whom we last saw climbing Gunung Agung in Bali, runs out to give us a welcome hug. Although Surakarta is a city of half a million, it is not a total surprise to meet Donna and Larry. Surakarta is the beginning of the traveler's trail through central Java; most budget travelers stay in a small group of inexpensive hotels located in the same part of town.

We park our bikes for a few days to get a chance to use some of the local forms of transportation. We take our first ride in a *bemo*, a three-wheeled taxi reminiscent of a hybrid golf cart with no muffler. The driver sits in a flimsy sheet metal cab; behind is the passenger area, a small, canvas covered box with wooden benches on each side. Six people can cram into the back if they grind their knees into the legs of the passengers across the aisle. A full *bemo* sounds like a Volkswagon bug in desperate need of a tune-up trying to pull a Greyhound bus. The motor revs to full speed, the exhaust pipe vibrates against the undercarriage in protest, the entire vehicle shivers and shakes and, contrary to all laws of physics, somehow manages to pick up speed. By the end of the block it moves with the flow of traffic.

But it is the *becaks* we enjoy the most. They are rickshaw-like contraptions where the passengers sit in front of the driver/pedaler on a padded seat built for two but sometimes holding three or even four people. A canopy protects the passengers from the sun's heat and folds down to give a view of the stars at night. Fancy iron scroll work, like a brightly painted wrought iron fence, decorates the sides and back of the carriage.

The loads carried on the *becaks* are enormous. It is common to see the owner of a food stall being pedaled to work, along with huge pots of food, wash buckets, dishes, stools, tables and even the canvas awning for the stall, all piled in the passenger carriage. If there is room the stall owner perches on top of the supplies. If not he or she sits on the rear fender.

The streets are crammed with *becaks*, each one lumbering along, making painfully sharp corners to dodge other *becaks*, pedestrians, bicycles, cars, *bemos*, vendors with push carts on bicycle wheels and an occasional ox-drawn wooden *dokar*. Since *becaks* have only one gear, the driver must strain to regain the vehicle's momentum, like a great awkward insect, whenever he is forced to slow down or stop.

We quickly find the *becak* fares vary not only with the distance but also with the gradient of the destination. Since the drivers always charge us more when they have to pedal up a steep hill, we likewise insist they give us a discount when we are going to a part of town that is downhill. Some travelers think it strange to haggle over fifty or one hundred *rupiah*, the equivalent of five or ten cents. But we feel the locals respect us more when we enthusiastically bargain. Indonesians love to ask how much we paid for various items. Coming back to our *losmen* after being in the market, it is common for the owner to ask how much we paid for different goods. If we paid a low price, they smile and say "*bagus, bagus*" (good, good) while patting us on the back. Vendors, on the other hand, always ask how much we paid for our *losmen*. And everyone asks about the cost of our sunglasses, jewelry, clothes and bicycles.

Our rules for bargaining: never be demanding; bargain as equals; have a basic knowledge of prices so we don't insult people with an offer that is too low; and, most importantly, use plenty of humor!

Between sightseeing and visiting markets we head out on the streets for our favorite pastime: eating. Food shops and stalls come in various sizes and shapes, but our favorite food vendors have pushcarts on bicycle wheels. With a kerosene stove built in the bottom of the cart, an awning over the top, a big cook pot in the center and glass cabinets on the side to hold food, spices, and utensils, these restaurants on wheels travel up the smallest walkways and down the busiest streets bringing cheap food to all. To let everyone know what they are selling the vendors use gongs and clappers to advertise their selection. *Kacang hijau* (mung bean soup) vendors pound hollow sticks together, pastry vendors bang two solid sticks, fruit salad vendors ring little bells.

We stop a man pounding a low-toned gong. He sells lightly fried tofu sprinkled with onions and fresh bean sprouts topped with hot peppers and spicy peanut sauce. Our meal is served on an old china plate and costs 100-200 *rupiahs* ($.09-$.18 U.S.), depending how high the cook heaps the tofu. After giving us a plateful, the cook pulls out two little wooden stools. We sit on the sidewalk and have a feast. When we're finished the vendor washes our plates in a bucket of water, grabs his stools and resumes pushing his cart down the street, beating the gong.

We say good-bye to the Canadians and to Larry and Donna, with plans to meet everyone in nearby Yogyakarta, or else in Singapore, Bangkok, or even Kathmandu. We pedal out of Surakarta to head southwest and explore some tenth century temple ruins before riding on to Yogyakarta, the cultural and the tourist center of Java. We visit palaces, markets and museums, and also see traditional dances and a lengthy performance of the *Wayang Kulit*, the famous shadow puppets.

It is said foreigners cannot understand the Javanese until they understand the intricacies of the shadow play. Shadow puppets are more than entertainment. They are a medium to teach beliefs, morals and proper conduct. Through the dialogue of the various characters, appropriate behavior in social situations, and the virtues of loyalty, dedication and honesty are portrayed.

During the shadow play the puppet master sits behind a thin, white screen with a bright torch or light behind him. On each side is a long row of puppets, flat leather caricatures on a stick. The puppet master holds one or two puppets in each hand, moving them close to the screen and away again, creating an image of a hazy blob suddenly coming into sharp focus as the puppet touches the screen and dissolving into mist as the puppet is pulled away. The shadow is symbolic of the spirit, a vague thing that can be known but not touched. It is real, yet unreal. It is a mystery.

The *Wayang Kulit* is a mixture of slow moving dialogue, slapstick comedy, action, adventure and tear-jerking drama. A traditional performance has three parts. The first runs roughly from 8 p.m. until midnight. It is symbolic of the youthful period in human life. At this time the puppet master instructs the audience on moral behavior and ethics. Around midnight the great clash between good and evil is shown and the hero of the story finally makes an appearance.

The second part represents a young adult's struggles in society to find

Shadow puppets, Java, Indonesia.

his or her role in life. The ancient stories from India's *Mahabarata* are further spiced by three characters of Javanese origin. *Semar*, *Petruk* and *Gareng* seem at first to be the Javanese Three Stooges. They are deformed dwarves, recognized by jutting jaws and sagging stomachs. They create confusion and hysterics, yet add wisdom, philosophy and the unique Javanese view of life to each performance.

Near 3 a.m. the *gamelan* music becomes lighter, the hero slays the evil characters and good triumphs over evil. Peace and harmony are restored, symbolizing the appropriate end to human life when wisdom and contentment lead to an honorable old age.

Because of its effectiveness as a teaching tool, many groups have used the *Wayang* to spread ideas. Muslim philosophy has influenced the play; Christian missionaries used it to teach stories from the Old Testament. Politicians have also gotten into the act. In the 1970's the government's five-year economic plan and a nationwide birth control program were subjects of *Wayang* performances throughout Indonesia.

Not all theatrical performances are found on the stage. We leave Yogya for heavily populated central Java and continually find ourselves the center of attention. It is not long before we play our parts with a flare from the shadow play.

Rural highways are a focal point for social activity. In each village people sit in chairs or on the front stoop watching the traffic and chatting with each other. The whole country seems to be lining the highway as if expecting a parade. Then we come down the road.

We ride by a group of people and one person sees us, points and laughs. Then everyone turns, looks at us, and points and laughs. We start to wonder--what's the joke? They yell out to each other, "look at the *turis* on bicycles," a comment that doesn't seem particularly funny to us yet it brings the locals to hysterics. Sometimes, not wanting to be left out, we join in the gaiety. We laugh and wave as we ride past.

We never meet lone laughers, they always appear in groups. I guess it takes the security of a group to point and laugh at others. We also note laughers don't like confrontation. They come in noisy hordes to the side of the road to laugh or yell hello, but if we stop the exuberance ceases. Suddenly everyone becomes very shy and talks in subdued tones with each other.

Then, whether we are standing by the side of the road or halting for a cup of tea at a *warung*, one person steps forward to be the official interpreter. Like the puppet master in the Shadow Play, the interpreter choreographs our interactions. Even though we speak Indonesian fairly well, the interpreter and the rest of the crowd seem to think a liaison is needed. The interpreter asks a few questions and then turns to tell the group what he or she has learned. We find this rather comical as our entire conversation is conducted in Indonesian and everyone crowded around us can plainly hear both the questions and our answers. After each reply we pause to let everything be repeated through the throng.

The seven standard questions that start all conversations are: Where are you from? Where are you going? How long have you been in Indonesia? Do you like Indonesia? What is your profession? Are you married? Do you have any children?

If we are on our bikes the next series of questions centers around our transportation: Are these your bicycles? How much do they cost? How far will you ride today?

If we are in a *warung* the questions turn to food. Do you like Indonesian food? What are you eating?

It amazes us people ask this last question, especially since we simply eat what they eat. Yet many villagers cannot comprehend that two foreigners would eat the local food. If we are eating fried noodles, inevitably someone will ask, "Is that fried noodles you are eating?" Or they will simply state the obvious, just to let everyone know they have things figured out, "You are eating fried noodles."

In <u>Mysticism</u> <u>and</u> <u>Everyday</u> <u>Life</u> <u>in</u> <u>Contemporary</u> <u>Java</u>, Niels Mulder discusses the Javanese tendency to label things that are out of the ordinary. Labeling gives the Javanese a feeling of order. People on motorcycles ride up next to us, look, and state matter-of-factly, "You are riding bicycles." Or they will look at us with deadpan stares and say to themselves, *"sepeda,"* which means bicycle. When stopped, people often come up, touch our bicycles and say *"sepeda."*

This happens so often that Tass and I, in our best Rod Sterling <u>Twilight</u> <u>Zone</u> imitation, repeat the mysterious word as if it were an arcane chant. Instead of waiting for the locals to tell us what we already know, we tell them. We ride past groups of stunned Javanese, look them in the eye, and say the word as though revealing a dark secret. *"Sepeda!"*

Our next stop is the temple of Borobudur, one of the largest Buddhist monuments in the world. The temple is 1,100 years old, and took 100 years to construct. Four generations of dirt haulers, blocklayers, stonecutters and carvers spent their lives on the project, putting an economic drain on the entire region. After its completion, the population of Central Java suddenly dropped drastically and Borobudur was abandoned. The site was buried under the ash of volcanic eruptions, then rediscovered in 1814.

Borobudur has nine levels and is shaped like a tiered cake. Each layer, or galley, is bursting with carvings, statues and designs. A pilgrim walking around each tier will travel over three miles by the time he or she arrives on the upper level. Along the way 1,500 panels carved in relief depict scenes from the life of Buddha, with each successive tier showing more heavenly beings. On the upper levels deities float beside and above the people on earth and smile benevolently at the righteous actions of the enlightened Buddha and his followers. The expression of each face is serene, the bodies posed in relaxed contentment: hips sway gently to the side, arms reaching out as in a ballet.

In the evening we ride into the nearby hills and camp near a family who offers to feed us for a small fee. We sit in their house under the light of a roaring kerosene lantern drinking tea and waiting for our food. Fifteen neighborhood children sit in polite rows on the floor staring at our every move. Thirty alert eyes follow our every fidget and yawn. At last the meal comes. Now our audience gets to see some action: the *turis* eating.

We return to Borobudur early the next morning to experience the temple without a horde of Javanese tourists. The surrounding mountains are covered in mist, the light is eerie and the temple has a mystical mood. We meditate in a corner next to silent stone Buddhas. By 7:30 a.m. the guards arrive, followed by the first trickle of tourists. We cast our last glance at the statues, descend the ancient temple steps, and head for the bicycles.

Central and western Java has a large fundamentalist Muslim population. Each day we notice more women covering their heads. A few wear veils. We are amazed at the effect of the Muslim dress code on many of the young girls. Girls in normal school uniforms wear short blue skirts and short sleeve blouses. They have unencumbered freedom of movement; they run, skip and laugh on the playgrounds. By contrast, the Muslim girls wearing shrouds and veils are quiet and reserved. Their clothing is like a leash physically restricting the way they can move and interact with society.

Even though we don't agree with some Muslim customs, we adapt our clothing and actions so we will not offend anyone--after all, it is their country. We pack away our tight fitting biking shorts in favor of loose cotton touring shorts. Tass wears blouses that cover her upper arms. I try not to look directly into the eyes of any veiled women. Yet we also remain true to our own ideas and beliefs about equality. I make a point to never get ahead of Tass when riding through towns; we ride side by side to display our respect for each other.

On the southern coast we visit the Cagar Alam Pananjung Nature Reserve. We stay in Pangandaran, a small fishing village, and spend three days tramping around the tropical forest scouting out Pied hornbills, Leaf monkeys, Bentang (water buffalo) and Sambong deer. In the evenings giant fruit bats fly out to their feeding grounds. With a five foot wingspan, they are the largest bats in the world. One night a continuous stream passes overhead. By counting sections of the colony we estimate nearly 10,000 bats fly over in a 45 minute period.

Dried fish for sale, Java, Indonesia.

But our most memorable sighting occurs as we walk home along the beach after a morning spent birding in the jungle. A snorkeling *balaclavite* emerges from the water. Wearing a swim suit, T-shirt and a neoprene hood/face mask designed for diving under the polar ice cap, the *balaclavite* splashes out of the tropical ocean and walks onto the hot, sunny beach. In true *balaclavite* form he stands chatting with a friend without removing the headpiece. The thick neoprene covers his head, face and neck down to his shoulders. I can't imagine how he can move his jaws, yet he carries on a conversation with his buddy. We spot him half an hour later, still in full regalia, walking along the beach.

At our *losmen* we analyze maps of the last section of road to Jakarta. Our two-month visa has almost expired; we fly to Singapore in five days. Even though I am getting another boil, we head out for the last 250 miles to the capital. We don't get far before my health completely falls apart. Tass is riding strong so I draft behind and try to forget how miserable I feel. I stare at my handlebars, my front tire and Tass's back. As we climb a small mountain range the strain increases. It is hot and humid, but there is no rest. We are on the marathon ride.

As we near the capital the roads are more and more crowded with diesel trucks carrying oversized loads. The drivers give us plenty of room and we have little fear of being hit. The big problem is air quality. The truck engines, desperately in need of tune-ups, belch out thick, dark smoke that hangs over the highway like black death. After just a few hours our bodies and clothes are dirty and black. Big goobers of muck fill the corners of our eyes.

Hills are the worst. As the truck engines lug up the incline, the vehicles pour out smoke in increased quantities. We huff and puff from the work, raising our consumption of the deadly air to dizzying levels. Sore throats, burning eyes and queasy stomachs are the result. Still we struggle on.

I battle diarrhea for two nights, spending my evenings squatting over a toilet. Thankfully, while I am on the bike the diarrhea stops. The last day our only enjoyment is knowing that by day's end we will have made it all the way across Java. Neither diarrhea, boils, nor diesel fumes can stop us now!

The next morning we head for the airport. Without checking the exact address, we foolishly ride to the airport marked "international" on our map. We arrive to discover our plane leaves from **another** international airport not on our map, but on the other side of the city.

Since we are leaving the country we have little Indonesian currency left; it is questionable whether we can pay for a lift across town. Luckily we still have over two hours until our plane leaves. We take off at a mad dash that becomes a grueling race against the clock. After an hour and a half of stressful, high-speed biking, we still have not reached the airport.

Suddenly, the flange on Tass's rear hub cracks. Two spokes dangle in the air; her wheel wobbles terribly. We stop by the side of the road. All the buses, taxis and trucks are coming out from the center of town and look too full for us and our gear. We are afraid if we take the time to flag down someone with room for the bikes, bargain for a price, and load everything up, we will miss our plane for sure. We think we are only three miles from the airport. We push on, broken hub and all.

We turn off the main road onto the airport highway only to find the guards at a toll booth will not let us ride further. Bicycles, a symbol of backwardness to the politicians of Jakarta, are not allowed on the last few miles of road to the international airport, a symbol of progress and status. The guards describe an alternate route, a narrow road through the back slums of Jakarta, three miles longer than the straight, uncrowded highway before us. By this time we have lost all sense of humor. I tell the guards what I think of their stupid toll road, their stupid ideas about progress, and their stupid suggestions for a detour. They are unswayed. We jump on the bikes in search of the back road.

The road is a maze through a land of squalor and open sewers. *Becaks*, vendors pushing carts and pedestrians fill the road. There are no taxis or buses to bail us out of our predicament. Besides, a vehicle could not get through this congestion any faster than we can on our bicycles. To make matters worse, suddenly no one understands our Indonesian when we ask for directions. Perhaps we are putting out stressful, angry vibes and are simply getting the same in return. We try to be cool but things continue to fall apart. Tass's bike is going down for the count; the rim hits the brake pads on each revolution of the wheel. If we miss the flight we will lose the cost of the ticket, and also have to pay a fine and hassle with immigration over our expired visas.

At a confusing intersection we ask directions for the tenth time. For the tenth time in three miles we are told the airport is three miles away. The man also tells us it is easy to get lost on the road. No kidding. A man arrives on a motorcycle and offers to show us the way. No sooner do we say O.K. than he tells us he wants 2,000 rupiahs ($1.80 U.S.) to help us. Even in our panicked state we refuse to succumb to such extortion. I turn to the first man and ask which road leads to the airport. He also decides he will not give us directions without payment. Across the street a policeman sits on a motorcycle. We make a beeline to him and ask directions. The crowd follows us across the street and the two men tell him not to help us unless we pay. He clams up. It seems the entire city is in league against us.

We are hot, sweaty and exhausted from our stressful ride. We are out of water and dying of thirst. Tass is on the verge of tears. We don't know which road to take and we are going to miss our plane. With no idea of where we should be going we simply take off. One hundred yards later we do a U-turn because, for some reason, the road we are on doesn't seem right. I stop beside a man loading a truck and ask for directions one more time. He instantly describes the way. We ride past the crowd that wouldn't help us and give them a thanks-for-nothing look and head down the right road, we hope, to the airport.

Two miles later the tarmac ends and the road becomes a rutted cart track. Unbelievable. We ask two more people if this is the back road to the airport. They say yes. For another mile we bounce across the bumps and ruts frantically trying to keep up our speed. Tass yells from behind telling me to stop. She is sure we are on the wrong path. I keep going, not because I think we are on the right road, but because I don't know what else to do. If this road comes out at anything other than an abandoned rice paddy it will be a miracle. But miracles happen! The path crowns a hill and suddenly we are back on the toll road, half a mile from the airport! We sprint the last stretch and arrive covered with sweat, our faces filthy from pollution and exhaust.

At the airline counter we are totally out of breath and can barely tell the ticket agent where we are going. The attendant panics, waves his hands in the air, and yells at us to hurry. He is certain that we are going to miss the plane. My hands shake from exhaustion as I dig out our tickets.

Every piece of paper I touch becomes soggy from the dirty sweat dripping from my hands and arms. We rip the panniers off our bikes and send them through the luggage check without I.D. tags. There is no time to prepare the bikes, so they too are whisked away without tags. Will we ever see our gear again?

We run down the hallway to customs. We look terrible, yet there is no time to clean up before we meet the stern-faced customs officials. More sweaty palms and soggy papers. Nothing seems to be in the right place. I lose and find my passport and visa three times before the ordeal is over. The humorless official is glad to see we are leaving his country.

Another run down a long hallway. We reach the gate and with tremendous relief see that our plane has not left. Since no one is boarding, we collapse into chairs, totally stressed out--headaches, dehydration, the works.

Now we learn the final irony. Our plane is late. We wait in the lounge for an hour, dying of thirst, with no drinking fountains in sight. Our iodine, which could be used to purify the bathroom tap water, is in a pannier with the bikes.

Finally we board the plane. Within seconds the flight attendant brings us ice cold orange juice. Our ordeal is over. No hard feelings. We toast Java.

8

Ruth And The Bank

We arrive in Singapore on November 29th, and so does all our gear. It is a six mile ride to downtown, through a pouring rain. We are soaked before we even get out of the parking lot. Our first impression of the island, viewed through the water dripping off our raincoat hoods, is how clean and beautifully landscaped the grass and gardens are along the road.

Once downtown we search for a *homestay*, a flop house for budget travelers. No signs advertise their location. Instead, an employee stands on the street, ready to pull in any foreigners who look like they are in search of cheap lodging. We get a dormitory room with six other people on the fifth floor of an apartment building, and have an amusing time getting our loaded bicycles into the tiny elevator and up to our room.

We stop at a bank to transfer money from home and then head out to explore the city. We walk through shopping center after shopping center where everyone carries huge bags of merchandise they have purchased. Yet we find the shopkeepers the rudest and most unhelpful in the world. The sales pitch consists of a constant nagging: "Do you want? Do you want?" Tass tries to buy running shoes but the salespeople are unwilling to let her try on the shoes. They want her to simply state her size and buy the product. In the stores where she is allowed to try on the shoes, the salespeople try to persuade her to buy shoes that don't fit.

I spend a few days looking for bike parts, visiting bike shops piled full of parts and accessories. Disassembled bicycles lay with their innards spread all over the floor, others are piled in corners. Employees bluster about at full speed, throwing things right and left, digging in piles of merchandise, kicking about for parts left on the floor. All interactions are brisk and to the point. At the first three shops, when the salespeople realize they do not have the part for which I am searching, they wave their hands back and forth. "No have." I ask where I can get the parts, but they now have no hope of selling me anything, and lose interest in trying to talk with me.

I finally find a shop with a good mechanic where I get a new rear hub for Tass and our bottom brackets and headsets regreased, jobs I don't have the tools to do properly. We visit the shop during a violent afternoon rain storm. The floor quickly begins to flood. Two employees yell and scream at each other as they scramble to move piles of boxes out of the water. The mechanic makes no move to help. He sits relaxed on a tiny island, working on Tass's bike.

We came to Singapore for two reasons: to get money and to get visas for the Indonesian island of Sumatra. We get the visas without problems but run into difficulty with the money. The telex transfer from our bank back home is supposed to take 24 hours. Five days later the bank announces the money has come addressed to Ruth Junek. The bank refuses to hand over the funds. We call home and discover the error occurred between Minneapolis and Los Angeles. We start the process over. To make matters worse, Tass now calls me Ruth.

In the meantime we scour English bookstores and stock up on books on the language, culture, history and wildlife of a variety of southeast Asian countries. Most evenings we end up in the Indian district. We haven't had good south Indian food since Fiji. We also enjoy the Indians' company. Many are fluent in English and have a wonderful melodic way of speaking and a good sense of humor.

In December more and more banners go up each day proclaiming "Merry Christmas," and "Enjoy Christmas in the Tropics." It is interesting that a non-Christian population should be so enthusiastic about Christmas. Yet it is not a religious holiday that is being celebrated, but a secular event. Santa is the focal point on the signs and banners, which is probably not that much different from the holiday season at home. It is a time for gifts, feasting, family unity, and, most of all, a time for businesses to promote their products. Before long there are more decorations up than found in most U.S. cities.

After four more days our money finally arrives. We fly to Sumatra the next day, eager to resume traveling.

121

9
Christmas With The Bataks

The monsoon season covers the Indonesian island of Sumatra, the fifth largest island in the world. The unpaved roads in the south are bogged in mudslides and floods. We fly into the northern city of Medan, whose streets are more crowded and polluted than the cities of western Java.

Mopeds with sidecars swarm around us. Each of the motorized bicycles has a centrifugal clutch, which requires the pedaling help of the driver to get the loaded carriage moving. Engines scream at the highest possible rpm--pouring out hot, smelly clouds of smoke--while the drivers pedal like crazy. At each intersection we race crowds of the vibrating mechanical marvels off the starting line and on down the street.

Trucks and buses in Sumatra are equipped with not one, but six air horns, which are used at every possible occasion. With all the wild traffic around us I wonder why there are no famous race drivers from Indonesia.

"There are no horns on race cars," Tass jokes. "No self-respecting Indonesian would drive without a horn. Besides, after driving these roads, driving on a race track would be boring."

Luckily the traffic drops drastically as we travel into the sparsely populated countryside. One of our reasons for coming to Sumatra is to see orangutans. Since holding hands with a zoo orangutan in Java, we have wanted to see a "man of the forest" in the forest. Our first stop is the Gunung Leuser nature reserve, Indonesia's largest national park.

We arrive at a toll booth one mile from Bukit Lawang, the closest village to the reserve. In one breath the guard tells us we must pay 100 *rupiahs* ($.09 U.S.) to ride the last bumpy stretch of road, and, if we are going to stay in Bukit Lawang, we can lodge "*sangat murah*", at the lowest price, in his home. We take him up on the offer. He abandons his post and leads us down the rocky road to town.

We are ushered, bicycles and all, into the family's living room. A flurry of activity follows as two teenage daughters are moved out of their bedroom to make space for us. While our room is being prepared we take off on a hike. A mile away, on the other side of a river, is an orangutan research station.

At the bank of the river we are stunned to find a tent city of college students, a Sumatran Fort Lauderdale. Everyone is having a party. A ramshackled collection of lean-tos, dilapidated shelters and ragged tents lines the river. Giant portable stereos blare out the latest Indonesian hit tunes. Litter and garbage cover the ground. Caught off guard, we are outraged by the scene and stomp past each campsite ignoring the calls and questions of the revelers.

The trail ends at the river. Although the river is narrow, it is deep enough to stop encroachment by the campers. We wait for a *prahu*, a small, dugout canoe, to ferry us across. The orangutan reserve employee wants to see our permit before allowing us in the boat. A few students who get in the boat are not asked any questions. They can come and go as they like, but foreigners can only stay three days--and have to purchase permits, which are only available from a government office back in Medan, the capital. We show our permits and cross the river.

The center was started in order to return baby orangutans to the wild. Poachers make big money shooting a mother orangutan, capturing the young and selling the babies on the black market as pets. When police confiscate illegally owned orangutans, which are usually under a year old, they are brought to the reserve to learn to survive in their natural environment. For the young this can be a quick lesson. Others, having been in captivity longer periods of time, re-adjust slowly.

When orangutans arrive they are temporarily held in cages and monitored for illnesses. If healthy, they are released into the forest to learn to forage and build sleeping shelters. At first the orangs are fed twice a day but are given only small amounts of food, not enough to sustain them. In this way the orang is also forced to find more food. During feedings workers continue to monitor the orang's health. When the orang feels secure in the forest, it simply moves into more secluded parts of the park.

Since the reserve must remain a safe and quiet haven, no one,

Indonesian or foreigner, is allowed to hike into the park unless accompanied by a government guide--a good policy in view of the hordes of people whooping it up on the other side of the creek. The next morning we hire a guide and hike in to view the feeding ritual.

The path through the rain forest is narrow and slippery. We are surrounded by a thick growth of trees, vines and creepers. We strain our necks, staring up into the forest canopy in search of orangutans or any of the six primates found in the area. We hike slowly up a muddy trail and arrive on a hill 30 feet from the feeding platform as two orangs make their appearance.

A young orangutan, Gunung Leuser nature reserve, Sumatra, Indonesia.

One by one the solitary orangutans work through the rain forest canopy to the tower. Unlike their monkey cousins, who race and swing through the trees, orangutans move with deliberate actions. Every movement is planned and executed in a masterful style. The orangs have no tails, but their feet are nearly as dexterous as their hands. They prefer to hold on with all four appendages at all times, using more than one branch for support whenever possible.

The best moves come when the orang ends up in a tree where no other branches or trees are within reach. Instead of retreating, the orang rocks the tree back and forth like a giant, wild pendulum. We wonder how often branches, and even entire trees, break from the stress. The orang sways the tree until it is able to reach a branch on a neighboring tree. This is a critical moment. If the branch it grabs is too thin it will break off. If it is too thick it will not bend, and the orang will be unable to hold on when the tree it is rocking sways the opposite direction.

If the orang grabs the right size branch, it ends up holding two separate trees, bent together by its grasp. Then, ever so slowly, the orang moves out to the end of the branches of the tree it is in, branches that would be unable to hold its weight without the orangutan also holding the branch of the destination tree. Finally, stretched out in space, the orang stops all movement and hangs quietly, patiently, in limbo. At last the orang commits itself to the move and releases its grasp of the first tree. Immediately, both trees spring to their original shape, lobbing the orang, who never lets go of the new branch, into the center of the new tree.

We make two trips into the reserve, but because we have to pay an hourly wage for a guide, we spend most of our time in the rainforest outside the park boundary. Following a hand-drawn trail map given to us by a local teenager who wants to be a naturalist, we hike into a secluded canyon. We stop when we find a clear view of the upper forest canopy, a great place for birding and spotting primates.

The mosquitoes come first. Although we wear long pants for just this reason, they bite through the material wherever it is pulled tight against our skin. They bite our ears and the backs of our hands and fingers as we fiddle with the binoculars.

After half an hour the animals and birds in the forest who were initially alarmed by our presence quiet back down. Birds begin to flit in close. We try to shuffle into position to get a view, but it is difficult birding. Due to the thick growth and shadows, we often spot birds only 15 feet away and have to follow their movements for five minutes before getting a split-second-view in the right light to show a key identification mark. Sometimes we watch a bird for much longer, maybe narrowing the species to two or three possibilities, only to have it slip out of sight before we make the final identification.

We have the best luck with primates. We sight five of the six species found in the area. Other than the orangutans, our favorites are the gibbons. Unlike the slow and cautious orangutans, the gibbons are daring aerial acrobats who swing fearlessly at high speeds through the topmost canopy of the forest. We spot one group moving rapidly through the trees when suddenly their "highway" ends in a giant tree overhanging a steep ridge. They congregate on the last limb, 30 feet above and 20 feet away from the closest tree down the ridge. We are convinced it is a dead end, yet they look down as if they consider jumping.

Suddenly, to our utter astonishment, one of the animals leaps into space. As it falls, the gibbon makes a giant arc in the air, its arms and legs splayed in all directions, ready to grab the nearest branch it flies past. Only because of the distance it drops is there enough time for the gibbon's momentum to carry it across the enormous gap. It makes a perfect four point landing, and the branches bend another 15 feet from the weight of the impact. Single file, the rest of the troupe follow suit.

We spend six to eight hours each day in the jungle, and retreat to the house during the afternoon rains. The family is a typical middle-class Sumatran household. With a family of eight, and two guests, the mother works full time at home. Each day starts early, when half an hour before sunrise the household comes to life. A fire is lit in the cooking hut in the

After watching orangutans and gibbons swinging through the trees all day, Bruce decides to give it a try, Sumatra, Indonesia.

126

backyard. The giant boombox in the living room is turned on to full distorted volume with Indonesian top tunes. The daughters use hand-made brooms to sweep the house, the yard, and even the road in front of the house.

Next, the cement floor in the living room is scrubbed with rags. Food is prepared and breakfast served. Afterward, the dishes, along with numerous loads of clothes, are hauled to the creek and washed. The clothes are hung out to dry and later pressed using a monster iron heated by placing hot coals inside. Water is hauled, firewood cut, and more food prepared and served.

The house remains full of activity until the afternoon rains quiet things down. This is when we return from our hikes, study our bird books and read or write. We peek in the bedrooms to see family members splayed out on the bed catching a few zzz's. The mom often naps on the couch with a granddaughter in her arms. Those who are not sleeping do little but stare quietly into space. Everything is wonderfully peaceful.

The rich smell of rain fills the air. I stand under the covered porch and watch the rain pour down. I love the rhythm of the monsoon. Everyone is busy each morning, knowing when the rain starts it is time to relax.

During meal times we eat at the table, alone. The family never eats meals communally. Each person dishes up a plate of rice and vegetables whenever she or he is hungry. When eating, family members sit privately on the floor of the kitchen or squat on the sidewalk out back. We find it interesting that there is a cupboard in the living room full of plates, glasses, and silverware, yet everyone eats traditionally, with the fingers. Like fine china that is seldom used, the utensils in the cupboard are for status, to show guests the family is modern.

The father does not eat any of his meals at the house. He leaves for work before breakfast and spends his evenings at a *warung*, a little restaurant, many of which are full of similar men, nursing cups of coffee, chatting or staring into space.

Shortly after nine everyone heads to bed, and falls asleep with clothes still on and the lights glaring. We are the only ones who sleep in the dark, a fact that causes a disturbance on our first night when the mother repeatedly knocks at our door to give us candles because our bedroom light is off. Each night, as we lay in bed half asleep, we hear the father come home at about 11:00 p.m. He pushes his motorcycle into the living room, where it is parked for the night. He locks all the doors and shutters but leaves the lights on. Since we have displaced the daughters, they sleep with the mother. We are not sure where the father sleeps, maybe in the living room or in the kitchen. No matter how early we rise he is already up.

Since the home has no *mandi* for bathing, nor a toilet, each morning

127

we head to the neighborhood creek, which functions as both facilities for most of the villagers. When bathing, the women wrap a *sarong* over their clothes, walk into the water, and somehow remove their wet clothing from under the wet *sarong* to bathe, while still wearing the *sarong*. Men wear *sarongs* or just underwear. Soap is used in massive quantities, covering the body from head to foot. We bathe at the creek daily, and try not to think of the people upstream using the creek as a toilet. We scrub quickly, keeping an eye out for anything offensive bobbing past.

We leave Bukit Lawang and ride toward the Karo highlands on a road full of switchback and hairpin turns. We pedal through virgin rain forest, something seldom seen in heavily populated Java and Bali. Since it is warm we ride through the afternoon rains, and camp each evening in isolated fields.

As we gain altitude we ride into cloud forests. After the sweltering humidity of the lowlands, the cool mist is wonderfully refreshing. At the top of a pass we meet two women selling corn on the cob. An old, betlenut-chewing grandmother stokes the fire under a gigantic pot of boiling water. The other uses large wooden tongs to fish us corn out of the pot. We ask where they live. The old woman points off into the mist. We eat more corn and ride into the mist ourselves.

In planning our route through northern Sumatra we asked a number of people about road conditions. During monsoon season most unpaved

Bruce riding on backroads during the monsoon season, Sumatra, Indonesia.

128

roads are impractical for riding long distances. We were assured by many locals that the route we plotted was over tarred highways. The roads turn out to be a collection of golfball to baseball sized rocks with a half-inch coat of asphalt spread over them, fifteen years ago. Where the tar is holding up, the road is as smooth as corrugated tin. Where the asphalt has worn down, the road is coarse, bare rock with enormous mud holes. The only traffic in the highlands is big, smoking, 1950's-vintage Chevrolet trucks carrying vegetables to market.

Like neighboring Java, Sumatra is a land full of volcanoes. We climb Gunung Sibayak, a volcano shrouded in mist, and make it half-way up Gunung Sinabung before torrential rains and leeches force a retreat.

Just before Christmas we pedal to Lake Toba. Unlike most Sumatrans, who are Muslim, the Bataks who live on Lake Toba are devout Christians, and that is where we want to spend Christmas.

Lake Toba was formed 20,000 years ago when a giant crater, 60 miles long and 20 miles wide, was blown out of the Sumatran highlands in the largest volcanic explosion to ever occur on the face of the earth. Lake Toba formed inside the crater and, after more volcanic activity, an island formed in the middle of the lake. Samosir Island is our destination.

We take a ferry to the village of Tuk Tuk and rent a traditional Batak house on the edge of the lake. Long ago the Bataks were pushed out of Burma and Siam by Mongol and Siamese tribes; they have been living in the Sumatra highlands for 1500 years. Their homes are built off the ground on large wooden stilts. The walls of their dwellings are only four feet high and cantilever outward at a 70 degree angle. Topping the walls is a 20-foot high thatched roof, shaped like an A-frame, which gives the ceiling plenty of height to make up for the short walls. The roof also cantilevers out 12 feet in front and in back of the house creating two porches for rainy days. The center of the roof is much lower than the two ends, giving the structure a graceful, swayed appearance.

Our house is at the lakes edge. The door is only three feet high, with a one-foot stoop at the bottom. I really have to crouch to get in. Inside is one long living room with a *mandi* bath and a toilet built onto the back. We even have electricity--a great bargain for 1,500 *rupiahs* ($1.30 U.S.) per night.

The next day I head out in search of a little Christmas tree, but I can't find anything that would not be missed if I cut it down. Instead, I borrow a hoe and a can from our landlord and look for a plant. I settle on a two-foot high cassava. Back at the house I spend the afternoon cutting out paper snowflakes, stars, and angels, while Tass colors them and strings each one with thread. By evening we have a fully decorated Christmas plant.

Despite my care in transplanting the cassava, the next day it starts

129

Our Batak house (second from left) on the shore of Lake Toba, Sumatra, Indonesia.

wilting fast. Our landlord's son comes to the rescue with leftover pine boughs he brought down from the mountains for the family's own Christmas celebration. We arrange the boughs into the shape of a tree, restring our decorations and add some colored popcorn I buy in Tuk Tuk.

On December 24th we spot Russ, one of our Canadian friends, in a *warung* eating breakfast! We last saw the Canadians in Java, almost six weeks ago. They have since shipped their bikes home from Singapore and have split up for a few months. Russ thinks Kevin is in Thailand, but he has no idea where Tom might be. They all hope to meet in Bangkok in a few weeks.

In the evening the three of us walk to a local church for the Christmas Eve service. The building is absolutely packed. Despite our attempts to blend in at the back of the church, a commotion soon arises, with calls made to clear a spot for us at the front. Moments later we are pushed and shoved through the throng, but even our hosts can't get us all the way to the front of the crowded building. Halfway up the aisle it is decided we have gone as far as possible. A place for two people is somehow cleared in one of the narrow pews, and the three of us are crammed into it. The small, hard wooden bench is not made for long legs. My knees jam into the pew in front of me.

The service begins with a group of kids putting on a Christmas pageant. The kids are good actors, and the audience loves the show. Three of the performers have excellent poise in front of the crowd, especially two girls who capture my heart. It makes me wonder about their future. How many of these girls with bright and inquisitive minds will have any chance for further education, and how many will spend their lives toting back-breaking loads of vegetables to market with troops of children behind them?

Shortly into the performance we discover the church is also full of low-flying mosquitoes. Since we are wearing only thongs, the mosquitoes soon zero in on our bare feet. We ignore the bites for the first half hour, but then things get desperate. We bounce and shuffle our feet under the pew to keep the little bloodsuckers off, but it doesn't help. The pageant continues, as does the mosquito torture. Packed in the middle of the crowded church, there is no escape. We are here for the duration.

The pageant lasts two hours--then the regular service begins. We get a reprieve from the mosquito torture whenever we stand to sing hymns, which is a comedy in itself. Most of the songs are familiar, but, of course, sung in Indonesian. Since the church is too poor to have hymnals, everyone sings by heart. Without a written script we are unable to translate the words at a singing pace, and since everyone around us is singing with such gusto in Indonesian, we find ourselves unable to remember any of the English lines after the first verse. All we can do is hum. Near the end of the service the collection plate is passed around. After being handed through half the congregation, when it gets to us there is only 150 *rupiah* ($.13 U.S.) inside.

Despite the church service and our decorated pine boughs, it is hard to believe it is Christmas. Still, the next morning we check under the "tree" to see what Santa brought. The big surprise for me is a small bottle of Pustifix bubbles which Tass has been secretly carrying since we left home! I am a bubble connoisseur and Pustifix is my favorite brand. Colorful bubbles fill our house and drift out over the lake.

Russ leaves the following day, and we make plans to meet in Nepal for the spring trekking season, three or four months away. Feeling the need for a break, we stay at the lake for two weeks. Each day we get up before dawn, do our morning meditation and stretches while the sky grows light, and then eat breakfast out on the porch. Fishermen pass by in dugout canoes, holding the lower end of a single paddle in their hand and cradling the upper handle in their armpit. Paddling one-handed leaves the other arm free to put out nets. Sometimes we spot fishing *balaclavites*.

After breakfast we lay in the sun, swim laps to another dock on the lake, read and study, go for daily runs, take another swim to get the stink off, and then eat supper at our landlord's *warung*. Later, we relax with a cup of coffee and eat Khian Gun Butter Chocolate Cream cookies and read until bedtime. It is a luxurious vacation.

Our Lake Toba holiday ends on January 6, 1985. With sadness we shut the little door on our house for the last time and say good-by to the family that was so kind to us. The boat ride to the mainland takes an hour. We arrive on market day, so we dally and eat a second breakfast before climbing back on the bikes. As we pedal out of the giant crater, we are surrounded by swirling mists. At the rim it begins to drizzle. We spend the rest of the day descending out of the Karo highlands in a rainstorm. Because of the monsoon season, we don't go any further south. Instead, we head northward, back down to sea level where the landscape is covered in rice terraces.

As darkness falls, we come to a series of little villages. After much searching, we finally spot a place next to an abandoned building to pitch our tent. We use our flashlights to see as we set up the tent in the wet grass. Moments later a man comes out of the ramshackled structure, which we find out is his home, to see what we are doing. We ask if it is O.K. to sleep here. He smiles nonchalantly, as though foreigners on bicycles are always camping in his yard, and returns to his house.

An hour later, as we sit in the tent reading by candlelight, a group of six teenagers shows up. They sit inches from our tent door with their faces up against the mosquito netting giving us the fish in a fishbowl routine. We put down our books and chit chat. It is rather bizarre to have the mosquito net up as we talk to each other, yet we don't want to open the door and let in the bugs--from the way our audience is swatting their arms and legs there must be a swarm of mosquitoes outside.

After the conversation runs its course, Tass and I speak to each other in English. We are exhausted and simply feel like being quiet and reading, not entertaining guests. They speak to each other in Indonesian, and we listen as they discuss all the items in our tent. Finally, they ask if we want to sleep. We reply yes, and they take off into the night, joking and laughing.

Near midnight we are jolted from a deep sleep. Someone is squatting at the door yelling into the tent. At first we can't tell if the man is mad, drunk, or just inquisitive with a very loud voice. Luckily it turns out to be the latter. He asks all the normal questions. Where are we from? Where are we going? Are the bicycles locked to the tent ours? Are we hungry? Do we want to sleep in his house?

We explain that we are happy in our tent, and since we are already in bed and were already asleep (hint, hint), we will just stay put. After a few more questions and a barrage of *selmat malams* (good nights), he disappears into the dark.

No sooner do we get back to sleep than the whole side of our tent erupts into a bright glow, as if there is a bonfire next to us. I bolt up and look through the mosquito net door to see the loud man has returned and is fumbling with a chimneyless lantern next to the tent. Trying not to panic, I quickly let him know the tent is highly flammable. He expresses concern about our sleeping without a light. We assure him we like to sleep in the dark, and he retreats to his house with the light.

As we cook breakfast the next morning, our friend reappears. We imagine what he thinks of us, camping in a nylon tent that looks like a U.F.O. He sits, smiling, watching us load up the bikes. Tass takes a picture of him with his family, and we head back out onto the highway toward Medan and the airport. Whatever lies ahead, Indonesia will be a hard act to follow.

10

Mercedes and Monsoons

We fly into the island of Penang, two miles off peninsular Malaysia's northwest coast. Penang was established as the first British settlement in Malaysia in 1786 when Captain Francis Light came to the uninhabited island. According to one account, he loaded up the ship's canons with silver dollars and fired the charge into the island's thick jungle to encourage workers to clear the land.

Today the island's largest city, Georgetown, is a popular tourist destination due to its strong Chinese atmosphere and historical flavor. Since Malaysian and Indonesian are nearly the same language, we easily speak with everyone. We check into the Eng Aun Hotel, and for ten Malaysian dollars ($4 U.S.) get a large room on the upstairs floor. The hotel employees, older Chinese men wearing baggy shorts and sleeveless T-shirts, shuffle around in ill-fitting wooden sandals that clap noisily on the wooden floors with each dragging step. During lulls in work they sit around a big table in the lobby, smoking cigarettes and cigars while playing with small cards that look like flattened dominoes.

We visit a number of Chinese temples on the island. All are full of glass-covered altars packed with pictures and relics of ancestors. In the Temple of the Azure Cloud, commonly called the Snake Temple, our eyes take a moment to adjust to the darkened interior before we spot two deadly Waglers pit vipers on the front altar. A sign disclaims any responsibility should a visitor get too close to the snakes. Seconds later, a woman standing nearby lets out a cry and points to a similar group of snakes curled around the table leg behind us. We glance around and spot snakes in other nooks and crannies and even hanging from the top of a picture on the wall. The snakes appear calm and relaxed, much more so than some of the visitors. It is said the smoke from the incense puts the snakes in a semi-trance state, and because of this they are not so aggressive. Perhaps that is just a sales pitch to sell more incense.

After three days exploring the island we cross the bridge to the mainland and turn south. Our plan is to ride down the western coast of Malaysia to the capital, Kuala Lumpur, pedal east across the interior, and then turn back northward to Thailand. Since much of Malaysia has the same monsoon pattern as Indonesia, we will be in rainy weather until we cross the central mountains and drop to the eastern side of the peninsula. We are getting tired of the monsoon and soon hope to be in Thailand, and out of the rain.

Malaysia is the third most prosperous of the eastern Asian nations, after Japan and Singapore. Even though we travel through back-road villages, we see a big change from Indonesia. The rural homes are built of milled

A nearly life-size paper Mercedes-Benz decorates the street-side funeral ceremony for a Chinese businessman, Penang Island, Malaysia.

lumber instead of bamboo; there is a TV antenna on nearly every house and a car in most driveways. It is said that due to a local Mercedes-Benz factory there are more Mercedes in Malaysia, per capita, than any other country in the world. Whatever the reason, we see plenty of the cars.

We ride through giant plantations of rubber and palm oil trees and find scenic places to camp each night. During the day we keep an eye out for south Indian restaurants where all-you-can-eat meals cost just one Malaysian dollar ($.40 U.S.). The meal is served on a banana leaf, without silverware, so we eat with our right hands. The leaf is piled with rice, curries, chutneys, sauces, vegetables, and yogurt. We eat helping after helping. When we are totally stuffed and can't eat another bite, we fold the leaf in half to show we are through.

One afternoon we stop to get out of the rain at a roadside restaurant. Three Chinese businessmen sit at one table, two plantation workers at another, and a group of orthodox Muslims wearing *sarongs* and white skull caps calmly sip tea behind us. They all face a TV, watching an All-Star Wrestling video. The boisterous wrestlers yell and hype up the crowd. The camera zooms in on each blow as the TV audience screams for their favorite wrestlers.

This is not the first time we have seen bizarre American videos playing to a captive audience. Grade B Hollywood movies full of violence and a sordid view of American life are heavily marketed in third world countries. The videos give a distorted view of our culture, beliefs and lifestyles, which prompts many people to ask us strange questions about our country. We leave in the middle of the tag-team finals and climb back on the bikes.

After three wet days we arrive in Kuala Lumpur. The city is full of buildings with beautiful Arabic architecture: domes, onion shaped archways, and inlaid tiles with graceful geometric patterns. Although Malaysia is a secular state, the government is heavily influenced by Islamic law and strongly protects the rights of the indigenous Malays who live mainly in rural areas. Four out of every five people hired for government service must, by law, be Malayan. (A Malayan is a Muslim descendant of a specific ethnic group--a Malaysian is any resident of the country.) This means 80% percent of all government employees are Muslim. Yet only half of the nation's population is Muslim, and less than a fourth of the population of the capital, Kuala Lumpur, is Muslim.

Like other Malaysian cities, Kuala Lumpur has an assortment of jewelry stores specializing in goldware. Each store has two guards, generally good-sized Indian fellows, most often Sikhs, wearing maroon uniforms, big black boots, and packing giant shotguns. No messing around with puny pistols for these guys; they go for the heavy artillery. Because of the small size of the stores and the large size of the shotguns, if one of the guns ever went off, everyone in the store, robbers, customers, clerks--even the guards themselves--would have a good chance of being wounded or killed.

We leave Kuala Lumpur to ride northeast over the Genting Highlands. We ride through beautiful rain forests. Although the interior of Malaysia is still undeveloped in many areas, the primary traffic is big logging trucks carrying out massive sections of trees. The rain forests of Malaysia, like rain forests all over the world, are being decimated rapidly.

The highway through the mountains ends at Kuala Lipis. The only way across the section of jungle in front of us is by train. We check into a *losmen* to escape the rain, and I spend the evening overhauling Tass's squeaky rear hub. There is not a drop of grease in the bearings. Since the hub was rebuilt in Singapore, I can only guess the mechanic used cheap, water soluble grease. This wet weather riding is hard on our gear.

The next morning the train clippity clops through forests of thick vegetation past huge limestone walls and cliffs covered with trees and vines. I ride with my head out the window and look up and down the length of the train as we arc around giant corners and roll out of tunnels. We devour a bag of 20 rambutans, one of our favorite Asian fruits, as the gentle sideways rolling of the cars lulls us into relaxation.

All too quickly the ride is over. We rush to the baggage car to get our bikes before the train workers throw them out onto the ground, as they do

Bruce getting ready to chow down on a favorite south Indian dish: rice, dahl and assorted chutneys served without silverware on a banana leaf, Malaysia.

137

with everyone else's luggage. We are in Gua Musang, a booming logging town in a strong Muslim area. The Malayan spoken here has a different slang, and we suddenly have a hard time communicating.

The worst is trying to speak with Muslim women who occasionally work in shops or restaurants. They are unable to talk with us. Any attempt at conversation is short-lived--some break out in nervous laughter, or else they freeze and are unable to even use sign language. Others simply turn and bolt into a back room. Admittedly, it is unusual to have two foreigners on bicycles stop and walk into the stores, but it is not like we came from Mars. The interactions are especially irksome to Tass, who begins to rant about the obvious outcome of a religion which blatantly puts half the population in a subservient role. Many of the women seem programmed to be mental juveniles.

And what must the locals think of us? We pedal up to the open store fronts on loaded bicycles, covered with sweat if it is not raining and soaking wet if it is. We mosey in, take a seat, order huge amounts of food, and drink enormous quantities of tea. In contrast, the men in the restaurants (we never see women) all move slowly. They nurse a single cup of tea for hours while calmly puffing on hand-rolled cigarettes. They don't speak much. We, on the other hand, talk with each other while we wait for our food and then continue to talk as we eat. Imagine, a man sitting at lunch, talking with a woman! They must think I am hopelessly foolish. Their wives and daughters are working out of sight, washing laundry by hand and nursing babies. Virtually everything we do is different from their lives. Yet once the initial shock is over they all smile, and usually by the time we are half way through our meal, we have a friendly conversation going with some of the men.

We drop out of Malaysia's mountainous interior near the northern border town of Kota Bharu, our last stop before Thailand, and check into a guest house run by a friendly Chinese woman who insists we call her Mummy. She speaks broken English at a rapid pace and makes up for the words she does not know by repeating the words she does know three or four times in each sentence. Mummy gives me a free haircut on the lawn in front of the guest house, and we pronounce ourselves ready for the Thai border. After 10 weeks of traveling in monsoons, it is time to get out of the rain.

11

The Garden Of Liberation

We spend our first week in Thailand riding 90 miles per day up the Thai peninsula. The southern part of Thailand is much like Malaysia; in fact, the present boundary between the two countries was not established until 1909. It is not until the third day that we leave the Islamic influenced southern provinces and the last of the people who speak Malayan.

For the last two weeks I have been trying to learn the Thai language, which has five tone variations: low, medium, high, rising, and falling. The same word, spoken with a different tonal pitch, can have a variety of meanings. The word *mai*, if spoken in a low tone, means "new." If spoken with a falling tone it means either "burn" or "no." If spoken with a rising tone it means "to be able to" or "to have."

It is hard for me to divorce my emotions from my speech, which can change the meaning of a word just by talking in an excited tone, or a frustrated tone. Our first attempt to order a meal is a complete failure. No one has the slightest idea what we are trying to say. We are not sure what we've ordered, and when it comes we are not sure what we've been served.

As we ride northward, the last of the mosques disappear behind us. Giant statues of Buddha begin to dot the countryside: cement Buddhas,

*Spirit houses for sale, Thailand. Many Thais place these ornately decorated
houses in their yards. By providing the spirits with such a nice home, they
hope that the spirits won't be tempted to live in the people's homes.*

some covered with gold mosaic, stand or sit in meditation and even lie in
repose. Buddhist temples, called *wats*, appear everywhere. It has been
estimated there are 20,000 Buddhist monasteries in Thailand. We take
breaks at many of the *wats*, to rest on little shaded benches and refill our
water bottles with cool water from large clay urns set out for travelers.

Buddhism is such an integral part of Thai life it is impossible to
understand the people without an awareness of their beliefs. So we have
made a "date" with a Buddhist monastery. In Bali, we were told of a *wat*
that runs a meditation retreat for foreigners. Since then we have been
planning to arrive at the monastery for the February retreat.

In the late afternoon we pedal up to the entrance of *Wat Suan Moke*,
"The Garden of Liberation," and enter the monastery through a group of
buildings arranged like a small college campus. A monk guides us down a
path to a two-story building, the kitchen and women's dorm.

A short woman, Mrs. Patum, collects our money--we pay 300 *baht* ($12
U.S.), for room and board for the entire 10-day retreat. Mrs. Patum shows
us a place to store our bicycles and then gives us a few items for our stay.
We each get a burlap meditation mat, a small pillow to sit on (my pillow,
obviously donated to the monastery, has two fat babies embroidered on

140

one side with the words "Little Twin Stars" beneath them) and a three-inch high wooden suza bench to help relieve the pressure on our knees and ankles during long periods of sitting on the floor.

Tass follows Mrs. Patum to her room. I follow Phillipe, a Frenchman who has been at the monastery three months, on a trail through the forest. The monastery is located on 100 acres of land. Other than the buildings at the entrance, *Wat Suan Moke* is more of a hermitage than a typical Thai monastery. Seventy monks live here, each one alone, in small huts scattered throughout the forest.

We stop at a building on the edge of a meadow. On the outside It looks like a barn; inside a single room holds ten wooden beds. Three of the beds have thin, woven reed sleeping mats. No one else is in the room. Phillipe shows me a water spigot for washing and a small pit toilet. I put the thin mat I was given over the wooden planks of an empty bed, hang up my mosquito net, and head across the meadow to the meditation hall for the introductory meeting of the retreat members, nearly 40 people.

An American monk gives a brief orientation in English. The rules are simple. We are to take a 10-day vow of silence. That means no talking, no writing notes to each other, no sign language, no body language. We are even to refrain from having eye contact with each other. If we are confused about anything we can ask questions after the daily lecture each morning. If we have further difficulties we may talk with a monk who sits each afternoon under a large tree.

We are to follow the daily schedule posted on the wall. A bell will wake us and will ring each hour to keep us on schedule:

4:30 a.m.	wake-up
5:00-6:00	sitting meditation
6:00-7:45	Hatha Yoga (stretching exercises)
8:00-8:45	breakfast
9:00-10:00	work
10:00-11:00	lecture
11:00-12:00	sitting meditation
12:00-1:30	individual practice
1:30-2:30	sitting meditation
2:30-3:30	standing meditation
3:30-4:30	sitting meditation
4:30-5:30	standing meditation
5:30-6:15	supper
6:15-7:00	individual practice
7:00-7:30	chanting
7:30-8:30	sitting meditation
8:30 p.m.	individual practice/sleep

We are introduced to Ajan Po, our meditation master, who tells us through an interpreter about the Buddhist techniques used at the monastery. We must only think of the present moment. No thoughts of where we have come from or where we are going; no worrying about the past or the future.

We are to learn the art of awareness by being conscious of everything we do. When we sit we must learn to realize **with our entire being** we are sitting. When we walk we must realize **with our entire being** we are walking. When we eat we must realize **with our entire being** we are eating. We must watch our every movement. From the first moment we wake up to the last second before we fall asleep we are to be totally aware of each task, as though it were the most interesting thing in the world.

The object of this is to learn to concentrate, to develop the mind to be one-pointed, so when we meditate we will know how to focus our total energy--body, mind, and spirit. Ajan Po asks if we have any questions. No one does. We are excused. The retreat has begun.

I walk, alone, across the meadow to my dorm. One more bed is made. I will have four roommates. As each of them comes in the door I divert my gaze to their feet. Since we were never introduced I have no idea of their names, nor what country they are from. Each of us takes our turn using the toilet, and then we all climb under our mosquito nets and go to sleep.

> Yesterday is but a memory
> Tomorrow is the unknown
> Today is the knowing

At 4:15 a.m. the beeping alarm on my digital wrist watch wakes me in the darkness. I crawl out from under the mosquito net, light a candle, and listen to the sound of the flame as it grows bright and then soft again. I put on soft, cotton draw-string pants, a long-sleeved T-shirt, and wrap my Balinese *sarong* around my body like a shawl. The night is cool, the air damp.

Inside the meditation hall the glow of oil lamps softly illuminates one large room. Each of us lays our gunny sacks and small pillows on the concrete and sits on the floor. Each time I think of how long ten days is I drop the thought from my mind, likewise the thoughts about the last week, last month, last year. I sit, and think of nothing but sitting in a dark room on the hard floor, and all is quiet.

I have always been fascinated with the eccentric religious hermits of history. At the age of sixteen I joined the Self-Realization Fellowship and began doing yoga and reading the Hindu *Vedas*. Over the next four years my interest shifted to Buddhism, and soon I was studying first Tibetan and then Zen Buddhism. In my mid-twenties I began to feel that many of the authors who made the most sense in explaining Buddhism were Christian monks and theologians. At that time I rediscovered the depth of my own religious tradition and found that my study of other religions had helped me to better understand my own culture's teachings.

At times in my life I have considered a vocation as an ascetic, so a 10-day retreat didn't seem intimidating. I envisioned scenes from the writings of Thomas Merton. Somehow I had skipped over his frequent references to difficulties and had convinced myself everything would be peaceful and, more importantly, full of meaning.

So, with some surprise, I find the euphoria of the first two days disappearing as I begin my sitting meditation on the afternoon of the third day. What value is there in what I am doing? The feeling of futility follows me

We take a 10-day vow of silence at Wat Suan Moke, Thailand. We are given a gunny sack, pillow and wooden bench to use during our sitting meditations.

to my standing meditation. My legs are so tired all I want to do is lie down, but I force myself to keep standing and walking. My hips ache, my knees hurt and my ankles are sore. I try not to think of the what lies ahead. I am starving, and I still have an hour of standing meditation, an hour of sitting meditation, and another hour of standing meditation before I can relax in a chair and eat supper.

The romantic in me is stunned that things are not going well. Here I am in a monastery, surrounded by meditating monks, and I feel useless and barren. Halfway through the slow walk back and forth on my little section of trail, I finally admit to myself that I am miserable.

I walk slowly, barefoot, down the narrow dirt path that is swept clean of leaves each morning. I refocus my mind on my feet, on how my heel comes into contact with the earth, how the outside arch comes down and the weight shifts to the ball of my foot until my toes push the foot slowly back off the ground. Each step is a smooth flow. The steps, taken together with a relaxed breath, move me slowly, steadily, down the path. Parts of the trail are in the shade where the ground is moist and cool. Other parts are in the sun, the dirt is hot and powdery; dust rises between my toes and envelopes my feet in soft warmth. With each step the earth feels more secure, more sacred. I breath deeply and think about how the path is like life itself. Sometimes we walk in the sunshine, other times in the shade. There are lessons in both.

On the fifth day Tass passes me a note. It has no greeting, no "I love you" at the end, just the emergency message: "need papaya salve." She must have a boil. After supper we meet on the trail, alone. I hand her the salve and a short note asking if she needs help--and telling her I love her. I struggle whether to talk. So often with boils we need each other to nurse and clean the wound. Tass looks at my note, gives me a little smile, shakes her head, and without saying anything, turns, and walks back down the trail.

The next day we allow ourselves to glance into each other's eyes for a moment, just long enough to make contact, a brief acknowledgment of the other's presence, and then turn away. It is hard for me to walk past people and not give them a grin, not only with Tass, but with everyone at the monastery. I have spent five days with my dorm partners, never acknowledging their existence. Five of us started, now there are three. I didn't see the others leave.

Each day we have two and a half hours of individual practice, a time to continue meditating, do laundry, take a shower, or whatever--as long as it is done with total mindfulness. I walk the swept paths through the woods and watch the birds and the sunlight on the leaves. Sometimes I stand and stare at the isolated monks' hermitages, one-room huts on stilts. Each has a covered porch with a table and a chair for reading. Potted plants

144

surround each dwelling, brightly-colored saffron robes hang on the clothes line. It is a bucolic, peaceful existence.

The following afternoon a short walk in the forest turns into a contemplative meandering through the hermitage grounds. During the morning lectures, Ajan Po has been telling us we must not think of anything, but simply concentrate on the breath alone. The last few days I have been rebelling. Concentrating solely on the breath feels too sterile, especially during the marathon meditations of the monastery. The long hours of sitting quietly have stripped me to the bone. I have been going deep into the core of my beliefs. More and more I am turning to prayers out of my Christian heritage to commune with God in a more personal way.

In the afternoon sitting meditation I focus on positive energy and love coming into my being with each inhalation, and a similar flow going out into the world with each exhalation. Suddenly, as if someone flicked a switch, my awareness becomes crystal clear. Everything in my mind is stilled, there is no dialogue of words or thoughts streaming through my brain. I feel as though I am floating. Still, a part of my consciousness observes myself. My breath comes much quicker and only out of the top of my lungs; my heartbeat increases, I sense a flush in my face. I feel a tremendous euphoria.

After a time the thought occurs that I shouldn't waste the energy I am connected with in simply feeling good. I begin to direct the energy to dark places in my psyche, in my soul, needing light and love. But as I acknowledge my own deficiencies the power overcomes me. Like a shock I see my own vulnerability, the fleeting nature of my life. I feel naked, defenseless. Standing utterly exposed before God, how can I, a mere human, ever hope to be worthy of what is before me? Without help I am lost. I beg God to transform me into a better person.

An hour later the gong announcing the standing meditation rings, but I remain seated. I feel as though I am going through a spiritual purge. With each exhalation there is an elimination of negative energy and emotions from my body. My face distorts as though I am about to vomit.

After another hour the next gong of the bell brings me back to earth, exhausted. My emotions are wrung out. I sit in numbness, then go outside and lay under a tree.

After evening meditation I walk back to my dorm and take a quick *mandi* bath. Another roommate is gone. Only two are left; both are asleep when I come out of the bathroom. My bed creaks as I crawl under the mosquito netting. Even though I am used to sleeping on the ground, the bed feels hard and austere. I lay awake for an hour, jotting notes in my journal and reading <u>The Cloud of Unknowing</u>. The author, a 14th century Christian monk, seems to be speaking directly to me. I write a final note and blow out the candle:

> I stand before a dark abyss
> What do I have to offer you, my Lord?
> Nothing but my tears

On the eighth day Tass and I meet, alone, on a trail. We catch each other's eye. Suddenly I want to tell her what I am experiencing, to hear her feedback, and to find out how she has been doing. I speak first.

"I've been using my own prayers."

"So have I," Tass replies. "I started a few days ago."

The branch of Theravada Buddhism taught at *Wat Suan Moke* is a rational philosophy well-suited for a logical, scientific mind. The meditation techniques--focusing on quieting the mind through the breath--are methodically laid out. But for us there is not enough emphasis on intuition and emotional feelings. We both need an intimate relationship with God to survive an encounter with God, or even with ourselves, sitting all day long meditating, as if on the edge of eternity. We talk for an hour about what we have experienced, and then walk down separate trails to the meditation hall.

During individual practice on the ninth day we are allowed to talk with other members of the retreat. Of the forty people who started nine days

Ajan Poh in standing meditation, Wat Suan Moke, *Thailand.*

146

ago, twenty-five have stuck it out. We socialize on the front porch of the meditation hall. It is interesting to find out what everyone's voice sounds like, and what they have to say after nine days.

The retreat ends the next day. A group of us meets at a tea shop outside the monastery to further discuss our experiences and exchange addresses. We make a diverse group: Maggie and Laura, two jokesters now that the vow of silence is over, just finished four years in the Peace Corps in Nepal and are now traveling home through southeast Asia; Caroline and Kadish, a Jewish couple from America who moved to Israel a few years ago, but have been on the road for nearly a year; Renate Lehmann, a woman from Germany who is traveling back through Asia after spending a year working in Australia and New Zealand; and Simon Benson, a professional singer in a Protestant cathedral in London.

The group decides to catch a third-class train to the capital that evening. Since we have only five weeks left on our two-month visa, we join in. The time we save will enable us to pedal northward from Bangkok through central Thailand and up into the mountains of the Golden Triangle.

12

Living Beneath A Fat Buddha

In Bangkok we stay in the oldest part of the city, north of Chinatown, near Khao San Road, the favored hangout of budget travelers. Each time we go downtown we ride through the crowded Indian and Chinese sections, where vendors and food stalls take up so much room that crowds of pedestrians spill out onto the streets. Stereo shops and movie theater speakers blare so loudly I can't hear the roar of diesel buses revving up inches from my shoulder.

Bicycling in Bangkok is like riding in the middle of a stirred up ant pile. Like drivers in many southeast Asian cities, no one pays attention to lane markings. Everyone weaves from side to side--wherever there is an opening in traffic. At the immense queues of buses and cars backed up at traffic lights, we join the motorcycles and cruise between the snarled vehicles to the head of the pack.

After six days in Bangkok we get our Burma and Nepal visas, see enough shrines to satiate even the most die-hard temple visitor--namely, me--and study enough maps and books to finalize our 1,200-mile route through northern Thailand. As usual, we plot more things to do than we have time. Rather than waste a day riding through the suburbs of Bangkok, we take a two hour train ride to get out of the city. Our first destination is Khao Yai National Park, east of the capital and a bit out of our way, but we would like to see some elephants.

The train drops us off in the lowlands, 3,000 feet below the park. It is the hot season in central Thailand. The combination of heat, hills and stopping to bird, slows our momentum. It takes all day to ride 30 miles up into the park, where we camp in the forest.

The first morning is devoted to birding. The trails wind through thick forest with low visibility, so we search out overlooks where we can see the forest canopy. By mid-afternoon we spot 23 new birds.

I am amazed how each bird species retains its uniqueness. Take for example, the Long-tailed minivet, a dazzlingly bright red bird with a black face, throat and wing section. The male Scarlet minivet is almost exactly like the Long-tailed minivet, same size, same color everywhere--except for a tiny red line on the bird's secondary wing feathers. The females of the two species have even less distinction: the female Long-tailed minivet has a bit more gray in the cheeks, or so our bird book says, but you have to be in a lab under controlled light to see the difference. Yet the Long-tailed minivet and the Scarlet minivet know they are separate species and never crossbreed.

Compared with many animals, the distinctions birds make in choosing their mates is remarkable. Consider dogs. Imagine if, like birds, an Irish setter would mate only with an Irish setter; a Doberman with another Doberman. Or, like the Long-tailed minivet, if a twenty-three-spot Dalmation would romance only with another twenty-three-spot Dalmation.

In the afternoon we pedal out on an old dirt track to a blind where we hope to see elephants. The thirty-foot observation tower has been gutted by fire and now has no floor or walls. We climb up a rickety ladder and shimmy out onto the narrow concrete beams, all that is left of the floor. The seating is precarious, but the view of a watering hole down the hill is excellent.

We sit quietly and watch the sunset. A flock of twenty hornbills flies past at close range, our first sighting of the giant, colorful-billed birds! But no elephants. Undaunted, we set up camp in the tall grass near the tower.

In the morning we climb back in our perch before dawn, but again no elephants. At mid-morning, when it is too late for animals to come to the water hole, we walk through the area and find enormous piles of elephant droppings in softball to nearly basketball proportions. We also find tiger scat. We spend another night at the tower, spot a nesting tree with forty-one hornbills, and see a few Sambah deer. But still no elephants.

The next day we have no choice but to abandon our search for the pachyderms and begin riding northward. The weather is hot and dry, the air full of dust and smoke. The haze parches our throats and stings our eyes. At dusk we begin looking for a place to camp, and leave the main road and ride into a side valley surrounded by limestone cliffs. We spot a monastery sign and head to the *wat* to get water. The smoke and haze in the air gives the place an eerie feeling. At the temple, the monks have tatoos covering their arms. Tass looks at me out of the corner of her eye and jokes about stumbling upon the <u>Twilight</u> <u>Zone</u> monastery.

I ask a monk for water; instead, he takes me to an office where I meet an administrator who speaks English. It turns out we are at *Wat Tham Krabok*, Thailand's only monastery to rehabilitate drug users. It is great luck. We accept an invitation to spend the night and are given a tour of the facility. Our first stop is the herbal steam sauna. The air is laden with fragrant smells of oils and lemon grass. It is so hot we cower on the lowest bench and take chipmunk breaths to keep from scorching our lungs. We sweat out all the grime picked up on the dusty road.

Afterward, we sit on stone benches under a grove of trees and drink a bitter herbal concoction to help our bodies eliminate toxins. Our guide sips her drink and tells us the story of the monastery. In 1957 a small group of monks moved into nearby caves in the limestone cliffs. Within two years there were thirty monks and an abbot. A Buddhist nun who had

Thailand is famous for the beautiful architecture and upswept roofs of its temples.

been working with traditional medicine in the area gave the abbot a recipe for a drink that she said would help cure an addict's physiological craving for drugs. People began coming in for treatment, and within a few years the entire focus of the monastery turned to drug rehabilitation.

The next morning we watch a group of patients receive the medicine. A big, burly monk stands at the end of the row, arms folded on his chest, supervising the operation. The patients, each with a spittoon in front of him, line up in two rows, facing each other. One by one they drink the bitter tonic. Each makes a grim face as he swallows, and then guzzles from a water container to wash it down. Other patients, further along in treatment, chant with drums and cymbals to get the drinkers psyched up for what comes next.

Within minutes several of the patients begin to cough and spit up phlegm. Soon the whole group is gagging and throwing up. This ritual is performed each morning for ten days to detoxify the addicts in a radical cleansing to end their drug cravings. Patients also get plenty of rest and constantly take showers and herbal saunas to help the body cleanse itself.

The monastery claims a 50% success rate with patients who take the 10-day course and 70% for those who stay a month. Forty percent of the men who go through the month-long program remain monks for one to five years.

After an audience with the abbot we head back out on the highway. Central Thailand in the dry season is like a post-nuclear landscape: a scorched wasteland of smoke, dust and heat. Fires burn everywhere. The farmers practice a thorough slash and burn agriculture. Not only are the fields burning, but the ditches along the road and even the yards around many of the homes are blazing or smoldering. The countryside seems full of pyromaniacs.

A blistering headwind blows out of the north. It is a blast furnace, sucking the moisture from our bodies. We guzzle water, yet we feel terribly dehydrated. As we ride we frequently pass groups of monks on pilgrimage walking beside the road, robes billowing in the wind. Some carry a *kraton*, an umbrella to shade the sun. Others walk without any protection from the sweltering heat, bald heads shimmering in the sunlight.

The monks often walk for weeks, even months. Some have destinations, others just wander until the beginning of the rainy season and then find a temple to wait out the wet weather. One old monk wearing a big pair of sunglasses gives us a wave and a large smile as we ride past, but most do walking meditations and seem oblivious to us and the traffic. Like us, they stop for rest breaks in the small roadside shelters built by the government. People living along the highway also put clay urns by the road to keep cool water for pilgrims and travelers. We stop and use silver dippers with wooden handles to refill our waterbottles. But by the time

Bath time, Thailand.

we wait for our iodine drops to purify the water, it's as hot as the sun and wind.

In the city of Lop Buri I get my first flat since Australia. We pull over next to a man walking down the sidewalk, who immediately begins talking to us in English, with a distinct American accent. His name is Dhama, Dang for short. As a young boy he learned English by hanging out with GI's on leave from the Vietnam War. Dang now works at a nearby *wat* as a cook and helper for a locally famous monk. As I fix my tire, Dang tries to persuade us to spend a few days with the monk. It sounds interesting, but we have already spent lots of time in monasteries. We're ready for hill-tribes. But Dang is persistent.

"You won't get another chance to see what rural Thai villagers believe." Dang continues his salespitch while I pull out my punctured inner tube. "Luang Poh is one of the holiest monks in all of Thailand."

We explain that we can not squeeze another stop into our schedule. But Dang will not give up.

"Luang Poh has healing powers. He is a very interesting." As I put the wheel back on the bike, Dang tries a different tactic.

"You will be sorry later if you don't come. This is a unique opportunity."

By the time I put my panniers back on my bike we are convinced. We ride out of town heading east instead of north toward the mountains. Dang takes a bus while we ride our bikes to the village where the temple is located.

Although *Wat Tha Khae Nauk* is a small temple, it is easy to find. In the middle of the temple grounds is a 40-foot statue of a fat Buddha meditating with a sly grin. Dang meets us at the Buddha's feet and escorts us into a room under the statue where Luang Poh Thep has been living for the last two months.

Luang Poh sits on a pillow on an elevated stage, giving advice and dispensing herbal remedies to a group of ten people sitting on the floor before him. Rather than interrupt the group we slip into a corner with Dang and watch Luang Poh interact with the people.

The monks at *Wat Suan Moke*, where we took the 10-day vow of silence, represent a no-nonsense school of Buddhism that is trying to remove what they believe to be superstition and cultural baggage that has accumulated around the original Buddhist doctrine during the last 2,300 years. Like the school of higher criticism in Christianity that attempts to see religion through 20th century eyes, the monks at *Wat Suan Moke* are trying to de-mythologize the Buddhist scriptures.

At *Wat Tham Krabok*, the drug rehab monastery, the abbot is in the forefront of changing the way monks can act. The monks at *Wat Tham Krabok* are very strict and follow many traditional rules, such as never riding in cars or trains (if they want to go anywhere, even across Thailand, they must walk). Yet they also do work with drug rehabilitation, a task many other monks view as non-religious. Because of their work, they do not receive government subsidies, as do all the other *wats* in Thailand.

The monk now before us represents another group. Luang Poh is a "forest monk" of the *Aranyika* sect, which embraces a mystical view of Buddhism--including the use of psychic powers during healing ceremonies. Luang Poh spent the last two and a half years alone, meditating in a hermitage in the woods. A few months ago he left the wilderness on a pilgrimage and chose to take up temporary residence at this out-of-the-way, empty temple. Being a charismatic person, he quickly began to draw large crowds who come to pay homage and seek guidance.

Poor old women with tattered clothes and army colonels with starched collars and spit-polished shoes come for healings, blessing and even predictions about the future--including questions concerning the winning number in this week's lottery. Luang Poh talks quietly with some, with others he jokes and laughs, a few he teases and tells them they are asking the wrong questions. It is an informal time full of laughter and socializing.

An hour after we arrive a group of 20 people, mostly women, gathers for an intense healing session. Luang Poh leads the group in a radical deep breathing exercise. For fifteen minutes the crowd huffs and puffs using deep, rapid breaths. The women begin to rock back and forth, some with wild abandon. Others heave and shake.

One of the women cries out as her body trembles, then she curls up in a ball on the floor, her forehead pressed to her knees. Luang Poh stands before her, his eyes intense, his face rigid. He takes a large breath and blows forcefully at the woman. She has her head down and is not looking in his direction, yet she responds immediately. Her cries cease, she murmurs softly and then gently rocks back and forth, her face still bent over her knees.

This scenario is repeated as Luang Poh walks through the crowd. Dang leans over and whispers to us that Luang Poh is "getting rid of the baddies." It is a psychic and spiritual showdown as Luang Poh rebukes the evil spirits in each person. Some of the confrontations are quite dramatic.

After the session we join a relaxed group sitting before Luang Poh. With Dang as an interpreter we have a pleasant conversation. Luang Poh asks us about America, about our bike trip and about our plans for the

We spend three days living with Luang Poh beneath the statue of a fat Buddha, Thailand.

future. It is interesting that of all the monks we have met he is the first to ask us questions about our lives. He takes an immediate liking to me and tells me I should shave my head and become a monk.

One hundred people gather that evening in a temple building for a hour-long guided meditation. It is an impressive number for an isolated monastery in the countryside. Afterwards, we sleep under the fat Buddha on a raised platform next to the monk.

The next morning, when there is just enough light to see the green color of tree leaves--the time Buddhist tradition says the alms round is to begin--I join Luang Poh on his daily rounds. As we walk to the village we meet another, older monk from a nearby temple. Due to seniority, he takes the lead. Luang Poh is next and, because of respect given to foreigners, I follow in third. Behind me is an older temple helper.

Although the monks carry large food bowls, called begging bowls in English, the alms round is not considered by the monks or the lay people as begging. *Therevada* Buddhists believe people gain merit by giving to monks. Even if there is more food in the bowl than the monks can eat, the monks will never refuse food. To do so would deprive someone of merit.

We walk through the small village on a predetermined route. Those giving alms stand before their homes, waiting for the monks. As we walk up they bow or kneel on the ground in reverence and hold out bowls of beaten silver. Many hold the offerings to their foreheads. When the monks stop, the villagers scoop the food into the monks' bowls. Both monks stand quietly, without helping--Buddhist doctrine states the monks should be indifferent to what is placed in their bowls.

Within half an hour the begging bowls are full of rice. The two monks stand patiently while the other helper and I pack the rice down to make room for more. Each bowl, held by a thick strap over the shoulder, holds nearly two gallons of cooked rice--they are more like begging buckets. In addition, the other temple-helper and I carry tiered food containers, each with five compartments for separating sauces, delicacies and treats. We also tote large plastic sacks for fruits and sweets wrapped in banana leaves.

Back at the temple, while Luang Poh does a walking meditation, we help Dang arrange the food into an elaborate smorgasbord. Dang knows what foods Luang Poh likes and places his favorite dishes neatly in the front row. After everything is ready, Luang Poh comes over and loads up a large plate of food. He eats slowly, thoughtfully. Other than a small snack of fruit just before noon, he only eats this one meal a day.

Yet even the hungriest monk could not put a dent in all the food we collected. After Luang Poh is finished we have a wonderful breakfast with Dang and two other temple helpers. We sample a variety of food and have enough left over to feed everyone lunch. Dang tells us it is Luang Poh's popularity that is responsible for such an abundance of delicious food. Other monks, especially in poor rural areas, can go days or even weeks and eat only rice.

Even though Luang Poh eats a gourmet breakfast, he lives a strict life-style. Originally, Buddhist doctrine stated a monk could own only eight items: an undergarment, toga, belt, shawl, begging bowl, water filter, razor and needle. Over the years that list has been modified, but monks like Luang Poh still own few possessions.

Luang Poh also has a *krot*, which is used as an umbrella in the rainy seasons and a shade during dry season pilgrimages, a mosquito net, and a woven mat for a bed. He has a few books, some pictures of famous Buddhist monks, an assortment of amulets and prayer beads, and a satchel of herbal tonics which he gives out to people.

In the afternoon we show Luang Poh postcards of our home in the Black Hills: snow skiing, buffalo and American Indians. We are stunned when he sees a picture of Mount Rushmore--and tells us the English name of the monument. He remembers it from a picture in a Thai school book! Later, he twice remarks how much he admires the enormous carving, which may be only natural for a monk living under a huge statue of Buddha. That evening we give him the picture. It is a strange gift but what

Bruce with Luang Poh and another monk on the morning alms round, Thailand.

else can we give him for his kindness? He places the picture on a shelf with his photos of Buddhist saints.

Luang Poh periodically calls for me and, with his limited English and my faltering Thai, we discuss my future. He repeats that I should become a monk and stay with him at the monastery. When I laugh and ask what he thinks Tass should do, he replies she can bicycle by herself back to the States.

His suggestions are less surprising when we learn of Luang Poh's past. Dang tells us Luang Poh came from a wealthy family, was married and had a number of children before he became a monk. He left his family just a few years ago. The precedent for such action was set by Buddha himself, who abandoned his wife and son to seek enlightenment.

I thank Luang Poh for his offer but refuse. I have never felt Tass is standing between me and my spiritual destiny.

The timetable of our visa demands we move on. Luang Poh loads us up with gifts of medicinal herbs, balms and even pickled vegetables--his favorite. We receive his blessing and ride out of the monastery grounds.

13

Water and Roasted Nuts

Feeling pressed for time, we ride 90 miles a day as we work our way northward. The heat takes its toll. Each evening we feel dehydrated and exhausted as we lay sweating in the tent. In the mornings we wake groggy and lethargic. We long for the mountains and, hopefully, cooler temperatures.

Yet when we reach the base of the mountains, things get worse. Tass has another boil, the temperature is just as hot, and now the roads are steep. At a village clinic she has a culture taken. The doctor foolishly squeezes the boil, rupturing the wound. For three days it drains blood as well as pus.

Finally, we arrive in Chiang Mai, the cultural center of northern Thailand. It is a beautiful city with more than 300 temples, plenty of good restaurants, bookstores--and lots of tourists. After seeing few foreigners since Bangkok, we now ride down streets full of travelers. Everywhere signs in English advertise treks into the Golden Triangle. We check into a quiet little guest house and spend a few days visiting the National Museum, the Tribal Crafts Center, the Tribal Research Center and various trekking agencies. Our research is a crash course in hill tribe history.

The diversity of tribes up in the mountains is astounding. There are six main groups: Karen, Hmong, Yao, Lahu, Lisu, and Akha. Each has its own language, history, customs, religious beliefs, political views and even agricultural practices.

During a break in our studies we visit a temple in the nearby city of Lampun and meet Veerasak Yodrabum, Yod for short. Yod and his wife, Oy, have taught in the hill country and are now working on a book about the mountain people. Yod invites us to stay at their home.

Like most rural Thai homes the living quarters consist of a small group of buildings surrounded by a banana grove, vegetable garden and chicken pen. The house is a tropical dwelling with thin cracks between the wooden planks to allow a light breeze to drift through the rooms. The windows have no glass, only wooden shutters.

We share living quarters with a Karen man. The tattoos on his arms are to keep him from being reborn as a woman, Thailand.

159

The kitchen is a large bamboo building next to the house. It is built in the style of the Karen tribe, with wider, half-inch cracks between each piece of bamboo in the walls, a raised bamboo platform for eating during meal times and napping during other times, and a large rock structure beside the firepit for smoking and preserving foods.

Two Karen men live in the kitchen building. One is a young man who helps cook and does work around the house, the other is an older man who is writing his memoirs about Karen life and history. Oy, who is a teacher, translates his notes into Thai. Yod, who is a freelance writer, edits the script to make it flow smoothly. Yod tells us that little of Karen history from the Karen's viewpoint has ever been published.

The old Karen man is a real character. He has sparkling eyes and a wide smile with three-quarters of his teeth missing. His arms are covered with tatoos in Karen script, applied over the years as he grew and fulfilled certain cultural and religious obligations. Although he is a strong Christian and leads us in a Karen grace before every meal, the tattoos are to insure that he will not be reborn as a woman--which shows he also believes in reincarnation, and that life in the mountains is very hard for women. Like most Karen, he is a chain smoker and always has a six-inch long, hand-rolled cigarette or a pipe in his mouth.

After reading about all the hilltribes, we decide to first visit an Akha tribe. Rather than going through a trekking agency, Yod offers to arrange a trip for us. He has been planning on visiting a Black Lahu village near the Laotian border and encourages us to come along. From there he will get us a guide to visit an isolated Akha tribe.

At the Lahu village we are introduced to Benjamin, a 17-year-old Black Lahu whom Yod convinces to take us into the mountains. Benjamin has never been a guide and speaks little English. Furthermore, he has never set foot in the Akha village we want to visit, or any Akha village for that matter. Still, Yod assures us everything will work out splendidly. We load up our backpacks and follow Benjamin into the hot, dusty mountains.

Akha tradition bars outsiders from strolling through the villages. The Akha believe if you don't know anyone who will invite you in for a glass of water, you should not set foot in the village. The man we are hoping will invite **us** in doesn't know we are coming. Although he grew up in Benjamin's village, Benjamin has never met him. He left five years ago to live as a teacher with the Akha. We hope he is home.

After walking up a canyon and then hiking through a steep bamboo forest, we arrive at the outskirts of the Akha village. In front of us a group of three large wooden totems guard against evil spirits coming into the village. We stop at a nearby wooden trough filled with spring water, splash our faces to clean up, and walk past the totems, into the village.

Immediately we meet a woman walking up the hill toward us.

Surprisingly, she pays no attention to us. We, on the other hand, can't take our eyes off her and stand gawking as she climbs a notched log ladder to a house on six-foot stilts. She wears a loin-cloth of stone beads, silver coins, and sea shells over a blue, knee-length, embroidered cotton skirt. Her blouse is also covered with embroidery, but I hardly glance at it, for on her head is what we have hiked into the mountains to see--the famous hat

Wearing her family's wealth on her head, a young Akha girl will have more silver and beadwork added to her hat until, by adulthood, it may weigh ten pounds, northern Thailand.

of the Akha women.

The headdress is covered with beadwork and silver coins pounded into concave buttons. A silver slab, six inches high and four inches wide, pokes up behind the hat. Tassels of dyed chicken feathers and thick strands of stone beads and hand-beaten coins drape from the hat to her chest. The hats of the Akha women can weigh as much as ten pounds.

The hat, along with the embroidered clothing, shells and beads, is not part of a traditional costume reserved for special occasions--it is her everyday dress.

She ducks inside the door as we walk into the village. Forty bamboo homes, built on stilts, cover the steep hillside below us. Other women, sitting on elevated bamboo platforms, momentarily stop their work to watch us. No one smiles. Only a small band of children, following twenty feet behind, pays any lasting attention. Occasionally one or two get brave enough to run by us. Then they stop along the trail and jump up and down in nervous excitement before scampering back past us to rejoin their friends.

At the bamboo house of the man who is our contact in the village, we receive a cool greeting. Our hoped-for host speaks a few curt words in a Lahu dialect to Benjamin. He doesn't acknowledge us. After a few moments of uncomfortable standing around, he turns and goes into his house. We hesitantly follow. Inside we sit in a corner while the two Lahu men strike up a slow conversation.

Actually, the word conversation is misleading. Benjamin mumbles a few words, followed by thirty seconds of silence. Our host answers briefly. Two minutes of quiet. Benjamin speaks again. More silence. At last the teacher hands us a gourd of water, a sign that we can spend the night. We take a drink and are ignored once again.

We sit for an hour and listen to the lack of conversation, and then excuse ourselves to walk through the village. This time we begin to make brief eye contact with some of the people. The women pound rice, kids haul water, a few people gather to chat. We try to blend in, an impossible task.

An old woman with a mouth full of betelnut walks past. She stops and stares at our plain clothing and Tass's long, blonde braid. Passing by us, she walks to the gate of her yard, turns, and motions us to follow. We climb the short bamboo ladder to the platform in front of her hut. She brings us water and a plate of roasted peanuts and then sits down to clean the kernels off a pile of dried corn cobs. Again we are ignored.

The Akha are known for their strong self-image and resistance to change. The woman has no interest in ogling over us, in coveting our western-style clothing, our camera, our watches. We are not Akha. We are strangers, adults without the correct social signs of success. Tass is a woman without a hat, without jewelry, without children. I have no pipe, no dogs and no pigs.

A small, dirty-faced boy comes up the ladder. It is a warm day yet he is shivering. He sits meekly next to the woman. She ignores him. Finally, he holds up an arm to reveal a large abrasion. She responds by swatting his head. He huddles next to her and continues to shake. She finishes her work and then, with a scowl, grabs his arm and spits a mouthful of betelnut-filled saliva on the wound. This relieves the boy. Akha first aid.

A few minutes later the woman holds up the boy's arm to show us the wound. I excuse myself, using sign language she probably doesn't understand, and run to the teacher's hut for our medical kit. When I return the boy sits with a deadpan face while I clean the dirt and sand out of the wound. With more sign language I try to explain the importance of cleaning an injury. By the time I finish a group of people has gathered to show us various health problems. We soon have a full clinic. Infections are drained of pus, slivers pulled out of feet, and other minor ills treated. In the seven years the village has been located on this ridge, no doctor has

In the seven years the Akha village has been located on this ridge, no doctor has ever visited the tribe. The first-aid kit is put to use as Bruce treats minor cuts and infections, Thailand's Golden Triangle.

ever visited the tribe.

The Akha originated in the Yunnan province of China. They move their villages whenever the soil in their fields is depleted of nutrients. Like the other hill tribes who have migrated into northern Thailand, the Akha have their own unique language, customs and religious beliefs. The Akha commitment to their tradition has kept their tribal culture strong, but is also responsible for an intolerance to new ideas. The tribe's resistance to change causes problems with the Thai government, especially in regards to agricultural practices. Besides growing quantities of opium poppies, which annoys the government, the Akha use destructive farming techniques on all their crops, both legal and illegal. As a result, they are causing widespread deforestation in an area of Thailand that is more and more crowded each year.

The village has been grazed clean of grass and shrubs. Dogs, pigs and chickens scour the area for food. Ever on the alert, a pack of animals follows us when we take the trail to a barren hillside, the village toilet. They eye each other nervously, ready to fight over our waste. I grab a stick to fend off a big pig while I squat. It's nerve-wracking to continually parry his advances, and the stress gives me momentary constipation, further prolonging the ordeal. The dogs are more cautious and wait for me to move away before rushing forward. By that time the pig has gulped down the meal. Hot lunch.

In the evening we are invited to a marriage ceremony in a large thatched-roof dwelling on stilts. Inside, one room is divided by a tall partition. Our host motions for us to sit on the bamboo floor. Six men squat beside us, each with a cup of tea and a glass of home-made whiskey. We are likewise served whiskey and tea but politely decline the small, hand-rolled Burmese cigars passed around on an enamel plate. In the corner a small fire burns on a hearth of dirt packed on the floor. The fire on the men's side of the house is for brewing tea and cooking meat. On the other side of the partition, the women's side, are two more cooking fires: one for preparing vegetables and rice, the other for cooking the animals' food.

We sip our whiskey and watch the men cook pig on the fire. The Lahu teacher, who has ignored us all day, comes over to greet us. Much to our surprise, he speaks in broken English. Since we are vegetarians, he tells us to eat in the next room, on the women's side of the house. Men are seldom invited into the women's area, so I am excited for a chance to go on the other side of the partition.

The women are dressed in their finest clothing. The bride is in a corner, covered with embroidered blankets and strands of coins and beads. She sits with her back to the room, her face to the wall. We sit at a small table while the teacher graciously serves us fried rice, vegetables and eggs in a delicious broth. Everyone else gets plates of rice and bowls of either burnt, greasy pork or lightly cooked meat oozing with red juices. The women, with great delicacy, use chopsticks to pick out raw tidbits.

After a lengthy meal the tables are cleared, and we return to the men's side of the house to wait for the main event of the evening. In preparation, women place bowls of cooked rice throughout the house. Having read about Akha marriage customs, we find a seat in a protected corner. An old man sitting by the fire takes a bowl of rice and climbs on a bench near the partition to look over at the women's side of the house. Moments later an old woman sticks her head above the wall to face him. The two elders recite blessings and marriage instructions, then scoop out a

An Akha woman getting water piped through bamboo from the village spring, northern Thailand.

handful of cooked rice from the bowls they hold. Without pausing his chant, the man tosses his rice onto the women's side of the house. The old woman responds by throwing a ball of rice onto the floor before us.

Thud.

The two elders throw another handful, and another. For a few minutes the men out in the middle of the room sit stoically, sipping whiskey while the shower of rice continues to grow. Finally, with mischievous grins, they take sticky handfuls of rice from nearby bowls and pack them into lethal-sized, four-inch balls. We back further into our corner.

A major battle erupts. At first it is men against women but then everything degenerates into a free-for-all. Heavy, gooey, globs of rice hurl through the air to hit their targets with resounding thuds. Old men and women put all propriety aside and scamper around the room ambushing each other. By the end of the fight the entire house is a complete mess--the floor, walls, furniture and guests are covered with rice.

The next day Benjamin is eager to move on to our next stop, a Red Lahu village. He doesn't like the way the Akha cook their rice. As we walk out of the village we wave to the woman who gave us the water and roasted nuts. Dressed in clothing fit for a queen, she will probably spend the day working in the fields.

14
Among the Hmong

We return to Yod and Oy's house, read all the English books on hill tribes in their library, and prepare for another trip into the mountains. We want to ride our bikes on a loop along the Burmese border and take a few side trips into villages.

We head out on the Mae Hong Son highway and take our first detour to the village of Doi Kum. The road to the village is a mountain track, 18 miles of rocks and ruts with a 3,500-foot climb. Not the terrain for fully loaded street bikes, but that has never stopped us before. I break a spoke after only three miles. Luckily we carry plenty of spares.

The hills get steeper, the road rougher. We sweat and groan, riding in our lowest gears, and sometimes pushing our bikes on the steeper sections when our tires spin out in the loose gravel and powdery dust. We arrive dirty and exhausted. A crowd of inquisitive villagers immediately forms around us.

Doi Kum is a Blue Hmong village. The women wear thick, quilted, *batik* skirts and jackets covered with embroidery. Like the Akha, the most distinctive part of their dress is on the head. Hmong women wrap their hair in giant buns; some even shave the front half of their head to dramatically emphasize the mound of hair piled in back. The men wear

167

calf-length black baggy pants with billowy legs and embroidered shirts. On special occasions, the men wear caps topped with huge red pom-poms.

In contrast, we wear faded biking shorts and rather dusty T-shirts. We pull out a letter of introduction for the village teacher, an old friend of Yod's. Twenty people accompany us to the front gate of Suwanee Siroros's house. Suwanee, Mu for short, meets us at the door. We give her the letter, which she slowly reads as we and the rest of the twenty people stand patiently to see what will happen next. Mu finishes the letter and stands quietly before us, thinking. We ask if she speaks English. To our relief she replies yes. We explain why we came to the village. She makes no reply to us, but speaks in a Hmong dialect to a few villagers.

We are used to the Western style of welcome, where the hosts immediately give feedback to the guest, "Oh, I am so glad you came" or "It is nice to meet you," even if the hosts are not yet sure that they **are** glad to see you. In Thai culture, meetings and relationships start off at a slower pace. The Thais believe that if true friendship is to develop it must be nurtured carefully. After more contemplating, Mu tells us we may move our belongings into her house and suggests we walk around the village before supper and watch the women grind corn.

The Hmong came to Thailand from China in the 1850's. Today they are one of the most widespread of all hill tribes, with communities in south China, Vietnam and Laos. To us, they look more Tibetan than Chinese. Approximately 60,000 Hmong live in Thailand.

Unlike the Akha village, none of the homes are built on stilts, and few are made of bamboo. Most are built of hand-hewn planks and have tin roofs instead of thatching. Mu's house even has a cement floor, a gift to her from the village. We watch the women grind corn at a communal stone mill hooked to a two-person hand swing. Tass gives the grinding a try and works with another woman, grinding corn until after dark.

We return to Mu's house to sit on a woven reed mat and eat supper. Mu tells us much of the wealth in the village comes from growing opium, a fact we guessed when we rode through fields of poppies just before arriving in the village. The government has been pressuring the villagers to stop growing opium. Mu tells us three years ago the villagers planted cabbage instead of poppies, but they lacked ways of getting their crops to markets. Despite government promises to help transport the crops to lowland cities, much of the cabbage rotted before it was sold. The villagers nearly starved that year and are now reluctant to grow other crops. When the villagers grow poppies, opium traders come to the village to pick up the unrefined drug so there is no worry about getting crops to far away markets. Yet selling opium also has its problems. Some of the opium traders don't give fair prices and others intimidate villagers with threats. This is especially true close to the Burmese border where opium kings roam the countryside with large private armies.

As an alternative and legal form of income, Mu has been working with the villagers to put on performances of traditional Hmong singing, dancing and storytelling for tourists. As of yet, no foreigners have been in the village. But Mu is confident once word is out in Chiang Mai there will be a steady flow of tourists who will pay to spend the night and see a Hmong festival. Now we offer a chance for a dress rehearsal; Mu tells us we will be guests of honor at a special dance tonight.

It seems the entire village gathers to perform for us. We sit on a bench in the village square and watch group after group come forward to sing, dance and perform skits that tell of Hmong life and traditions. In one skit the village healer does a hilarious impersonation of his peer, the village *shaman*, curing a person who has seen a ghost. The old man walks around the quaking victim doing various rituals and chants that bring riotous laughter from all the villagers. Then, in a dramatic finale that could win an Oscar for special effects, the *shaman* circles the victim with a bowl of burning coals held on a long pole. Every few steps he spits a mouthful of

Hmong children dressed for a festive evening, Thailand.

highly flammable liquid into the coals, causing a huge fireball to erupt which nearly singes every hair on both his and the patient's head. The children in the audience first cower in terror and then jump with nervous excitement as the old man does his tricks. It is an impressive performance.

The singing and dancing goes on until midnight. When the show is over we are taken to the home of the assistant village chief. We are ushered into a large room with a cooking fire and a long bamboo sleeping platform. Our host is reluctant to believe we will stay warm in our sleeping bags, and lays out beautiful *batik* quilts for us.

It is pitch dark when we awaken to the thumping sound of rice being husked in a large stone pestle. Without checking my watch I know it must be very early, the roosters have not even started to crow. Ten minutes later the pounding stops and we smell smoke as the mother fans the coals to restart the cooking fire. When the fire catches, a faint glow illuminates the room.

The rest of the family begins their morning chores. A young boy, with the dexterity of a professional chef, slices two cabbages while the mother cuts up a large section of the heart of a banana tree. The food is sauteed in a frying pan, mixed with ground corn, and boiled to a thick mush in a giant, four-foot wok. This nutritious meal is prepared twice daily for the family's herd of pigs.

Pigs are a sign of status. Like many tribes, Hmong households have separate fires for cooking the animal's food, a practice requiring a tremendous amount of work, and also putting a burden on tribal resources and causing further deforestation.

Once the food is cooking, the mother and daughters step outside to take down their large buns and brush their hair. When Hmong women comb their hair, they save any hair that comes out in the brush and use the hair to make a natural wig, which is then added to the hair on their head to create their large distinctive buns. Tass watches the process with interest and is soon asked if she would like to be dressed in Hmong fashion.

The women scout the village for extra clothing. Within minutes Tass is the center of attention as a group of women fusses over her, while another group offers comments and suggestions. She is dressed in a traditional *batik* skirt and blouse covered with embroidery. A beautiful needlepoint sash is tied around her waist. When it is time to do her hair, a black wig is added to her blonde hair, giving Tass a multi-colored bun. Stone beads are also woven into the bun of hair and a thick, solid silver necklace is placed around her neck. She looks striking.

Next, I am attired in traditional men's clothing. Since I am much taller than the Hmong men, my T-shirt sticks out between the bottom of my short-tailed, embroidered shirt and the top of my billowing knicker pants.

170

When we put our own clothes back on they feel drab and boring.

We thank Mu for her hospitality and leave a donation to help the village kick the opium habit. As we pedal away a group of children runs beside us to the first steep descent on the road. I am not sure if they are politely escorting us or if they just want to see if we'll crash on the big downhill out of the village.

We make the first hill but then run into trouble. The deep ruts and bumps, combined with the soft, powdered dirt, make it impossible to brake and steer at the same time. Both of us take our first major crash: Tass does a prolonged slide on her hip; I execute a somersault, removing half of the skin on my back.

Back on the main highway the weather is once again stifling and the road steep. The sun beats down on us. We work like slaves up each pass. Sweat drips in our eyes, and we can't keep sun screen on our perspiring bodies.

By the second day we climb high enough that the temperature drops to a bearable level. We stop in two Karen villages. One we simply pick off the map; in the other we have a contact and another letter of introduction from Yod.

The Karen have lived in Thailand the longest of all the hill tribes and have settled into the most stable agricultural lifestyle. They are the most ecologically minded of the hill people and generally live at a lower altitude. Both Karen men and women wear large turbans and are avid smokers. If there is not a pipe hanging out of their mouths, they puff on huge, hand-rolled cigarettes with corn husk wrappings, or green cigars smuggled from Burma. Many Karen women also chew mouthfuls of betelnut which produces stained, red lips and black teeth--of which usually a number are missing. They laugh and grin and their eyes sparkle.

The first village we stop at is just off the main road. We spend the afternoon sitting on open porches watching women weave clothing on back-strap looms. We buy a beautiful blouse for 160 *baht* ($7 U.S.) even though the cloth to weave the blouse cost the woman 92 *baht* and the weaving took two weeks. She tells us she will use the money to go to a Christian meeting in another village next week. Many of the Karens were converted to Christianity when they lived in Burma during the 1800's. Since then they have been actively evangelizing other hill tribes.

At the second village no one speaks English. Unfortunately, even after nearly two months of practicing Thai, we have barely mastered the art of small talk. Rather than limit our interactions to two and three word sentences, smiles, and confusing sign language, our host thoughtfully sends off a note with a man who returns an hour later with an interpreter. Surprisingly, the interpreter went to college with Yod. His name is Saranyou, and he now works for the government. He is on the opposite

Karen woman with two of her children, Thailand.

side of the political spectrum from Yod. Yet even though he and Yod have different views, it is obvious he still respects his former classmate.

Yod and Saranyou parted ways in 1976, when, after repeated demonstrations by students and intellectuals against a series of ultra-right wing governments, many protesters grew tired of being hounded by the government and dropped out of Thai society. Some became apolitical, others moved to the hill country to do humanitarian work. A few joined insurgents living in the mountains. Yod and Oy left the university to teach in a Karen village and help the tribe to strive for political rights.

Saranyou's job is to travel to remote villages and teach anti-guerrilla doctrines. In some areas he helps arm the people so they can protect themselves from robbers and drug lords, which are a real threat, and from communists, which are a questionable threat since many who are labeled communists are simply trying to get basic rights for the people.

The whole problem is complex and, to us at least, both sides have justifiable complaints. The guerrillas claim the Thai government does not really represent or even help the hill people--which is true. The government's primary interest is to suppress anyone who questions its authority.

The government, on the other hand, complains that the guerrillas are supported by opium lords and do not have a political infrastructure to offer a better alternative--which is also true. The government believes the guerrillas are merely puppets of the smugglers. The guerrillas reply they will take arms from whomever they can.

Our host, like most of the hill people, is caught between two unfavorable options. He doesn't like the government's policies, yet he is fearful of the alternatives offered by those who take up arms. Until the government brings the hill tribes into the social and political infrastructure of the country, which is no easy task considering the cultural and ideological differences, there will continue to be tension in the mountains.

Even though we are getting culturally overloaded from hill tribe encounters, we can't pass up squeezing in a visit to one more hill tribe group, the Lisu. The highlight of our stop at a Lisu village is the successful attempt by one of the villagers to ride Tass's Trek (my bike is too big for anyone to try). The entire village watches the proceedings as I run up and down the trail beside the Lisu man, coaching him on.

Back in Chiang Mai we stay with Yod and Oy one more night, share stories, take some final notes in their library, and then catch the first train to Bangkok. In the capital we check into our old guest house, dig out some gear we left behind, and spend half the night repairing and reorganizing equipment. We leave for Burma the next day.

15

Sell Whiskey? Cigarettes?

Even though we bicycled along the Burmese border while in northern Thailand, we could not cross into Burma. All land borders into the country have been closed since the 1960's. Tourists are allowed to enter and leave Burma only by flying into the capital, Rangoon, and are given only seven day visas.

We land in the capital and stare out the window as our plane taxis past the terminal and comes to a stop nearly a quarter mile from the building. Everyone walks, toting bags and carry-on luggage, back across the hot pavement in the scorching sun to the terminal. Inside, not surprisingly, there is no air conditioning. In fact the ceiling fans don't even work. We stand in line in the suffocating heat for three hours before getting our passports stamped. An even bigger holdup occurs when we finally get to the official checking luggage.

"No bicycles in Burma," he tells us sternly as he waves an admonishing finger at us.

We had been warned that our bikes would be confiscated at the airport. Since we just get a seven day visa, we don't have enough time to see the country by bicycle anyway. But the official wants to impound only our bikes, not our panniers, which are still piled on an airport pushcart.

We don't want to haul all our bicycle gear around Rangoon looking for someplace to store it, so we try to persuade the official to confiscate the panniers as well, which we consider a part of the bikes. We argue long enough for the guard to get exasperated and call for his superior, whom we follow to an office to plead our case.

After fifteen minutes the official finally gives in. We hook the panniers on the bikes and stuff everything we don't need inside. After filling out numerous forms we push our loaded bikes into a vault. With a great flair, the official slams the metal door, drops a giant metal bar across the door, and clicks an enormous padlock shut. We shoulder our backpacks and head out onto the street, the last ones through customs.

"Sell whiskey? Cigarettes?"

A short smiling fellow and his large, fat friend descend upon us as we walk out of the terminal. When we shake our heads they try another angle.

"Taxi?"

This time we say yes. They escort us to an old decrepit vehicle. We hop in and go less than a block before the two entrepreneurs try again.

"Sell whiskey? Cigarettes?"

Unlike nearly everyone else on the flight, we did not bring in Johnny

Bruce playing hacky sack with a group of Burmese children.

Walker black label and five-fifty-five brand cigarettes. Travelers are legally allowed to bring in a quart of alcohol and a carton of cigarettes. If you bring the right brands they can easily be sold for double or even triple the purchase price on the thriving Burmese black market. But neither of us felt like cashing in on the alcohol and tobacco trade. However, we do respond to the next offer.

"Change money?"

The socialist government's attempt to regulate all business transactions has resulted in an increased Burmese determination to barter and trade on terms outside of government control. We sell the driver a fifty dollar bill at black market rates, 20 *kyats* to the dollar, more than double the exchange given by the government run Bank of Burma. It is a good deal for both of us. It makes our stay cheaper and gives the driver an investment in a currency of stable value in a land of economic uncertainty.

The Burmese government's restrictions are designed to isolate the nation from the modern world. Because of this policy Burma is a land where time stands still. The streets are nearly empty of vehicles. The few cars and buses to be found are of ancient vintage. Old Chevrolets are a major status symbol.

Once inside the country, visitors find travel extremely restricted with exasperating regulations governing everything. Our taxi stops downtown at a government approved hotel. The tourist hotels are just like regular hotels except they cost three times as much. We book a room in the hot, noisy building and then head for the government travel agency, the only place foreigners can purchase train tickets north to Mandalay.

The grumpy bureaucrat behind the counter checks the schedule and announces she can't book us any seats for two days. With a seven day visa we can't afford to wait even one day. We have two options. We can get together with a group of foreigners and hire a truck to drive us northward, or we can ride the overcrowded second class train. Most foreigners opt for the private truck. However we decide our stay is so short we would rather spend our time squished into a train full of Burmese than packed in a pickup with a group of foreigners.

The train to Mandalay is crowded to standing room only. The toilet is a simple hole in the floor to the tracks below. There is no water in the bathroom tap. Food and drinks are supplied by vendors who clamor at the windows during brief stops. During longer stops the vendors crowd on board to squeeze up and down the aisles selling their products.

After a few hours on the train, a family of six scrunches together enough to make room for one of us on their bench. For the next 18 hours we take turns, one of us sitting, squeezed into the spot, while the other stands. The seat has no cushions, just hard wooden slats. Still it feels wonderful to sit. The father is a large man who speaks fluent English--before World War II

Burma was a British colony. Like most Burmese, he is eager for contact with the rest of the world and unhappy with the government's policy of isolation. He is an astute observer of his country and very entertaining. The family shares their food with us whenever they eat, and occasionally buys us treats from different vendors.

We get off the train in Mandalay. The city, which is smaller than Rangoon, is considered the cultural center of Burma. We travel around in the Burmese version of the bicycle taxi, with the two passenger seats built back to back on one side of the bicycle. We visit a number of temples where exquisitely carved marble statues of Buddha wear garish garlands of tinsel and colored blinking lights. Iron gates seal off many of the shrines, making the altars look like bizarrely decorated prison cells. Las Vegas Buddhas behind bars.

Again we stay in a government approved hotel and get the required stamp in our visa lodging certificate. Our room is on the second floor, one of a number of wooden cubicles built into a large room, with the roof high above the 10-foot walls. To keep people from climbing over the walls into another room, chicken wire hangs over each room in place of a ceiling.

Two days later we head for the ruins of Pagan. Since there is no train to the area, we leave Mandalay in a compact pickup converted into a shuttle bus. Those uninitiated in third world buses might guess the truck will hold eight people. I figure they will pack 16 of us into the pickup. We

A Burmese woman puffing on a cornhusk cigar.

leave Mandalay with 24 passengers.

It seems no matter how close or far we have to go in Burma, it takes a day and a night to get there. We ride across the hot, dusty plains, drifting in and out of consciousness, taking cat naps squeezed between the other passengers, with everyone using each other's shoulder for a pillow.

The ruins of Pagan fill an immense plain in central Burma. Hundreds of temples built in the 11th and 12th century dot the landscape. We rent ancient clunker bicycles and ride on backroads of soft sand, exploring temples. Our favorite is Manuha Temple. Built by a king held captive in the city, each of three buildings houses a large statue of Buddha, with the walls hemming in the statues from all sides. The architecture chosen by the king represents his own life experience, and the expressions on the statues show the king's response to his imprisonment. We squeeze down narrow walkways to get cramped access to the statues. Serene expressions cover each face, showing the statues are unconcerned about their crowded living quarters.

The temples epitomize the nonchalant Burmese philosophy of life. The Burmese don't seem to let anything get them down. Patience might be Burma's greatest natural resource.

After another ride crammed into the back of a pickup, we catch a train for a stifling hot night ride back to Rangoon. The train doesn't even have lights, and this time we don't get a seat.

One of hundreds of abandoned temples dotting the plains of Pagan, Burma.

We spend one last day in Rangoon before heading to the airport to retrieve our bicycles from the customs vault. Our whirlwind tour of Burma is over. Our next stop is Nepal, where the trekking season is already underway.

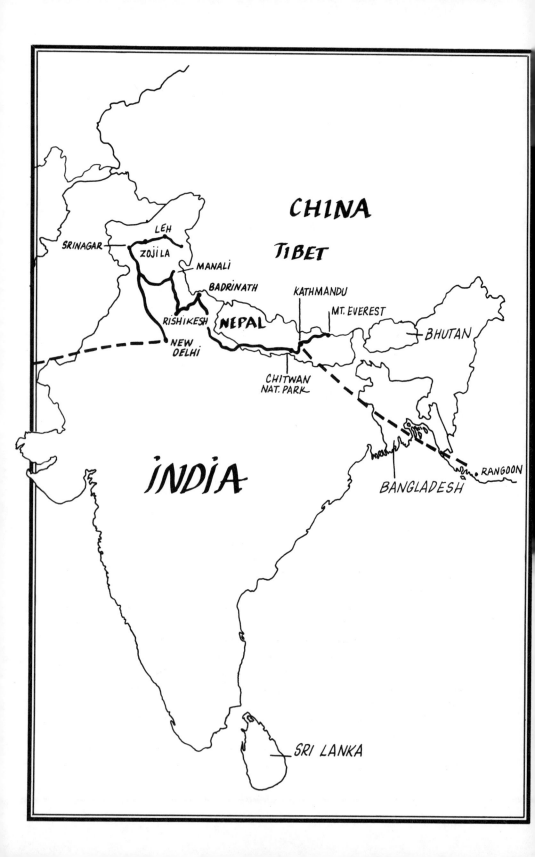

16

The Mother Goddess of the World

Moments after boarding the Air Nepal flight to Kathmandu, I spot an attendant at the back of the plane struggling to put Tass's bicycle on the two rear seats. Startled, I squeeze down the crowded aisle to see what's happening.

"Baggage compartment finished," the steward explains as he stuffs the dirty front tire of Tass's bike on the window seat. I quickly reach out and give the pedal a spin to keep the greasy chain off the seat as he drops the bike in place.

"Bicycles fit good here," he continues as he grabs my bike, which has not been cleaned since the dusty roads of the Golden Triangle, and tries to shove it in place. Spokes ping as my pedals grind into Tass's wheel. Not enough room. Undaunted, the steward demands the two Indian businessmen in the next row move their seats forward. Apparently their comfort is not a concern. My bike is hoisted back into the air, dropped into place, and we take-off for Nepal.

Kathmandu is considered by many travelers to be one of the dirtiest cities in Asia. After months of traveling in Thailand and Indonesia where immaculately dressed people sweep houses, yards and even streets daily, Kathmandu is a shock. In the alley outside our hotel the open sewer is

Tass shopping for masks, Kathmandu, Nepal.

clogged, forcing us to sidestep nasty puddles whenever we take the short-cut downtown. Because of the low standard of living, many people have soiled, torn clothing. Most of the kids on the street have a few day's accumulation of snot dribbling from their noses.

However it is not long before we forget about the dirt as the legendary charm of the city takes hold. The smell of open sewers gives way to the delicious aromas of restaurants and food stalls. Kathmandu is also famous for its cuisine--Italian, Mexican, Tibetan, Indian, and, of course, Nepali restaurants line the streets.

At lunch we get a table in a south Indian restaurant overlooking a bustling street, eat *roti chani* and *dahl* with our fingers, slurp down *lassies*, a yogurt drink, and discuss our preparations for our Mount Everest trek. By the end of the meal we have compiled two lists of errands, one for each of us. We eat dessert and split up to do our designated chores.

Our plan is to hike through the Solo-Khumbu region to the base of Everest, climb a small peak, explore a few side valleys, and hike out through the Arun Valley. The trip will take approximately 32 days. Since the area is a popular trekking route with places to get lodging and food in many villages, we decide not to carry a tent or cooking gear. Rather than hiking into the mountains to be alone, we want to stay in lodges and homes and eat with the locals in tea shops--to get to know the people. Since we are not using porters, staying in homes will also help us learn Nepali.

Running errands in Kathmandu is a time-consuming process; some of the items on our lists require endless searching. We sent all our winter gear home after leaving New Zealand. Now we scour the trekking shops for cold weather clothing. Each shop is full of equipment to rent or sell. The gear has been accumulated over the years as large climbing groups sell, give away, or abandon gear after their expeditions.

Because there are only two trekking seasons in Nepal, travelers across Asia migrate to the Himalaya each spring and fall to hike. Besides making new friends, we bump into people we have met throughout the last year of traveling: Larry and Donna, whom we met on the volcano in Bali and again in Java; Renata, who slept next to Tass at *Wat Suan Moke*, the monastery in Thailand; and Paul and Deb, whom we first met in a hut on the Routeburn hike in New Zealand, again in a museum in Sydney, next on Penang Island in Malaysia, and last at a bustling market in Bangkok.

But the biggest surprise is meeting Phil and Georgette, two friends from Tass's hometown, Deadwood, South Dakota. We are in a mountaineering shop, bargaining on the rental price of a pile coat, when we literally bump into Georgette, who is trying on boots.

Socializing turns out to be our favorite pastime. We meet friends for nearly every meal and during breaks for cake and pie as well. Everyone

Used false teeth for sale, Kathmandu, Nepal.

has tales to tell. We swap info on routes, illnesses, places to see and places to avoid. After each meal Tass and I pull out our errands lists, scratch off the things we have accomplished, add items we suddenly remember we need, and go back to the search.

After four days of bargaining, we nearly have our gear and permits together. We pack up our bikes and everything else we don't need, and store it all in a luggage room at our hotel. Then we hear that the bus to Jiri, the town where our hike will begin, has gone on strike. I go to the bus station to find out what is happening.

"Finished. Jiri finished," says the 16-year-old kid sitting on the log railing next to the closed ticket window.

"Will it run tomorrow?" I ask. He shakes his head. "Jiri on strike. Finished!" he states emphatically, as though the bus will never run again, at least not during my lifetime.

We go to the bus station early the next morning anyway. The Jiri bus is definitely not running. We buy a ticket to Lamosangu, the closest town. We arrive at noon and join a group of people waiting for a ride the last 70 miles to Jiri. After an hour a man drives up in a truck and announces he will take us all to Jiri for 4,000 *rupiahs*, an exorbitant sum. We count the crowd and figure it will cost 200 *rupiahs* per person, almost $10 U.S. The bus that is on strike only charges 67 *rupiahs* to go to Jiri all the way from

184

Kathmandu. The crowd of local businessmen, farmers, laborers and porters stands around, unsure what they should do. Tass and I get together with three other foreigners and loudly announce we will spend the next three days walking before we pay 200 *rupiahs* for a ride.

The rest of the crowd agrees, and the truck driver lowers his rate to 125 *rupiahs* per person with a discount for the farmers going half way. It is still steep, but then so is the road, and the truck will use lots of fuel. After some debate we all agree to the new price. Everyone climbs into the back of the truck, and the driver's helper begins working his way through the throng collecting money.

It is like pulling teeth. A lengthy discussion must be held before each passenger hands over any money. As the representative of the foreigners, I join a group of five Nepalese who follow along through the entire process, watching the exchange of money and counting each bill out slowly to insure everyone pays fair share and no one is overcharged. Each name is listed in a notebook along with the amount paid.

An hour later the awesome task is finished. Everyone has paid and there is a big wad of bills in the collector's hands. Once more the money is slowly counted, 2,090 *rupiahs*. No sooner is the amount tallied than the truck driver announces he will not budge for less than 3,200 *rupiahs*. We all look at each other in disbelief. The thought of going back through this penny-pinching group to raise more funds is too terrible to contemplate. No one knows what to do next. Just as we are about to demand our money back and unload our gear, another bus, stuffed full of people, with twenty-five extra passengers clinging to the luggage rack on top of the roof, careens around the corner with the horn honking and everyone waving and yelling for us to wait.

A large group of people gets off the bus and comes over to join us. The money collecting resumes. This time the task is even more difficult as all the new arrivals squirm around, trying to duck out of paying. An hour later the funds are retallied. Everyone is stunned when it is announced there are only 2,900 *rupiahs*. The truck is now packed, yet the coffers have grown little. Everyone accuses someone else of not paying. The driver refuses to start the engine.

We sit another hour in the hot sun in the back of the crowded truck, waiting for more passengers. When no one else shows up the driver finally decides he has enough money. We start up the road to Jiri in the late afternoon.

The highway is steep and full of switchback and hairpin corners. The back of the truck is crammed to standing room only, so we perch on the luggage rack on top of the cab. We have more room but also more wind chill. When the sun goes down, so does the temperature. We pull out our sleeping bags, use our packs as back rests, and try to get some sleep.

185

At 1:00 a.m. we pull into Jiri. The passengers all climb out to find someplace to spend the night. We simply move our sleeping bags to the back of the empty truck and fall asleep.

At dawn, the air is cold and crisp. We eat a quick breakfast of porridge, *chapatis* and milk tea at a nearby food stall, hoist our packs, and head off on a wide trail leading into the mountains.

The trek from Jiri to Everest follows a well-established route into Namche Bazaar, the market center for the entire Everest region. Most foreigners traveling into Everest fly into the high altitude airport at Lukla to start their hike. We take the extra seven days to hike in from Jiri so we can spend more time in the 6,000 to 12,000 foot level, the "foothills" of the main range, where most of the people live. Although we will be hiking at lower elevations, the first week will cross the steepest terrain. We will be hiking against the grain of the mountains, which means we will repeatedly climb high passes only to descend into low valleys, cross rivers, and begin the ascent of the next pass.

Hiking in Nepal is unlike hiking anywhere else in the world. The back country is not a wilderness. It is the home of millions of people. We pass groups of porters and Sherpas carrying loads up and down the steep valleys. Some are somber under their burdens, others yell out greetings and flash big smiles.

The Nepalese are famous for the weight they carry. Everyone totes

Tass starting our 32-day hike to Mount Everest, Nepal.

enormous loads in wicker baskets held on the back with a tump line, a strap across the forehead. Each porter also carries a wooden cane which doubles as a luggage rest during breaks. With the loads still on their backs, the porters prop their burdens onto the wide T-handled cane and then lean back to transfer the weight to the cane. A Nepalese kickstand.

The second day of hiking we reach the top of a high ridge. Below lies the first of a series of deep valleys we must cross. We descend the 9,000-foot pass to a suspension bridge on the Liku Khola river at an elevation of 5,000 feet. After crossing the bridge, we begin the ascent of 11,600-foot Lamjura Pass. The following day we crest the pass, descend 3,000 feet to the next valley, and hike up Tragshindo La Pass, where we spend the night at one of the region's two cheese factories.

The Tragshindo Cheese Factory is a large stone building with a roof of massive wooden timbers hauled up from the lowlands on the backs of porters. The family living in the corner of the building has turned their home into an inn. Travelers eat and socialize in the large kitchen and sleep outside in a small, unheated, wooden shed containing a bumpy mound of packed dirt and rock which serves as a communal bed. We share the hut with five other foreigners: three left Jiri the same morning we did; the other two are hiking out. We lay our sleeping bags out to claim a spot on the "bed" and head to the inn, eager to try some Nepali cheese.

Cheese is made in the spring. Since it is now early April, no cheese has been produced in nearly a year. But we are elated to find there is still cheese stored from last season. The menu choice is between cheese pie and cheese soup. After a day of hiking the decision is not what to eat, but what to eat first. We start off with the soup.

Unfortunately, it doesn't taste as good as it sounds. There is a slight moldy after-taste as the food goes down, and even moldier belches follow as the food settles into our stomachs. As we watch the mother prepare our second course, we discover why the soup tastes peculiar. After being stored in a cellar for nearly a year, the thick layer of protective wax on the cheese picked up a coating of dirt, dust, and mold. None of this, however, bothers our chef. She grates blocks of cheese, still wrapped in their dirty wax covering, into each recipe.

Later in the evening Aaron, a new friend from New Zealand, Tass and I sit in a small room off the main kitchen, huddled in front of a fireplace trying to ward off the evening chill. Before long we forget about moldy belches and order more cheese pie for a late night snack. We lazily watch a young girl bake the pie. She covers the inside of a large, cast-iron pot with three inches of ashes and then places the pie gently inside the pot. A heavy lid is put over the pot and covered with a pile of coals to create an oven. As the pie bakes, the girl, who is about twelve years old, keeps busy breaking wood, stoking the fire, boiling water, and doing dishes. She wears a peasant's scarf, a well-worn blouse and an old dress that just covers her calves. Despite living in the cold mountains, she is shoeless. We sit in silence as we watch her add more and more wood to the fire.

Suddenly, the reality of the situation hits me. This fire has been built for us. The cooking fires at this inn, and countless others along the trail, burn constantly to provide food for hungry trekkers. Each time the girl throws a log on the fire we can say good-bye to another chunk of Nepal's dwindling forests.

Before I can share my thoughts, the door flies open and the woman running the inn bustles in with more food for the oven. Although I was impressed by the care the young girl took in arranging the fire, it is apparent the woman does not share my admiration. She looks at the fire and begins to yell and then knocks the girl about the room. The girl, who may be her daughter or a hired servant from another family, makes no effort to defend herself. When the beating is over, the girl rearranges the burning logs with her bare hands. Tass, Aaron and I sit together in uncomfortable silence. I can't imagine the girl's life. She is working her childhood away and getting physical blows as a reward.

We eat the pie baked by slave labor over wood that should still be in the forest, and then belch our way to bed, uncertain whether our being here is helping the local economy or just adding to its problems.

The next morning we leave the cheese factory and hike through a light covering of snow toward the next pass. Near the summit we meet three groups of porters, each huddled around a smoldering fire cooking *tsampa*, a doughy mixture of barley flour and water. The porters wear worn and tattered western-style clothes. A few have tennis shoes full of holes, others have rubber thongs, the remainder are barefoot. They sit shivering, exposed to the wind. A few whimper from the cold as we pass.

I am astounded a group of people could live for generations in a mountain environment and still be inadequately prepared for normal weather conditions on a frequently traveled pass. The only way the porters have of obtaining warmth is to whack down a few trees and build a fire. We have yet to see any porters wearing wool clothing. Even though the porters come from lower valleys, they spend their days carrying loads over these passes. Yet no one thinks to bring an old jacket or blanket when going above 10,000 feet. I didn't expect the porters to drop their loads at each pass and hike to the nearest overlook to sing the theme from The Sound of Music, but I did think they would show more basic mountain sense.

On the other side of the pass we drop down to a small village with a large Buddhist *gompa*. Since it is the first Tibetan-style temple we have seen on our hike, we stop to explore the structure and eat lunch in the warm sunshine of the monastery courtyard. It feels so good to relax we decide to stop for the day.

When afternoon clouds appear we check into the Tragshindo Monastery Lodge, and spend the rest of the day sitting on a hard wooden bench watching the Sherpa proprietor nurse the fire under an assortment of blackened kettles. A Tibetan mastiff lies sleeping in the middle of the floor. Beside me sit a quiet group of trekkers reading, all bundled in down coats, hats, and mittens.

All the foreigners look up in consternation whenever anyone comes in or goes out--the locals never close the door and always leave a cold draft in their wake. The Nepalis don't seem to have any desire to keep the lodge warm. They huddle and shiver just like we do, but they seem to view being cold as a normal part of everyday life and do little to change things.

A well-groomed Nepali dressed in green tights and a down vest comes in the door. He has thick black hair, a long waxed mustache, and carries a shiny new ski pole for a walking stick. A Nepali politician. The man makes the rounds, encouraging everyone to vote for him. He eats a plate of boiled potatoes, gives us all a few more gold-toothed smiles, and heads out the door--without shutting it.

The next day we drop off the 10,000-foot pass to cross the Dudh Kosi River at 4,800 feet. Unlike the climbs, where we use the same muscles as bicycling, the long downhills are stressful on our legs. Despite the strain on our knees, the descent into the valley is enjoyable. We walk at a relaxed pace through moss-covered tropical rain forests and terraced fields clinging to the steep hillsides. Rather than racing to our destination each day, we take our time and savor each hike. Villages with lodging are separated in increments to accommodate the pace the porters' travel. Since the porters all carry 80-100 pound loads, and stop twice daily to build a fire and cook their food, we easily walk each section of trail in 4-6 hours. That gives us plenty of time to sit on overlooks and enjoy the view, pull out the binoculars and scout for illusive birds, talk with porters we meet on the trail, and take a few breaks in tea houses along the way.

We hike through a variety of ecosystems and travel through different ethnic villages as we climb up and down each pass . One settlement is mostly Rais, another Tamongs, and, as we get further into the mountains, another Sherpas. Some are a mixture of all three. Unlike the hill tribes of Thailand, the differences between each group are more subtle. Yet from village to village we notice changes in the architecture of the homes, styles of clothing and types of jewelry.

We climb out of the Khari Khola valley through steep terraces of golden-ripe barley. Old Sherpa women with braided hair coiled on the back of their heads work the fields, slowly harvesting each head of grain, one by one, with a sharp sickle knife. They wear large necklaces of

Enjoying the warm morning sun on the porch of a trailside tea stall, Nepal.

turquoise and red coral, ancient seashell bracelets and silver belts.

In the afternoon I crest a high ridge. Although Tass is ahead of me up the mountain, I stop to look at some *chortens*, Buddhist monuments built on overlooks and passes. By the time I resume hiking the sun has set behind the mountains and the air is chilled. Just before nightfall I come to a group of houses and find Tass standing in the trail talking with two hikers we have been leap-frogging since the beginning of our hike.

Tass, John, and Julius are discussing whether to spend the night here, at a little house that has a wooden sign tacked next to the door with the word "lodge" written in English, or whether to hike on to a big two-story lodge an hour up the trail. None of us feel like hiking in the dark, but we are also uncertain whether we will get much sleep here. Two drunken men and two topsy-turvy women are inside the home having a party. Another woman is vomiting in the front yard.

While we talk I watch two little boys playing nearby. They wear tattered and dirty clothes with the crotch removed so they can go to the bathroom without bothering to lower their britches. Potty training--Nepali style. Suddenly, the younger boy, who is about three years old, emerges from the house with a big kitchen knife and begins chasing his four-year-old brother around the yard. The weight of the knife, which is the size of a meat cleaver, makes the weapon an unwieldy tool in the child's hands.

He swings wildly and staggers when the momentum of the swing follows through. Luckily for his brother, he has poor coordination, and there seems little chance of a blow hitting its target.

The older boy escapes over a dirt bank while the swordsman relieves his frustration at losing his prey by spinning in circles and lashing out at piles of dirt and rock. In one wild swing he connects with an old tree stump with enough force that, had it been someone's leg, the knife would have easily slashed into the bone. Maybe the little terror can hit something after all! He works for a time to extract the embedded blade from the tree and then runs at high speed into the house--waving the knife above his head.

We watch the scenario with anxiety and visualize the inebriated adults performing first aid on one of the children. This household may need a clear-thinking adult before the night is over. We enter the building and take a seat by the fire.

The revelers soon stagger out the door and wander off into the night. A nicely dressed woman appears, sweeps our sleeping area, and cooks us a delicious meal of potato pancakes topped with yak butter and spiced curd. Even the hellions settle down as we sit around the fire after supper. By candlelight we show the woman and children our postcards from home, and then sleep on wooden pallets in a room next to the kitchen.

In the morning we begin a long descent down a mountain face that is permanently in the shade of a large peak. Mist swirls in the deep valleys below. We hike past moss-covered trees and blooming rhododendrons. Everything is cool and wet. The air smells rich and fertile. On an exposed ridge we watch two Lammergeiers, enormous vultures with nine-foot wing spans, rise up from the valley in smooth, exhilarating arcs. I call out to them as they soar past our overlook. They fly in for a closer view and then continue upward. Two more of the beautiful birds appear over another ridge. All four meet above the massive canyon and circle higher and higher until they are just black dots sailing on the wind.

On the eighth day we join the trail coming from the airport at Lukla where most of the tourists fly in and out. We wonder if we will see an increase in foreigners, but we hike all afternoon without seeing anyone. After a final climb out of the valley we arrive at Namche Bazaar, located at 11,300 feet on the steep face of a hill that closes in on itself like a giant amphitheater. The fields are bare. Potato planting season is still weeks away. The town is cold and windswept; there are no bright buildings, nor any trees.

In order to acclimatize we need to take a rest day before hiking further into the mountains. We take two days off, to be in town for the weekly market day which draws in people from all the surrounding valleys. The big event of our first day is taking a shower. Our last shower was with icy cold water, on the first night of our trek. After that numbing experience we adopted the local custom, which views the minor inconvenience of body odor to be preferable to bathing in frigid water. Now our hotel owner heats up water for a brief shower, which will be our last bath until we return to Namche in two or three weeks.

When the sun is out we explore town and sit in quiet corners of the narrow dirt streets watching the activity. A middle-aged Tibetan man walks past with his braided hair tied in loops around the top of his head. He wears a large turquoise earring with a chunk of reddish-orange coral dangling below it. Next, a Sherpa girl shuffles past wearing a Patagonia jacket and a bright yellow Jansport backpack. An enormous *dzopchuck*, a crossbred *yak* with horns two feet long, rounds a corner and saunters down the narrow street. He ambles by two stores and a lodge, then stops in front of a set of double wooden doors. He stands patiently in the middle of the narrow alley while pedestrians are forced to squeeze up against a wall to pass. Finally, the *dzopchuck* snorts loudly and steps toward the doors. With one powerful butt of his head the doors fly open, and the beast gingerly steps inside over the raised wooden threshold.

Early the next morning we hike up a ridge for our first view of Everest, which we refer to as "The Big E." The Tibetans and Sherpas call the mountain *Chomolungma*, "The Mother Goddess of the World." The sun's rays slice across the valley. White peaks surround us. Far up the valley is the black triangle top of Everest.

We drop back off the ridge and head for the Namche market, a terraced hillside where farmers and vendors sell their wares. It is an ideal market for people watching, but rather poor for shopping. Nearly everyone sells either potatoes from the highlands or rice carried in from the lowlands.

After a few hours we shoulder our backpacks and head out on a steep trail to the top of a different ridge for a stunning view of 22,493-foot Ama Dablam. Through our binoculars we spot Tengboche Monastery near the base of the mountain, our destination for the night.

When we arrive in the middle of the afternoon, the monastery is in a cloud of mist. The structure is surrounded by squat, windowless, stone houses. Long rows of prayer wheels line the outside of the main *gompa*. Each prayer wheel is two feet high with carved letters spelling out *mantras*. As I walk past I give each a turn. The Tibetan Buddhists believe the motion of the wheel sets off a vibration, sending the inscribed prayer to heaven. Some of the wheels rattle and quickly wobble to a halt on old worn-out bearings. Others turn easily in my hand and spin for a moment before stopping. For the same effort, I sometimes get one prayer, other times two or three. Prayer wheel jackpot.

Inside the courtyard, young monks scurry up the stairs next to the main temple. I wear a pile coat, overcoat, hat and gloves. They have only light sweatshirts and woolen robes which leave their lower legs bare. A few run past without shoes, bare feet slapping on the cold stones.

We spend a night in the lodge next to the monastery. The next morning we get another view of Everest poking up behind a massive face of snow and rock connecting 28,268-foot Lhotse with its sister peak, 25,771-foot Nuptse, the other two mountains in the Everest massif.

We follow the Dudh Kosi river to the settlement of Periche and stop in for the daily talk on altitude sickness given by the Himalayan Rescue Association. The doctor, Ellis Tobin, tells us that twelve years ago one of every ten people who climbed in the area died of altitude sickness. That has changed now with an awareness of symptoms and cures for the illness. In order to further acclimatize, Ellis recommends we sleep two nights in Periche.

So early the next day we leave our backpacks in the village and head out on a side-trip up the Chhukung valley. We walk less than two minutes before Tass stops to vomit. Eager to see the view up the valley, Tass resumes hiking. An hour later on top of a ridge, she stops to vomit again. This time she is left weak and nauseous. She decides to rest in the sun beside a *yersa*, a temporary shelter used by yak herders. I continue up the valley alone.

Tengboche monastery, Nepal. Everest is on the left, poking up behind the Lhotse-Nuptse wall. Ama Dablam is on the right.

Above me is the amphitheater of the Imja Khola glacier. Peaks with beautifully patterned ice flutings surround me. Huge bands of lightly-colored rock on the immense Lhotse-Nuptse wall testify that the formation originated as sedimentary rock. The colliding continents continue to push the Everest massif upward at the rate of three feet every ten years. I watch an avalanche come down the south face Lhotse-Nuptse wall. The enormity of the mountain is revealed by the length of time it takes the fast-moving snow to reach the bottom.

Back in Periche we talk with Ellis about Tass's sickness and decide it is not the altitude that is making her ill, she has giardia--again. We both had our first bout of giardia a few weeks ago in Kathmandu. It is a nasty illness of the upper intestines which causes nausea, vomiting, and dreadful tasting belches. The local remedy is to take a two-day dose of Tinaba, an antibiotic that is a borderline poison and not even sold in the U.S. It kills everything in the stomach, good and bad.

As we sit in our lodge drinking milk tea, Tass hears a familiar voice and looks up through the only window just in time to see Kevin and Russ, our Canadian friends, walk past. We jump up and run outside for a mountainous reunion. Meeting them isn't a total surprise. When we first arrived in Nepal we received a letter at the Kathmandu post office saying they had left for Everest. We also saw their names at the Sagarmatha Park entrance three days ago and guessed, if they traveled at normal hiking speed, our trails would cross either today or tomorrow. Tom is not with them, he flew home months ago from Singapore. We spend the rest of the evening eating, drinking tea and telling stories.

The next day Tass feels better, but we decide to take another rest day anyway. The Canadians, who have already made it to the base of Everest and are now hiking down, take a rest day with us. It is not long before we begin talking of food. Kevin and Russ, the original food hounds, have discovered a cache of left-over expedition food for sale in the lodge. We follow them to a storage room where we find boxes of gear and tinned foods left from climbing expeditions that either quit early or had overstocked supplies. We scrounge through bottles of ketchup, a case of throat lozenges, cans of olives, imported beer, boxes of food with undecipherable (to us) Japanese and Polish labels, a gallon of nacho cheese sauce, and, strangest of all, two five-gallon containers of toilet bowl cleaner! We split a box of pre-sliced Kraft cheese, get some cans of mixed nuts, and, for dessert, four boxes of Jello pudding.

The next day dawns cold, crisp, and clear. Tass has recovered, so we make plans to meet Russ and Kevin in Namche in one week and then head up the valley toward Everest. At mid-morning we ascend the terminal moraine of the Khumbu glacier. As we climb the switchback trail, we hear the gentle dinging of yak bells. The lead yak comes into sight loaded with blue bags and bright yellow ensolite pads. Red and yellow yarn hangs from his ears. He looks like a trim version of an American bison, dressed for a circus. Behind the animals is the *yak* driver, whistling and calling out repeatedly to keep the beasts moving. We step to the inside of the trail to get out of the way. We have heard of people passing cantankerous *yaks* on the outside of the path and being pushed off the trail.

We stop in the afternoon at a settlement of two buildings, 16,175 feet above sea level. We arrive just in time for a picnic with a group of climbers we met the night before. The expedition, led by Jeff Lowe, is doing a series of warm-up climbs throughout the valley to acclimatize for more difficult ascents later. We sit in the sun, drink tea and eat assorted treats from their provisions. They invite us to come to their basecamp in another valley after we finish our hike.

The next day is the final hike to Everest Base camp. The elevation gain is minimal, yet it is difficult walking. The Khumbu glacier is covered with loose stones and rubble. We pick our way through the uneven and jumbled rocks, watching for rock cairns marking the way. The sounds of small avalanches on the glacier, set off from the movement of the ice below the rock, surround us. Occasionally larger slides tumble down the mountains above us.

To our right the sheer wall of Nuptse rises heavenward; to the left Pumori stands like a white sentinel, almost too bright to gaze upon. The intense glare reflecting off the snow-covered mountains in the rarefied air makes us squint constantly despite the protection of our sunglasses. Ahead of us is Lingtren, with its huge hanging snow field suspended on the upper 3,000 feet of the peak. Beside it Khumbutse's sharp, rocky summit looks harsh and barren.

We hike past huge seracs, ice pinnacles glimmering in the sun. Like 50-foot high fangs, ice blue, cold and hard, they are a monument to the frozen world around them--a land of snow, ice, rock and wind. Half an hour before we reach Base Camp I begin to feel weak and dizzy. I'm not sure if it is the altitude or this morning's breakfast, but my stomach is churning. Tass coaches me on.

Below the Khumbu ice fall, in the middle of the rocky and barren glacier, sits Everest base camp. It is a jumble of rocks, tents, climbing equipment and garbage. Since expeditions are not required to haul out trash, the area is a junk yard. The view from the camp is not as spectacular as many of the places we passed along the trail. The camp is positioned for quick access to the mountain, not for scenic value. We sit beside a rock cairn, out of the wind, and eat lunch. Half an hour later we head back down the glacier for Gorak Shep.

At 17,000 feet, the outpost of Gorak Shep is a dark and smoky stone hut. Seven of us try to sleep on a mattress of cardboard and blankets thrown over an uneven mound of rocks. Besides the discomfort of sharp objects poking through the mattress, a procession of people getting up in the night makes sleep impossible. To stave off altitude sickness everyone forces fluids throughout the day. Now it seems every half hour someone is crawling out into the frosty night to go to the bathroom, shivering in the wind, beside the stone wall of the hut. At least the mountains are spectacular in the moonlight.

Groggy from the altitude and lack of sleep, we rise early. Our water bottles are frozen solid. I have a breathless meditation and do a few stretchs--Polar Yoga--and then head for the cramped, smoky kitchen. Breakfast is chapatis, eggs and copious amounts of hot milk tea. We share the tight quarters with an American, an Australian, and three Israelis who are concerned about the more serious symptoms of altitude sickness in one of their party. All of us suffer from slight headaches and nausea. Not even the well-acclimatized Sherpas live at this elevation. The proprietor stays here only for a few months during the trekking season. The name of the outpost, Gorak Shep, means "Crow's Death." Even birds don't stay long at this elevation.

After breakfast we head out to climb Kala Patar, the highest point of our trek. I leave the hut with an upset stomach, battling another bout of nausea. Tass, who is now in fine health, sprints up the mountain while I trudge further behind. I feel like I am walking through water. No matter how hard I try, I can't speed up and soon give up hope of catching her. Near the top I have to stop three times to regain my composure. Tass waves down to me and shouts words of encouragement. When at last I reach the summit at 18,450 feet, the wind is blowing fiercely. We crawl into a little niche in the rock and lay back to enjoy the view.

Below us lies the long wasteland of the Khumbu Glacier. On the other side rises the steep, snow-covered wall of Nuptse. The black, triangled top of Everest has a light halo from the wind and blowing snow. Close to us on the right stands Lobuche's east and west peaks. Behind us is the shimmering wall of Chumbu; to our left Pumori, Lingtren, and Khumbutse. On the horizon, countless other peaks, each breathtaking in its own right.

We stare at the mountains and say very little. Everything is dreamlike. We are both intensely happy. Tass shoots a few rolls of film. Finally, when we are both shivering violently from the icy wind, we head down.

At Gorak Shep we eat more chapatis and have a few cups of tea before descending off the glacier. With each step down the the valley we breathe more freely. Mists and cold winds buffet us all afternoon. Just before dark we arrive back in Periche. Now, at 14,000 feet, we know we will both get a good night's sleep. We eat a huge supper of *dahl bhat* and celebrate with a packet of chocolate pudding for dessert.

Mt. Everest, Nepal. The Sherpas call the mountain Chomolungma, *"The Mother Goddess of the World."*

Everest has been a goal for so long that we are unwilling for the experience to be over. We now want a view of Everest from another peak in a different valley. Our new destination is two days away. The peak we want to climb is 17,990 feet, but to get there we first have to drop through a valley at 11,650-feet.

Our new trail takes us around an enormous mountain face on a narrow path skirting over a sheer wall. A few thousand feet below lies the Imja Kosi river. The wind buffets us as we walk. We cross rock faces and small avalanche chutes where Sherpa maintenance crews have repaired the eroded trail in an unnerving manner. Due to the scarcity of wood each "bridge" across the cliff face is made with just one small log pole. Without any more wooden planks or even a supporting understructure, huge flat stones are set with one side resting on the rock wall and the other on the log spanning the cliff. The rock alone must be nearly enough to buckle the single wooden beam. We cross the structures one-at-a-time, certain our weight with our backpacks will break the single log, sending us tumbling down the mountain along with a dozen two-hundred pound stones that would knock us senseless long before we land at the bottom of the canyon, 2,000 feet below.

As we descend into the town of Phortse we discuss stopping for lunch. We are starving, but we have heard some weird stories about Phortse. According to an anthropologist we met, in-breeding has negatively affected the mental health of the locals. In addition, a number of *shamans* live in the town, and frequent poisonings have occurred.

Shamans in Nepal are chosen by spirits. This choosing is involuntary; in fact, it is generally not something a normal person would want. The choosing is often a painful process, preceded by symptoms Westerners might regard as signs of mental illness. Once a person becomes a *shaman*, he or she is above any system of earthly laws according to the views of the Sherpa villagers. They believe the *shaman* is no longer motivated by human drives; *shamans* act as they do because of the spirit who dwells within. Because of this, no effort is made to physically control them. A *shaman* may be either good or evil, depending on the controlling spirit. Those who fall prey to the evil manipulations of one *shaman*, simply seek help from a more sympathetic *shaman*.

The anthropologist told us it would be unlikely for a Westerner to be poisoned. But he also said he would not personally eat or stay in Phortse. Yet as we walk into town we are starving. We have not eaten since early in the morning and will not reach another village until nightfall. I look up the word for poison in my dictionary and joke that I'll order *Umaaleko aalu bina bikh dinos*, "Boiled potatoes without poison."

From a hillside we spot a long building with the word "Welcome" painted on its side. But as we make for the lodge we find the trail suddenly dead ends 100 yards from the house. We cut across a potato field, jump down a terrace, circumnavigate a vicious barking dog and end up in a plowed field that runs literally up to the front door of the house, again with no path in sight. Very strange.

We enter the door, find ourselves in a dark barn, and stumble around for a moment before locating the stairs to the second floor. The stairs are equally dark and very steep, and I smack my head on a rafter as we climb to the living quarters. We emerge in a large, clean, traditional Sherpa home. One small window lets in a dim light which casts a single beam across the room, illuminating all the dust in the air. A smoldering fire adds to the hazy atmosphere. One wall is covered with shelves containing beautiful, hand-beaten copper pots. Another section is full of sleeping bags in stuff sacks with the names of the former owners printed boldly in black letters.

Two women stand in a corner next to the fire. The older one wears traditional clothes and a wool ski hat that says "Snowbird," a Utah ski resort. The younger one is peeling boiled potatoes. No one moves. I ask for food, omitting the joke about poison. They stare at us without moving. I try again.

Suddenly the younger woman springs to life. She stuffs a potato into her mouth and practically flies across the room at us. With her face inches from mine she repeats my request for food, sputtering potatoes all over me with each word, and asks how many plates we want. Somewhat taken aback I hesitantly repeat our order and sit down on a dusty bench to wait for our food, which is served immediately. That, at least, is reassuring. Unless the poison was already in the pot we should be safe.

As we peel and eat our potatoes the young woman hovers over us and repeatedly asks if we want more. We assure her that even for hungry trekkers, one plate of seven potatoes per person is plenty. The woman continues to look and act very oddly. The other woman sits in a corner and smiles. Halfway through our meal the two collaborate as they hold a baby girl by the feet and hands while they make hissing noises, trying to teach her to urinate on command in the dirt hearth next to the fire. We finish our meal and leave. Good-bye Phortse.

Once again we descend to a river, cross the a bridge, and begin climbing back up the other side. The following afternoon we arrive in Gokyo, a settlement also built to accommodate the influx of trekkers over the last few years. There are three small lodges and little else. Two expeditions are passing through, so the area is full of yaks and foreigners. A French military group on their way to Cho Oyu wears bright down jackets. A group of Indian climbers in green army suits is busy with a load of gear nearby. Our lodge is full of porters and Sherpas.

Again we don't get much sleep. The air is filled with coughing, snoring and the sound of everyone fumbling around to go to the bathroom. In the morning we set off for the peak we will climb. This time I get the jump on Tass and manage to beat her to the summit, though not by much. At the top we have another breathtaking panorama of the Himalaya range. The view of Everest is spectacular, as are the views of many of the peaks in the distance despite the springtime haze. Most impressive is the massive wall of Gyachung Kong, with its huge snow fields and glaciers.

We descend out of the Gokyo valley, stop again at Tengboche Monastery, and then turn on a little-used trail to the base of Kantega and the camp of the American climbers we met a week ago. We arrive just in time to eat lunch and watch the climbers pack up and depart for a seven-day alpine-style assault of the peak.

A woman porter, Nepal.

After the climbers disappear into a mist covering the mountain, the friends and family left behind in base camp decide to cook up a treat. Two kitchen hands are sent to collect yak dung to make a fire for baking. A box of chocolate chip cookie mix is found, pots are procured from the kitchen tent and a Dutch oven is rigged up. While the cookies bake we play Pig Mania in a meeting tent with the Frost family. Our laughter soon attracts the inquisitive Sherpas working at the camp. It is soon Sherpas against foreigners in a hilarious game. Despite Dorene Frost getting a double-leaning jowler, an almost impossible throw with both pig dice landing balanced on their faces, it is the Sherpas, true gamblers at heart, who win. The cookies are delicious.

In the evening Tass and I sleep in the meeting tent, along with five Sherpas. Around midnight Tass wakes up shivering. We cuddle tightly, but she can't seem to get warm. She puts on her down jacket. It doesn't help. I lie directly on top of her so my body heat will warm her, but with all the clothing she has on my warmth can't get through anyway. We try the opposite technique and take off our clothes. Again I lie on top of her. She continues to shiver for nearly three hours and then, totally exhausted, finally falls asleep.

The next morning Tass feels tired and has a cough. We are camped at 14,000 feet and are descending today to Namche, at 11,300 feet. After breakfast we say good-bye to everyone and head down the trail. Within a few hours Tass becomes weak. The pain in her chest returns. We stop in Tengboche, eat lunch and then drop into the steep canyon to cross the Dudh Kosi. At the river we face a major climb, and Tass is feeling even worse. We stop a passing yak herder and pay him to have one of the yaks carry Tass's pack to the top of the hill. The yak walks slowly enough for us to keep up. At the summit Tass retrieves the pack and carries it the last two hours into Namche.

We decide to take a rest day to give Tass a chance to recover. The next morning she wakes up with severe chest pains. She can barely get out of bed. Something is seriously wrong. I head out to find our doctor friend, Ellis Tobin, who luckily just came down from the Himalayan Rescue Association's aid post for a few days of rest and relaxation. He does an examination and confirms our worst fears. Tass has pneumonia. Fortunately Ellis has antibiotics with him. He advises Tass to wait a few days before hiking to Lukla, where she can fly back to Kathmandu for rest.

Three days later Tass feels ready for the hike. I take as many heavy items from her pack as I can carry. Once we start walking she feels better and, since the walk is mostly downhill, we decide to make the trip in the usual one-day time period rather than dragging it out over two slow days. But in the afternoon Tass's strength disappears. Clouds roll in and before long it is raining. We walk in the rain for half an hour before finding a tea stall to take refuge.

A cup of tea later there is no sign of a change in the weather. We are now committed to hiking to Lukla as there is no place nearby to spend the night. We put our wet raincoats back on and head out into the storm. Things get worse. The wind picks up and the rain turns to sleet, then to a mixture of rain, sleet, and snow. The trail becomes a stream. It is impossible to walk without soaking our feet.

After an eternity we arrive in Lukla. We check into an unheated lodge and hurry to change out of our cold, soaked clothes. No sooner are we dried off and sipping hot tea than we begin hearing stories from other travelers about delays and problems at the airstrip. The valley has been covered with clouds for nearly a week. Since there is no control tower, radar or landing lights, the pilots from Kathmandu have refused to fly into the valley, much less land on the tiny airstrip.

The next morning we spot breaks in the clouds as we walk to the runway. The sky looks better, but the runway doesn't. The surface is eroded and full of large stones; one end is 180 feet lower than the other, ending at a 1,000 foot drop-off into the Dudh Kosi river.

Tass considers forgetting the flight and walking out of the Arun valley as originally planned. After reconsidering we both agree it would be best for her to fly out. Still, she encourages me to walk out the Arun valley where I can catch a much cheaper flight from Tumlingtor back to Kathmandu.

The clouds break enough for a group of three small planes to land, taking nearly all the foreigners in line ahead of Tass back to Kathmandu. Feeling certain that Tass will be able to catch a flight out the next day, I leave her at the airstrip and begin my own hike out.

I start out looking forward to a relaxed hike by myself, but the first evening I change my plans. Our trekking book lists shuttle flights from the Tumlingtor airstrip on May 4th and 6th. My birthday is on the 5th. The more I think about it the more I would like to spend the day with Tass in Kathmandu. If I hike fast I may be able to reach Tumlingtor in time to catch the noon flight on May 4th, four days away.

The next morning it is raining and visibility is minimal, which further encourages me to hike quickly. There is nothing to see anyway. I climb over 7,000 feet and descend more than 10,000 feet over a roller coaster section of trail that normally takes two and a half days to cross.

In the village of Guidel a ten-year-old boy responds to my questions of where I can get food and lodging by leading me to his home. His grandmother doesn't think much of the idea, and rants at him without so much as glancing at me. Unperturbed, the boy sweeps off a spot on the porch where I can sleep. Inside the tiny house the boy starts a fire and serves me milk tea while he cooks up rice, potatoes and vegetables in a large wok. Once again I am amazed by the amount of work and responsibility that kids can handle. My meal is delicious. The boy has a knack for using spices, and also for building a steady, controlled fire. His six-year-old brother helps cut vegetables and make tea. Both wear absolute rags, and endearing smiles.

The two boys sleep in the hay loft above a small cow pen, and descend the notched bamboo ladder at 5:00 a.m. the next morning, rubbing the sleep from their eyes and grinning sheepishly. Since I am anxious to resume hiking I pass on breakfast. I pay the boy for my lodging and last night's supper, and head out in a light drizzle.

In the afternoon the rain increases. I stop just before dark, cold and soaked to the bone.

Since the weather is getting worse I want to push on even harder. The next morning I decide to hike to Tumlingtor, which is still two normal hiking days away, in just one day. I gulp down a breakfast of old granola I find in my pack, and again head out at 5:00 a.m. The faster I hike, the more I am convinced I must go faster still. I don't even stop for lunch. Instead, I eat two small packages of biscuits while walking down the trail.

At the top of a ridge I meet two Sherpa boys, age 12 and 14. They are walking without packs, or accompanying adults, to a town three days away to visit an uncle and hopefully find work as porters. We drop off the ridge together, joking and laughing, and soon have a running race down the hill. Thirty minutes later the three of us arrive at a tea stall. My legs feel like quivering jello. The boys stop for a break but I am obsessed with pushing on to Tumlingtor. I'll eat later. I head on down the trail.

At mid-afternoon I catch up with the Canadians, who left Namche two days ahead of me. I am so commited to my march that I can barely slow down to say hello. Russ decides to join in on my high-speed hike while Kevin shakes his head and says he'll see us in Tumlingtor, which is only an hour away.

The last stretch is a killer. I am starving. I have three nasty blisters from my forced hiking, and the bones in my feet ache. Zombie consciousness.

Finally, Russ and I arrive in Tumlingtor, thinking we are one day ahead of the next cheap flight to Kathmandu. We stop at the first lodge and shed our backpacks. Without sitting down to eat, or even having a cup of tea, I decide to go straight to the airport, just to make sure everything is on schedule. I'll eat when I come back. Russ follows along.

At the airstrip we are told it will be three days until we can get a flight to Kathmandu. As we are digesting this unwelcome news, a small plane lands on the grass airfield. I ask where it is going next. The official tells us it is leaving in five minutes for the lowland city of Biratnagar, where it is possible to get an overnight bus to Kathmandu. There are two seats left on the flight.

Russ quickly decides to go with me. We run across the field to the lodge, grab our backpacks, and race back to the airport, arriving seconds before the plane leaves.

We land in Biratnagar and find the connecting bus to Kathmandu has already left the airport. A quick-witted bicycle taxi driver promises to take us on a shortcut through town and intercept the bus before it leaves the city. We ride past food stall after food stall, but there is no time to stop now. No sooner do we reach the main highway than a bus comes barreling down the road. Our taxi driver flags down the bus, and we clamber on board.

I am delirious from lack of food. Usually buses constantly stop to allow food vendors to come aboard. But now we pass through each little village without stopping. Finally, late in the evening, the driver takes a break and we get something to eat.

We arrive in Kathmandu the next morning, two days behind Tass, one day before my 32nd birthday, and three days before the arrival of my sister, Bobbi, and her husband, Don.

17

Giardia Blues

Tass says she has recovered from her illness, but she still looks weak. That evening, I come down with giardia, which I am convinced I picked up from my meal on the bus. I spend the next day, my birthday, squatting over a cement hole, the hotel's communal toilet. Once again I have to take Tiniba, the nasty drug that kills everything in the stomach.

Two days later we are feeling better as we head for the airport to greet my sister, Bobbi, and her husband, Don. At the airport we are met by a guard who will not allow us into the building unless we have tickets. When he finds we are here to meet someone, he points to a group of folding chairs under a canvas awning across the street. Recent acts of airport terrorism in Europe have caused a tightening of security everywhere. Still, this seems rather excessive.

We sit under the awning, and watch with a sinking feeling as the plane unloads without any familiar faces. I try to go to the airline counter and find out why Bobbi and Don didn't get off the plane, but the guard is unsympathetic. I can't even get in the door.

Maybe they are on the next flight coming in from New Delhi. Since we can't even get inside to find out when the next flight arrives, we stop anyone coming out of the terminal who looks like they might know. We talk with tour leaders, pilots, and well-dressed tourists. Everyone has a different guess as to when the next flight will arrive. We wait around for a few hours, and watch a few more planes unload. Still no Bobbi and Don.

Now comes the time of self-doubt. After numerous letters, postcards, and even a phone call, we thought we had everything synchronized. Did we somehow mix up the dates? I go downtown to the Royal Nepal Airlines office where I am informed Bobbi and Don cancelled their flight two weeks ago. Cancelled??

I ride to the India Airlines office, the carrier they were flying with into New Delhi. The woman at the counter acts as if I am prying into a national secret. After an hour she finally tells me a similar story. They were registered, but cancelled their tickets two weeks ago. We stop at the Kathmandu Guest House, where they were going to stay, but the clerk tells us they are not registered.

The next day, not knowing what else to do, we go back to the airport. The flight from New Delhi arrives, and again no familiar faces. At noon I go back to the Kathmandu Guest House. Again the man at the desk assures me that no one has checked in under their name. I ask again. He says no, and to prove it he shows me the register. On the top of the second page I spot their names. The startled clerk looks at the register and announces triumphantly, "Yes, they are here! They are in room C-5!"

I look at the shelves for room keys to see if they are presently in the hotel. Their key is gone but I spot two sheets of paper. Both notes were left for us, along with repeated instruction from my sister that we would be coming to ask for her, and that we should be given the messages. Bobbi and Don had simply rerouted their flight and came through Hong Kong rather than Europe. They arrived yesterday afternoon.

We finally meet up a few hours later. The four of us spend the evening at a Mexican restaurant discussing our plans for a week-long hike up the Langtang valley. Since this is to be a fun, relaxed vacation, Tass and I have organized an expedition style trek. While on the Everest hike we met Phu Tsering Sherpa, whom we have since hired as our *sirdar*, our expedition manager. Phu Tsering hires a cook and kitchen helper for us in Kathmandu, and will hire porters at the start of the trek to carry Bobbi and Don's packs plus the tents, food and kitchen gear. To keep our own costs low, Tass and I will carry our own gear.

We take a bus to the town of Dhunche where we will start our hike. But the next day Phu Tsering returns to our camp without porters, "Because of the boat."

We look at each other in confusion. The boat? Finally we make the connection. It is election time, no one wants to leave town until they vote. Many candidates try to gain support by staging big giveaways at the ballot box. Money and alcohol are commonly given out, along with empty promises, in an effort to win elections.

The next day Phu Tsering tries again. This time he returns with two brothers, a sister and a cousin to be our porters. They are *Tamangs*, a tribe spread throughout Nepal living around the 9,000-foot level. The elder brother, and leader of the group, wears a turban, a sleeveless tunic and a small piece of cloth wrapped around his hips like a mini-skirt. He has no shoes. A large knife sticks out of his sash and a serious expression is on his face. His brother and cousin are similarly dressed. The sister wears a thick cotton skirt, a velvet jacket, and a large coin necklace. She has a pierced nose.

Each of the porters is paid 40 *rupiahs* per day, less than $2 U.S. They provide their own food and sleep in rock caves along the way. We hit it off immediately and decide, even if they weren't carrying loads, they would be worth their salary just to spice things up.

Healthwise we get off to a slow start. Bobbi comes down with giardia the day before the hike, Don the day after. Tass and I are still weak ourselves. Luckily, it is luxurious camping. Each morning we wake at 5:00 a.m. to the soft voice of Hakpa, the kitchen helper, bringing hot milk tea to our tents. After our Everest hike, Tass and I love staying in our Walrus tent again, out of the smoky lodges with our own quiet, private spot to relax.

Tass trekking through the cloud forests of Nepal.

207

We hike through the moist cloud belt that, when not deforested, always seems to occur near the 9,000 foot level. Rolling mists move up and down the mountainsides full of lichen-covered trees and blooming rhododendrons. The taller mountain peaks of Nepal have a spectacular grandeur, but they are barren and devoid of life. Here the earth is bursting with a cool, wet fertility. Everything is green and alive.

We hike with umbrellas, strolling through the mist-covered valleys. Each day Siray, the cook, and Hakpa, the kitchen boy, race ahead of us to stop by the trail and cook lunch. Sometimes we only hike for an hour before rounding a corner to find a picnic lunch laid out for us. Other times we hike into the afternoon before getting our meal. Phu Tsering, in his usual humorous way, explains the discrepancy in meal times.

"Siray very bad gambler. Lose watch," he says with a laugh.

It is great to share another adventure with Bobbi, we were such pals when we traveled through Africa together, 12 years ago. After three days we arrive at the base of 23,770-foot Langtang Peak and have spectacular views of four other snow-covered peaks, all over 20,000 feet. Just when everyone is free of illness, it is time to start back.

Our Lantang valley trekking group, Nepal. Standing from right: the head porter is second, Phu Tsering third, Bruce fourth and Siray seventh. Kneeling from right: Tass is first, Bobbi third, and Hakpa fourth.

We spend one more day with Bobbi and Don in Kathmandu and talk with them about our bicycle trip. Seeing Everest has always been a major destination. Now with that accomplished, we are faced with new decisions. When we started our journey 20 months ago, we thought we would finish our trip in India or Nepal and fly back home. Since Thailand we have been thinking of bicycling home after India.

Bobbi and Don encourage us to follow our dream and give us a loan from my family to help us cover some of the extra expenses. Their support of our goal and their faith in us, two vagabonds who don't even know where we will live or work upon returning home, is very encouraging. The next day we say farewell as Bobbi and Don head for the airport.

We dally in Kathmandu, studying maps and discussing our new travel plans for India and beyond. Because of the war in Iran, Iraq and Afghanistan, we will fly to Egypt, tour Israel and sprint across Europe before riding from New York back to South Dakota. But no matter how we juggle our schedule, the timetable always ends with our riding across the States in November. We don't want to ride in the winter, but we don't have enough money to wait until spring. And we are unwilling to cut short our time in India to get home sooner.

Since it is the hot season in India, we plot a route through the cooler northern mountains following the length of the Himalaya to a region called Ladakh on the Tibetan plateau. But since there are no roads in western Nepal, we can't stay in the mountains when leaving Kathmandu. We must first drop south to the scorching plains of India before climbing back into the Indian Himalaya.

Yet we can't seem to get out of Kathmandu. Instead of packing up, we go shopping for presents to mail home for our arrival at Christmas. The monsoon rains begin and the marginal sanitation in the city gets worse. We each come down with giardia again, further delaying our departure. Perhaps we have had it all along. The advanced stages of giardia comes in waves; it is common to be ill, recover, and then repeatedly get sick days or even weeks later. Little do we know how long this will affect our health, not only on our trip, but even after we get back home.

When we finally leave Kathmandu we follow the old India-Nepal highway, a steep mountainous road with little traffic due to the newer, faster highway to the west. We camp near the top of the pass and descend the next day on a thrilling ride from nearly 8,000 feet to the lowland *terai*, a few hundred feet above sea level. The heat increases dramatically as we drop in elevation. The change in temperature is a shock after three months in the cold mountain air. By mid-afternoon the temperature is over 100 degrees. We stop at a tea shop and sit in delirium in pools of sweat trying to fortify ourselves by guzzling cold sodas. It doesn't work.

Tass outside the Snowman, our favorite pie shop, Kathmandu, Nepal.

We leave the main highway and take a side road that turns into a rough trail ending at a river, which we wade across, pushing our bikes, to enter the back door to Chitwan National Park. In the settlement of Saura we check into the New Dipak Lodge where for 10 *rupiah* ($.40 U.S.) per night we get a thatched hut with mud and cow dung walls.

Chitwan Park is prime habitat for rhinos, tigers, bears and a variety of birds. The next morning we hike on a bewildering maze of trails through the tall grass. Our guide, Rajandra, gives us advice on how to react to certain animals. He is especially concerned with the Sloth bear, which he considers the most dangerous of all animals in the park as it will not hesitate to attack humans. His advice is to stay together in a group.

"Even if bear attacks," he cheerfully tells us, "you can still have life." Rajandra elaborates on his strategy.

"Bear attacks. Friend run from behind, punch bear in nose. No problem. Bear run away." Rajandra claims the Sloth bear has such a sensitive nose, it actually turns its head to the side when attacking.

While his advice sounds rather dicey, a sign at the park visitors center is even more unique: "Usually, when you chance upon wild animals you will not be pounced on. If it does come after you, quickly clamber up a tree or else run and pray to God."

It is not long before we spot signs of rhinos: torn-up sections of grass and shrubs that look like someone got an army tank stuck.

"Rhinos mate here," Rajandra informs us. Once the male mounts the female, she often tries to dart away. The male responds by dragging his hind feet. The result is ecological disaster as grass, brush and small trees are uprooted wherever the female drags her lover through the bush.

Unfortunately, we see neither rhinos, tigers nor bears. By mid-morning it is too hot to see anything. All the animals bed down for the day. We retreat to our hut to try and escape the oppressive heat. We have little success. Our ankles swell until we look like we have elephantiasis.

The next morning we try a different guide, who promises to get us close to rhinos. After hiking for just a few minutes we can tell that Gito, the new guide, has much more experience and awareness of the forest and grasslands. We hike deeper into the park through eight-foot-high elephant grass. After an hour we stop, surrounded by grass and trees. Gito tells us to wait quietly. Moments later we hear grunts and splashes. Gito checks the wind one more time and then signals us to move forward.

Rhinos have incredibly poor eyesight; some species cannot see well beyond 15 feet. But they all have excellent hearing and an even better sense of smell. When approaching an animal that can weigh over 6,000 lbs., has a reputation for a disagreeable temper, and can run 35 miles per hour--faster than any human--it is important to take all these factors into account.

I have seen rhinos before, along with lions and elephants, from the inside of a landrover in African game parks. Being on foot is a different experience. Suddenly we look at our guide and wonder, how much do we trust this person's judgment? We point out a few trees to each other and whisper about an escape route just in case things don't go well.

We slowly move forward, adrenaline pumping, every sense alert to the slightest sound or movement. At the top of a small embankment we look down through the grass and see seven rhinos cooling off in a muddy creek 25 feet away. Gito points to one, a disagreeable old fellow, and whispers to keep a watch out for him. We stand quietly near the bank for five minutes, until suddenly the wind changes and the rhinos catch our smell. The cantankerous rhino makes a roaring snort and jumps in our direction.

Gito doesn't have to give us any warning. We turn and run--in record speed--through the tall grass to the base of the closest tree. But we both have enough presence of mind to look back before we begin climbing and find, to our relief, that the old boy was just giving us a scare and is now ambling off in another direction. We have a quivering laugh and ask Gito what he thinks is the best reaction when being charged by various animals. He agrees with the advice of our first guide, although he thinks the wild boar is the most dangerous animal. We ask about tigers.

"Tigers no problem," Gito assures us. "Get eye contact. Look with

One-horned Asian rhinoceros, Chitwan National Park, Nepal.

power. Don't let tiger think you are afraid." He proudly tells us he has never been stared down by a tiger, and that he can "have power" for as long as three minutes--during which time he simply psyches the tiger out. He demonstrates his stare, and I believe he has both the confidence and the power to match wills with any tiger.

During our hike we walk up to 16 rhinos. Only once did Gito advise us to stay back because "not so good if rhino charge us here." Later we laughed at his choice of words, as if in most places it is no big deal to have an animal weighing as much as a car chasing us through the forest. We learn to stand quietly when the rhinos look up at us; with their poor eyesight they often mistake us for tree stumps if we don't move.

On the third day we go with yet another guide. As former environmental education instructors, we want to see how the guides, many trained in programs set up by the Peace Corps, compare with each other. This time we hike outside the park boundary through an area of prime bird habitat. We also see three rhinos and spot some wild boar. But the main event is finding a small, fuzzy caterpillar on Tass's shirt. She pulls it off and we both hold it to look at its beautiful colors and then let it go in the grass.

Five minutes later we begin itching. Only then does our guide inform us that the hairs of the caterpillar cause a terrible rash. The microscopic hairs came through our clothes to cover our stomachs and then spread to our arms and all over our bodies. By the time we get back to our hut we are in such a miserable state we could strangle the guide.

We are tormented by the afternoon heat and the unceasing itching. The night is no relief. The temperature stays in the upper 90's, an impediment to sleep by itself. We both feel like screaming, which we occasionally do as an alternative to tearing off our skin.

We planned on leaving the next morning, but neither of us is in any shape to go anywhere but to the showerhouse, where we get 60 seconds of relief before the itching resumes. We sit all day broiling in the mud hut. The second night is so miserable that we get up at 4:30 a.m. and begin packing. The exertion of bicycling sounds agonizing, but spending another day baking in the hut sounds even worse.

We ride until delirium sets in and stop during the heat of the day for a few hours to get out of the sun. The air is so hot we cannot get our breath. Eighty-two miles later we stop at dusk in the town of Bhutwal.

We check into a lodge and get a room on the top floor of a three-story building. It is the oven hotel. The concrete walls are so hot they radiate heat all night long. The ceiling fan does nothing but blow the hot air on

108 degrees. Hot season on the Nepali terai.

213

us, adding to our withering and dehydration.

The next morning the heat shimmering off the highway bakes us from all directions. We drink bottle after bottle of hot, iodized water, but no matter how much we drink, it never quenches our thirst. Near midday, when the temperature is at its worst, we cross a section of the Mahabharat range. It is not a large climb by Himalayan standards, but in the heat it is a killer. When we stop to rest in the shade of trees along the highway, our bodies go into a pounding delirium.

Each evening we look at the map and mark our progress with a tremendous sense of accomplishment. For some reason the challenge of riding across the Nepali terai in the hot season has captured us. On the evening of June 7th, we ride into Nepalgonj, a dirty, noisy town near the Indian border. We have reached the end of the rideable roads in Nepal and have no choice but to head southward, across the lowlands of India.

18

Mother Ganges

The plains of India begin at the base of the Himalaya and spread out over one-fourth of India's heartland. The land is incredibly flat. The Ganges, as it runs through this immense plain, drops only 1,000 feet during its 1,000-mile journey from Haridwar, at the base of the Indian Himalaya, to Calcutta, at the Bay of Bengal on the Indian Ocean.

The temperature on the plain continues to hover at 105-110 degrees. The heat off the road sends shimmering waves dancing around us. Our tires make sucking noises as we ride through sticky sections of melting asphalt. The gooey tar covers our tires and then picks up loose gravel, which continually grinds between our tires, fenders and brakes. The heat melts the candles in my panniers into a distorted glob of wax. The only drinking water we can find tastes like rust.

Still, coping with the heat during the day isn't as bad as trying to survive the nights. We can never sleep. The area is too populated to camp, so we stay in cheap hotels. After our experience in the oven hotel, we now only stay in hotels where we can sleep on the roof. Each evening we carry our *charpoys*, wooden bed frames with a woven string mattress, outside and join other restless guests on top of the building where there is a slight breeze.

But no matter where we put our beds, something always keeps us awake. One night a celebration appears on the street in front of our hotel, complete with a brass band playing all night long. Another night two gentlemen beside us get up at 3:30 a.m. to have an animated discussion as they wait for the sun to rise. Although we always try to avoid hotels next to mosques, often that is not possible. One morning we are driven from our beds by a 4 a.m call to worship, which starts off with a man checking to see if the loudspeaker is turned on by rubbing the microphone first across a table, then his shirt, and then by giving it half a dozen whacks with his hand--all at ear-splitting volume. Next comes a loud gargling sound as he clears his throat for the start of the wailing prayer. I can't help wonder if he believes the neighborhood, and perhaps even Allah, is deaf.

Each morning we wake in a fog. Our eyes feel as swollen as our ankles. No amount of splashing water on our faces will clear our vision, or our brains.

We arrive at the the town of Pranpur at lunchtime. As usual, it is too hot for food. Instead we are infatuated with finding a cold *lassie*, a sweet yogurt drink. The narrow streets are full of people, and a crowd forms around us as we park our bikes. We are a big hit. We work our way through the throng to a restaurant, which quickly fills when half the crowd,

Crowds of friendly people mob us at every stop, India.

about fifty people, follow us inside. Because of the crowd, the waiter is unable to get close to our table. We order by shouting to the proprietor. The crowd continues to grow. The restaurant is in utter pandemonium. Finally the owner closes the doors to lock out the rest of the mob.

The temperature inside the restaurant, already insufferable from the mass of people, now skyrockets from a lack of ventilation. The force of the crowd pushes everyone in the front row to lean over our table. To create a diversion we ask a teacher questions about our route. I am soaked with sweat. Even though I repeatedly wipe my hands on my shorts, I drip all over our map as I unfold it.

As so often in India, I am asking unanswerable questions. The teacher's replies are long and drawn out, and have little to do with what I have asked. But the diversion works, the crowd relaxes and backs up enough for the waiter to bring our *lassies*. We guzzle a couple of the refreshing drinks, which the restaurant owner tells us are on the house. He also offers us free lodging for the night, but we politely refuse. It is only noon and we are determined to keep moving. We don't want to spend an extra day in the heat. The crowd follows us outside. Everyone smiles and waves. Although Indian crowds can get intense, it is great to be in a country where everyone is so enthusiastic. And, where so many people speak English.

We get a kick out of the Indian form of English. People commonly put "ing" on the end of verbs. One well-dressed man greets us saying, "I am thinking you are a tourist." Later he makes a route recommendation by stating, "I am thinking for me you must be visiting Corbett National Park."

At a *dharmsala*, a non-profit rest house for pilgrims and budget travelers, we ask the proprietor, as the sun is going down, if many mosquitoes come out at night. He replies, "Perhaps most certainly." Moments later a swarm appears that is so large we have to retreat to our room, light a mosquito coil, and cover our bodies with repellent as well.

After ten days of riding in the lowland heat we arrive at the base of the Indian Himalaya. We leave the back roads to join the main highway to Naini Tal, a popular hill station where wealthier Indians vacation to escape the summer heat. We slowly pedal our way into the mountains and finally leave the hot, dusty weather behind.

Now that we are out of the heavier populated part of India, we resume camping whenever possible. In the evenings we ride until darkness approaches and then begin looking for a tent spot. One evening I ride ahead of Tass. After a few miles I stop to wait for her.

Tass pulls up and asks, "What was wrong with camping on the hill after the valley we rode through?"

"I didn't see the hill so I didn't stop," I reply, feeling a little defensive. Somewhat testily, I quickly add, "If it looked so good, why didn't you stop?"

Bruce riding into the Indian Himalaya.

"Well, since you didn't stop I figured something was wrong that I didn't see."

We discuss if we should ride back or ride ahead and find another spot. Sometimes we feel oppressed by the countless daily decisions of traveling, often made without adequate information. Now, neither of us wants to be responsible for making the wrong decision. We both want the other to decide.

Five minutes of "I don't care, what do you want to do?" follow. Finally, since neither of us likes to backtrack, we decide to pedal onward.

More and more houses appear. Cultivated fields run up to the base of steep hills. We see no place to camp, and it is getting closer to dark. For the next three miles we accuse each other of failure to stop at the campsite at the hill, which has grown in our minds to become the perfect campsite in an otherwise uncampable section of road. After another mile we stop for a conference. There is no place in sight to camp, and now it is five miles to go back.

"What should we do?"

"I can't decide. **You** decide!"

"I don't care, what do you want to do?" We push on again at a faster pace.

It is almost dark when we spot a steep gully that may be a potential campsite. Now comes the tricky part. If anyone sees us going into the ravine our cover will be blown. After being surrounded by jostling crowds at every restaurant, market, and tea break, we are ready for a peaceful campsite--all to ourselves. We must move cautiously. Word of camping foreigners, multi-speed bicycles and a nylon tent could draw quite a mob. Camp then becomes a one ring circus, with us in the center ring.

To avoid circus camping we slip into espionage mode. Tass stands sentry with the bikes while I run up the trail into the forested gully on reconnaissance. The valley is full of trees and thick brush. One little spot, however, looks big enough for our tent and is just out of sight of the road.

Back on the highway I report my find, and Tass fills me in on the location of all the nearby locals. A few girls are down the road gathering firewood. Another is on a hill, chasing a goat. We decide to wait until the firewood collectors leave before establishing camp. But just about the time the girls are around the bend and out of sight, three boys walk around the corner from the opposite direction. They pass by but then begin to slow down. Their curiosity is stronger than their shyness.

We have to move on, or they will stop to watch us. We pedal in the opposite direction and notice a group of shepherds staring our way from a field below the road. It's hard to slip by unnoticed in India. We stop and wait around the corner, discussing our strategy.

"Have the three boys left yet? Shall we go?"

"No, I hear a bus coming. Let it pass first."

"When we go, don't let the shepherds see you!"

"O.K., let's go!"

We look around the corner and no one is in sight. Good. This time we ride close to the inner bank of the road, hunched low over the handlebars, so the people in the fields below can't see us returning. As we near the trail we shift to our lowest gears. Just before I turn to ride up the trail, Tass yells, "Don't turn!" In my mirror I see a man on a bicycle rounding the corner behind us.

We ride past the trail, get off the bikes, and pretend to adjust our luggage. The man on the bike clanks past without stopping. We wait for another two vehicles to go by and then sprint back toward the turnoff. This time no one comes. We make our break, turn onto the trail, and strain at the pedals as we ride high speed into the forest, trying to duck quickly out of sight. When the trail becomes too steep to ride, we heroically push the loaded bikes over a ridge.

While I set up the tent, Tass puts a pot of rice and lentils on the stove. A young girl walks through the forest, very close to our campsite, calling out to the cows she is herding home. She doesn't spot us. We take sponge baths in a little pool of water in a ravine near our tent. Voices down on the road pass by. Later, lying in our tent, we hear more voices on the road, but they too fade into the night.

The next morning I feel great until I go into the bushes to relieve myself. My stool is full of squirming worms. Since there are small pharmacies in every mid-sized village, I stop in a little shop in the next town, where a 12-year-old boy shows me a chart of six types of worms. I identify them as pinworms and buy a course of antibiotics from the boy, who assures me in a business-like manner that it will take care of the problem in five days.

We continue our climb into the mountains. After passing through a few of the popular hill stations, we see less and less traffic each day. On an isolated pass, Tass blows a sidewall on her front tire. We have had a string of bad luck with tires. It is the third one we have shredded since Kathmandu. We have no more spares, and we have yet to see a bike shop in India selling 27 inch tires.

Tires are not the only worry. Again we have stomach problems. Tass has cramps and diarrhea, and, after a week of good health, my worms are back. We should be eating bland foods, but the few tea stalls along the highway sell only poor quality *dahl baht* or an equally unappetizing mixture of potatoes and garbanzo beans in a greasy sauce. After nearly a year in Asia, we have become so accustomed to finding good food at the ubiquitous tea stalls that we did not bring enough supplies. We run out of oatmeal, and for a few days we have to eat the greasy food for every meal, even breakfast.

Our destination is the Alaknanda Valley, which will take us to Badrinath, at the headwaters of the Ganges. The last pass before the valley has a wild 28-mile downhill to the town of Karnaprayag. Much of the road is steep straight-aways with rollercoaster-like, rolling bumps. We coast full-speed, no brakes, standing up on the pedals with our seats off the saddles, riding like jockeys on race horses, letting the bikes lift and drop beneath us.

The bottom of the valley is hot and dusty, and 8,000 feet lower than our destination, Badrinath. When building the road the engineers designed the highway to follow the sacred source of the Ganges as often as possible. But the canyon is steep, and deep. Large, sheer cliffs rising from the river's edge repeatedly force the highway to switchback up for hundreds, sometimes thousands of feet, before crossing over the cliffs. Then, instead of traversing the hillside and staying at the higher elevation to rejoin the river further up the canyon, the road plunges all the way back down to the bottom of the gorge to follow the river for a few miles, and again climb back out of the canyon at the cliff face around the next corner.

The Alaknanda valley has a carnival atmosphere. The region is a sacred pilgrimage site for Hindus from all of India. Bus load after packed bus load

Countless switchbacks along the road to the headwaters of the Ganges, India.

of pilgrims make a constant flow up and down the narrow road. The switchbacks and exposed cliffs are terrifying to pilgrims from the lowland plains. We see pale passengers hanging heads out the bus windows; splashes of vomit cover the sides of buses. The crazy bus drivers only exacerbate the problem as they gun their engines around each corner, with little regard for the lives of the 100 people crammed on board.

Wealthier Indians make their pilgrimage in shiny Ambassadors packed with moms, dads, kids, aunts, uncles, nephews, nieces, grandparents and grandchildren--and whoever else can fit inside. The luggage racks are piled high with suitcases. The locally made cars are heavy-duty cruisers, with thick padded seats and velvety upholstery, complete with fringed curtains to keep out the hot Indian sun. Since Ambassadors have only four cylinders, the motors strain to get up the hills with their heavy loads. At every small creek or spring we ride past rows of cars with their hoods up, radiators billowing steam, giving the overheated engines a break.

The most fascinating travelers on the highway are the *sadhus*. Dressed in various shades of orange, Hindu holy men walk along the road with small bags slung over their shoulders or balanced on their heads. Most are barefoot. Many carry large, thorny walking sticks, others tote short iron staffs with a ring on one end. A few have iron tridents. They wear various types of *dhotis*, like a *sarong* with a batch of material tucked up between the legs. Some carry a spare blanket or sheet folded over their shoulders or piled on their heads. Others don't have any extra clothes and probably get cold at night.

Many of the *sadhus* have wild, unkept hair that sticks out in every direction. Others twist their hair into dreadlocks, matted strands that are knotted and snarled to resemble a braid, but unlike a braid they cannot be unraveled for washing. Some further twist their hair into buns or coils piled on top of their heads. The *sadhu* "do."

The majority of *sadhus* are avid smokers and constantly puff on *bidis* and *cheroots*, locally made herbal cigarettes. The followers of Shiva are often prodigious *ganga* smokers. Many have vacant stares and unclear eyes. A few smile and one or two greet us, but the other three hundred we pass each day are oblivious to our existence.

Since we have camped the last five nights, we rent a hotel room in the town of Joshimath for a change of pace, and a real shower instead of a sponge bath. At 3:00 a.m. the next morning the large Indian family next to us begins making more noise than a high school football team as they rouse each other up to catch the early bus to Badrinath. It takes them forever to get packed up; the racket doesn't end until 5:00 a.m. By that time the rest of the town is getting up, with the men starting their morning spitting and coughing routine.

It is a sacred ritual for Hindus to clear their throat each morning, which takes one to four minutes and is performed as loudly as possible. Laying in our hotel bed, we hear people clearing their throats at the hallway sink outside the room. We also hear noises coming up from the floor below us, and even in a number of houses on the hillside behind the hotel. Everyone makes gross noises, not only while clearing throats, but also when spitting. It drives Tass crazy.

We leave Joshimath and drop 2,000 feet, back down to the river, before starting the final ascent, a nearly 6,000-foot climb in 21 miles. The mountains are carpeted with the new life of spring; flowers shoot up everywhere, the air is clear and pleasant to smell, and the grass a vibrant green. Small pockets of mist hang between the rocky crags of the side canyons. We climb into pine forests and soon see coulairs of snow above us.

As we get closer, we can't help feel the sacredness of the area. This is the birthplace of a river held in reverence by 500 million people. Riding our bicycles here by our own effort and sweat adds to our feeling of pilgrimage. With each mile, more and more sadhus acknowledge us with a nod or a smile. We join the flow and jokingly call ourselves "the cycling sadhus."

Known in the west as the Ganges River, it is called Ganja Ma, Mother Ganges, in Hindi. A devotional book for pilgrims lists 108 different names for the river, including: Leaping Over Mountains In Sport, Dwelling In The Water Pot Of Brahma, Taking Pride In The Broken Egg Of Brahma, and Roaming About Rose-Apple-Tree Island.

In terms of size, the Ganges is not the largest river; the Nile and the Amazon are more than twice its length. In fact, when Aryan invaders first swept into India in 1500 B.C., they were more impressed with the Indus. However the Aryans soon realized the water from the Ganges has remarkable qualities and named the river Sursari, The River of the Gods. Countless cures and properties are ascribed to its waters. Despite having cremated and partially cremated bodies routinely thrown into the river, scientists say cholera is unable to survive in the water.

After a final set of eight switchbacks winding through a glacier, we come out in an open valley above tree line. Badrinath is in the center of the valley, a collection of tin roofs surrounded by snow-capped mountain peaks.

The town is packed with people. Since there are no hotels we check into a small ashram, a boarding house for pilgrims, and get a room on the second floor. The swamiji who presides over the ashram has taken a life-long vow of silence and does not speak except to chant prayers. When we talk with him, he replies by making wild hand motions and says, "hhmmm! mmmhh! mmhhmmm!" Two old mattresses are found in a storage area and thrown on the floor for our bed. We store our bikes in the room and head out to explore town.

The Hindu pilgrimage site at the headwaters of the Ganges, Badrinath, India.

People fill the small streets. Crowds pack in front of colorful shops selling religious paraphernalia, devotional pictures, paintings, prayer beads, incense burners, statues of Hindu gods, and piles of *tilak* powder, in all shades of color, to make religious marks on the forehead. Old men haggle with the shopkeepers while women finger piles of cheap costume jewelry trying on rings, bangles, bracelets, and necklaces.

The sidewalk to the temple winds down a narrow alley packed with shops to a footbridge spanning the rushing waters of the Alakanada, which cuts through the town. Although we had read and envisioned Badrinath as the "headwaters" of the Ganges, the true source of the river is a number of glaciers high above us. Even here above 10,000 feet, the river is already turbulent and violent. Stone steps built on the river bank allow pilgrims to climb down to the river, but few use them. The river is moving too fast; it would be suicidal to enter the water. Instead, everyone heads straight to a group of buildings on a rock cliff overlooking the river, with two hot springs in front. Before entering Badrinath temple it is the custom to cleanse in the pools.

Indians generally keep their bodies well covered. Except for the very poor, few men wear shorts, or even short sleeve shirts. Women wear *saris* with their midriffs exposed, but they are hesitant to show their legs, upper arms, shoulders or heads. Women often pull the *saris* down over their foreheads, and sometimes cover their faces. However at the Badrinath hot pool, modesty disappears.

Wealthy women undress to their underwear and join similarly attired men in the steamy pools. Poorer women with no underwear simply wear their *saris* into the water. *Sadhus* patter about in g-strings cleaning not only their bodies but also their clothes, by beating the clothing against the stone floor.

After being purified in the pools, everyone walks up the narrow, winding stairs to the temple. It is an ancient building painted in a kaleidoscope of colors, like an enchanted castle in Disneyland. We follow the shuffling line into the inner courtyard. Railings lead the crowd through a maze to keep the queue in order. We pass a variety of small altars on our way to the main shrine, a statue with a strange history.

A few centuries ago, some pilgrims fished the statue out of the largest thermal pool below the temple. It is made of black shaligram stone, but due to weathering is not well defined. Even though no one knows what the statue originally represented, it is now venerated. Pilgrims describe the rock

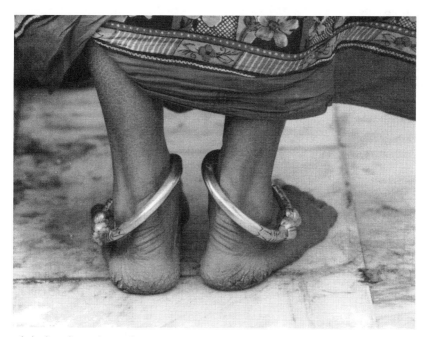

Solid silver bracelets adorn a woman's ankles, Badrinath, India.

as representing various Hindu deities: Brahma, Vishnu, Shiva, and Kali, among others.

As the queue gets close to the statue, things liven up. Small sweets of puffed rice are thrown toward the idol over everyone's head. Some people stand and pray, others sing and dance. Even though the room is packed, a few people lay prone on the floor, arms stretched above their heads in total obeisance. Many of the pilgrims have saved their *rupiahs* for years to come here, a place where they believe they can be purified of sin. Tears of joy stream down the cheeks of many of those around us.

We spend three days in Badrinath. Each morning we join in for a soak in the hot pool and then visit various shrines. At lunchtime we eat at a little restaurant overlooking the river and temple. A *sadhu* we met on the road has taken a liking to me and follows us around everywhere, so we usually buy him lunch. We also become friends with the restaurant proprietor, and answer his questions about America. He is astonished to learn that no one in our country speaks Hindi.

On our last afternoon, we sit overlooking the river and watch a man walk out onto the middle of the busy footbridge to dump a five gallon bucket of trash over the railing. The garbage catches in the wind as it falls, and scatters into the river, twenty feet below. To us it seems a blatant desecration, yet no one else even notices. Only in India could a river be sacred, worshipped by millions, yet also be a toilet, and a convenient place to dump garbage.

Bruce with his sadhu *friend, Badrinath, India.*

20

A Twist Of Fate

The Indian monsoon season, which has been traveling behind us, going about the same speed and direction, catches us in Badrinath. Storm clouds roll over the mountains bringing a biting wind and a cold rain. At the same time Tass, who has been fighting diarrhea and nausea again the last few days, takes a turn for the worse. We cancel our plan for a three-day hike into the Valley of Flowers and take a bus to the nearest town with a doctor. We have no choice but to drop all the way down to Rishikesh, 1,000 feet above sea level, where the Ganges meets the plains of India.

Since I don't feel well myself, we both want to be checked. At a health clinic, we ask the doctor if he takes stool samples.

"Most certainly," he replies, and hands us little specimen containers and wooden tongue depressors. "The bathroom here is too dirty," he apologizes. "It would be best to use the toilets at the Garwan Hotel."

Tass is white as a sheet, and not up for a walk in the broiling sun. I tell the doctor we have seen plenty of dirty toilets and would prefer to do the stool samples here. Still, he won't budge.

"No, no. I insist. It is only a ten minute walk and they have very clean toilets. Just order tea or some toast, and they won't mind you using the bathroom," he tells us with an accommodating smile.

In the afternoon we get the results. Tass has amoebic dysentery. I have a less serious bacterial infection. Unfortunately, we are in a poor place to recuperate. It is unbearably hot and extremely muggy. The beginning of the monsoon season means a month of hot, humid weather before the rains finally bring the temperatures back down. Our hotel doesn't have a roof to sleep on. We stay in a cement cubicle with no ventilation. The single window does not let in any breeze. The door opens onto a busy hallway, again with no breeze, only staring eyes. During the day, when it is the hottest and we need our ceiling fan the most, the electricity in town is turned off. We lay on our beds in the insufferable heat, moaning.

Each day we shuffle 200 yards to the main highway where we catch a horse-drawn buggy into town. The streets are filled with old piles of garbage, putrefying into compost. An open sewer runs next to the shops. Cows amble by, defecating as they walk, splattering on the hard ground. Moments later buses, traveling at full speed despite the pedestrians crowding the street, run over the mess and further splash it in all directions. Flies fill the air.

Luckily we find a restaurant owned by a friendly Sikh family. They pamper us with unspiced, yet delicious food, just what our stomachs need. We take our minds off our miseries by constantly reading. <u>Gandhi</u> is our favorite book during our convalescence. We spend hours discussing aspects of the book, especially Gandhi's belief that each of us can mold our personality in any way we chose. Like many great religious teachers, Gandhi taught that what is achievable morally and spiritually for one person is achievable for all.

We talk about the things we want to change in our own lives. It is sometimes hard for us to admit certain faults, or to tell others what we want to change about ourselves. Gandhi was just the opposite. He drove himself into changes by telling the whole world of his new directions, burning his bridges behind him, forcing himself to be held accountable to his own idealistic goals. The way he lived his life proved what he taught was true.

After four days in our broiling hotel room, we are ready to make a break. Even though Tass was bedridden with dizziness and nausea last night, this morning she is convinced she can ride. We decide to pedal to Dehra Dun, 30 miles away, thinking that will be as far as Tass can go. But once she is on the bike she prefers to keep going, and we ride seventy-five miles.

The next day we begin another climb into the Himalaya. How many hills have we ridden over in the last twenty-one months? How many times have we looked up to a distant mountain and chosen it as the day's goal? How many songs have we inwardly chanted to the rhythm of the pedals as our wandering minds seek escape from the slow work of riding up major passes? Look at the scenery. Stare at the road slowly passing under the legs. When it is really steep we stand up to pedal, and look over the handlebar bag at the spokes moving in a slow orbit around the front hub. First gear. Deep granola.

Then, on narrow switchbacks, we look over the side of the road, far down the valley where we started. One highway blends into the next. This turn reminds me of somewhere--was it in Malaysia that we stopped on a pass to eat boiled corn? Or was it Java? No, Sumatra. The view reminds me of a valley in New Zealand, or was it Fiji?

The next afternoon, in the middle of a heavy rainstorm, we arrive in Shimla, the summer capital of India during the days of the British Viceroys. We do a coin toss. I lose, and go off in search of a cheap hotel while Tass hangs out under a porch with the bikes. When I come back Tass is joking with a wealthy Indian couple who have stopped to chat. As I walk up they shake my hand and tell me, "Your madame is quite amusing."

It rains most of our two-day stay. We check into a musty hotel and, between downpours, explore town, which is full of Rhesus macaques. The short-tailed monkeys are everywhere, climbing up and down drainpipes and leaping across roofs. The territorial males chase each other and make wild displays to terrorize their opponents, and everyone else as well. A ferocious male with big teeth bounds down the side of a building and stops all pedestrian traffic as he bristles slowly across the sidewalk. Suddenly, with a loud growl, he lunges up over the entryway to a store, jumps on top of a large metal sign for a tailor shop, and bounces on it as if it was the branch of a jungle tree. The sign, which doesn't appear to be bolted well, rattles and sways on the verge of tearing out of the wall. Above us on a nearby building, another macaque responds by climbing a TV antenna to sway and screech in return.

Back on the bikes we continue our northwestern course along the length of the Himalaya, trying to stay ahead of the monsoon season. We get occasional dowsings, yet between rains we ride in beautiful, clear weather. On July 5th we ride into Manali under a banner welcoming the Dalai Lama to the city.

The Dalai Lama was both the political and spiritual leader of Tibet prior to the Chinese invasion in the 1950's. Since 1959 he has been in exile. To the Tibetans, the Dalai Lama is the embodiment of all that is Tibetan, a symbol of their cultural heritage. In exile he has taken a leading role in establishing schools, clinics, monasteries and *gompas*, and integrating Tibetan beliefs and lifestyles into the 21st century.

The next day, his birthday, we join 600 Tibetans crowded onto the lawn of a government guest house. Everyone is all dressed up; both men and women wear large necklaces and earrings of turquoise and coral. Since the

The Dalai Lama, whose name means "Ocean of Compassion," Manali, India.

Dalai Lama speaks to the crowd in Tibetan, a language we don't understand, we try to get an intuitive feel for the man by his interactions with the audience. He has a warm, endearing smile, and laughs and chuckles between speaking and chanting prayers. After the talk, we spend the day watching a festival of Tibetan dancing and music.

Neither of us has recovered from our illness. I wake each morning bloated with cramps from constipation, while Tass has cramps from diarrhea. We have another stool sample taken. This time we are told we both have giardia. We are beginning to wonder if we have had it all along since Kathmandu. I have lost 14 pounds, Tass 12. The giardia diet.

We relax in Manali for five days, until we get back to better health. By that time we are eager to do some exploring. Before leaving the area we want to take a side-trip over the 13,050-foot Rohtang Pass into the Keylong Valley.

The road is full of switchbacks and breathtaking views. At the top of a large glacier we catch up with a group of tour busses that passed us earlier in the day. Since many Indian tourists have never seen snow before, they rent rubber boots and wooden sleds from hawkers along the road and push each other up and down the glacier.

A sudden, violent rainstorm drives us into a tea tent, where we buy hard boiled eggs plucked bare-handed out of a boiling pot by the vendor. After a few cups of tea, the sky clears. We leave the crowds of tourists, who will go no further up the road, and pedal the last few miles to the top of the pass. We pitch camp on a grassy meadow to enjoy the afternoon sunshine, surrounded by 20,000-foot peaks.

The next day we descend the north side of the pass on a road that is open only from June through September. Landslides and avalanches have torn out the roadbed, which is under a constant state of repair. Every five miles we pass squalid settlements of moldy tents housing the road crews. The workers, brought in for the summer from other parts of India and even Nepal, have strange priorities. One crew uses brooms made from the branches of newly cut trees to immaculately sweep an isolated section of pavement, while 100 yards away the road is so washed out we must get off the bikes to push. Near huge mud holes workers patiently stack small stones into large, straight-walled piles, virtual works of engineering art, which, after it has all been neatly arranged, will be thrown into the holes. The only person doing anything useful is the guy tending the fire under the teapot.

We are now on the Tibetan plateau; the bottom of the Chandra River

Bruce riding over the 13,050-foot Rohtang Pass, India.

Valley is still almost 10,000 feet above sea level. The landscape is barren, with little grass and few shrubs. The houses have flat roofs; prayer flags flutter on the corners of each building. Everyone smiles and waves. The men wear woolen pillbox hats with embroidered designs and large gold hoop earrings in each ear. The women wear brown dresses with white trimmed borders, brown pants and brightly embroidered socks. Many of the older women shave the front third of their heads from ear to ear, like the Hmong hilltribe in Thailand.

By the time we come to our turn-around point, we are only 200 miles south-east of Ladakh, our final destination in India. The rough gravel road keeps going, but we don't. To go further, up along the sensitive border area of Chinese-occupied Tibet, we need a special permit, available only in New Delhi and hard to obtain. Since we have no permit, we have to go back over the pass to Manali and make an 800-mile circle around the mountains to enter Ladakh from the west.

Along the way, our next stop is Dharamsala. We spend a week in the mountain community studying about Ladakh and Tibet in a large library built by the Dalai Lama. One day we hike to the nearby Tibetan Children's Village, a combination boarding school, orphanage and nursery. Started as a single class in a small home by the sister of the Dalai Lama, the idea has grown into a number of well-respected schools emphasizing Tibetan studies. Inside the classrooms we are impressed by the quality of the work posted on bulletin boards. Outside 300 kids play games in a large field between two mountain ridges. The students built and leveled the field themselves over a two-year period, hauling all the dirt by hand during physical education class.

The Tibetans impress us as extremely hard workers. We stop at a rock quarry where Tibetan women in ornate dress, braided hair and large gold earrings, pound rocks into gravel with two-pound hammers. Other women carry loads of rock on their backs. As if that is not enough, as they trudge under their heavy loads from one part of the quarry to another, they keep their hands busy knitting clothes to sell,

We leave Dharmsala and climb further into the mountains towards Srinagar, the capital of Kashmir. Along the way a bizarre collection of poetic highway signs encourages drivers to slow down: "Don't die like fools, obey the traffic rules," and "Reckless drivers kill and die, leaving behind all to cry." The further we go, the stranger the signs: "I want you darling, but not so fast."

Five days later we cross the last pass and descend the switchbacked highway into the lush, green Kashmir Valley. Although Kashmir is politically a part of India, it is different culturally and philosophically from the rest of the country. The people are predominately Muslim. In fact, when Kashmiris talk of coming to their valley they speak of "coming from

India" as though Kashmir was not a part of that country.

The Kashmiris look central Asian, the cheekbones are higher, the face leaner, the nose longer. Many men use henna to dye their beards and chest hair a reddish color. The women, who seem more outgoing than most Muslim women, wear long pants, with skirts over the pants, and long sleeved, long-tailed blouses. They wear scarves tied tightly around the tops of their heads, gypsy style.

Srinagar is a holiday town. The region has attracted tourists for a long time. In the 16th century, the Moghul Emperors of central Asia chose Kashmir for their summer residences and built immense palaces and gardens around a group of lakes in the valley. When the British arrived they also wanted to build summer homes in the area. But the local Maharaja would not allow British citizens to purchase any land. The resourceful Brits came up with a clever way to get around the law. They built elaborate houseboats, which they simply moored on Dal Lake.

The idea caught on so well that today, when people think of Srinagar, they think more of the thousands of houseboats filling the lake than the city on the shore. Like most tourists, we come intending to rent a houseboat. We meet with three different men. Each tells us of an available room on a boat in our price range, and takes us on a long ride in a water taxi only to arrive at the houseboat and have the price of the room suddenly go up. After wasting half a day we get tired of the hype and take a boat to a hotel on a tiny island that is only a few feet larger than the hotel itself. We rent a room on the top floor, with a balcony overlooking the water out the front door.

Small boats called *shikaras* paddle past in a constant procession. Some are rustic, single passenger boats with a hard board seat; others are ornate taxis with bright, gaudy paint, big wooden awnings and gauze curtains over full-sized beds, complete with pillows so the passengers can stretch out and relax. Each boat has a sign extolling the comfort of its "Deluxe Spring Seats." Other *shikaras* pass by loaded with every imaginable household product, floating stores moving from houseboat to houseboat. Souvenir boats go past--one with jewelry, another has trunks of papier-mache boxes, a third with Tibetan *thanka* paintings. The aggressive vendors badger the houseboat occupants relentlessly.

Suna, the owner of our hotel, will not allow any vendors in the hotel unless we invite them in. Although Suna seems extraordinarily calm, the temperament of many Kashmiris is more volatile. Wherever we go someone is yelling and screaming at someone else over a business deal. One day two men in separate *shikaras* stop in front of the hotel to yell and scream abuses at each other. They appear ready to come to blows. We ask Suna to interpret the argument, figuring it is a major crisis. He replies there is really no problem, "The two men are just getting a bit of exercise!"

We leave Srinagar to ride over the three high passes into Ladakh, a portion of India on the Tibetan Plateau. As we pedal out of the city, a small convoy of Indian Army trucks overtakes us. The last truck swerves as it passes Tass. The back of the truck grazes her arm and gives her a nasty bruise. Somewhat shaken, we head out again, keeping a closer eye on our mirrors.

The air is fresh and clear. The pass ahead, 11,550-foot Zoji La, is the lowest of the three passes on the way to Ladakh. Yet it is the most difficult to cross. The Zoji La absorbs the brunt of monsoon clouds blowing up from India. The road is continually washed out from heavy rains in the summer and snow avalanches in the winter. Our goal today is the top of the pass where we hope to camp with a good view of the sunset.

After lunch we arrive at a traffic control post. The upper section of the pass is a narrow, single lane road with traffic flowing one way in the morning and the opposite direction in the afternoon. Due to road construction all vehicles are being held until 4:00 p.m. Beside the road a huge parking lot is full of loaded trucks, buses, taxis and jeeps--all with impatient drivers. We, however, are let through the gate.

We ride for an hour in peace and quiet, meeting only a few trucks, who shouldn't even be on the road, going the opposite direction. I get a flat tire. While I fix it, the convoy that had been waiting down the hill catches us. We sit by the side of the road and let the lead section of the pack--the high-speed drivers--zoom past.

After the trucks and buses comes yet another army convoy, each truck spaced 100 yards apart. They lumber up the road in low gear with engines roaring, pouring out great clouds of diesel smoke. We watch the trucks for a few minutes and then decide to resume riding even though the convoy is still passing by. If we wait any longer we'll never make it to the top before dark.

Sweating, dirty and exhausted, we pedal up the narrow switchbacks on the steep mountain face, choking on the dust and smoke from each passing truck. Like trucks throughout Asia, they are loud and close. As the road deteriorates, the rough but bikeable shoulder disappears. In its place is soft dirt covered with baseball-sized stones. Every few minutes a two-and-a-half-ton truck rumbles past.

I am riding thirty yards in front of Tass when I hear someone yelling. I stop and look back to see a soldier standing in the middle of the road waving his arms at me. He looks distressed. I get an uncomfortable feeling in my stomach. Once he sees me turn around and start back down the hill, he likewise turns and runs back around the corner. Neither his truck, nor Tass, is in sight.

I ride back around the corner to find the army truck stopped in the middle of the road. I hear Tass screaming, but she is nowhere in sight. It is not until I get to the truck that I can see Tass on the other side of the vehicle. She is hysterical. It takes me a few moments to find out she is uninjured. Beside her, in a mangled, crumpled pile, is her bicycle.

The truck tried to pass her on a narrow section of road overhanging a 200-foot cliff. The truck has a broken passenger mirror and a broken passenger window covered with cardboard, so neither the driver nor his sidekick was able to see Tass beside the truck. The truck was only halfway around her when the driver, thinking he had passed her and nervous about the cliff, swerved back toward the inner bank.

Somehow Tass jumped off the bike and kept from being crushed between the truck and the inside rock wall. But the truck ran over the bike from axle to axle, crumpling both wheels and hubs, flattening the derailleurs, shearing off one crank arm, hopelessly bending the other, and buckling nearly every piece of tubing on the frame. The front fork, rim, spokes, and low-rider rack are tangled like spaghetti.

The entire convoy behind us has stopped, and a number of drivers walk up the road to see what is the delay. We all examine the scene of the accident together. It is obvious the driver was too close to the inside shoulder when he hit the bike. The other drivers agree with our assessment and sadly shake their heads. The driver who hit Tass looks sick. We

Tass's crushed bicycle lies mangled on the road, Zoji La Pass, India.

sit by the side of the road and stare dumbly at the remains of the bicycle. Is this the end of our around-the-world trip?

No one moves until the company commander shows up forty-five minutes later. He hears everyone's testimony, agrees it was the truck driver's fault, and assures us everything will be rectified at the next military post. We load both bikes in another truck and catch a ride with the convoy over the pass.

The next morning we are ushered into a traffic control post, given a torn piece of paper, and asked to list the damages. The total is $650 U.S. The army officer takes one look at the amount and sends us to the convoy commander. We are given a better piece of paper and asked to write the entire story and re-list the damages. Two hours later the commander is still unwilling to make a judgment in the case. Instead, he advises us and the unlucky driver to go back over the pass to a larger army post where we can reach a settlement.

Luckily we don't have to ride with the driver who hit Tass. Obviously nervous, he has a terrible time turning his truck around. He looks like a candidate for another accident. We are escorted back to the guard post, where a civilian truck is stopped, and the army officer informs the driver he will give us a free lift back over the pass.

It takes six hours in a truck without shock absorbers to cross the 32-mile road. We stop for every imaginable difficulty. Trucks break down in the middle of the road in front of us. Road crews stop us while they clean up avalanches. Twice we have to back up to find a spot in the road wide enough to let an oncoming truck, which shouldn't be here this time of day, get around us.

We arrive in the middle of the afternoon, exhausted, and are led to an open tent full of officials. Although the convoy commander promised us restitution, we are now told the Indian Army doesn't even have insurance on its vehicles. Each driver is held responsible for any accidents. Since the driver who hit Tass is a poor man, we give up the idea of total restitution, which would only force the man, along with his wife and two children, into bankruptcy. Now the question is, how much should we demand?

For three hours we barter back and forth. A huge crowd of truck drivers who are waiting for the road to open, sits by the tent and listens to every detail with the utmost scrutiny. Each point we make is translated into both Hindi and Urdu for the crowd's benefit. Everyone is fascinated with our itemized list of damages. Most are incredulous about the cost of the bike until, exasperated, Tass gives a moving testimony on the quality of her Trek--highlighted by the fact that it has eighteen gears. Suddenly the opposition is muffled. The sympathy of the crowd swings to our side.

Just before dark we arrive at an agreement. The driver will pay us 1,500 rupiahs ($125 U.S.). To us it is a pitiful sum. To the driver it is two months wages. He is already in debt, and on shaky ground about losing his job. We can't in good conscience force him to pay more.

Once the agreement on the amount is reached, we think the ordeal is over. Far from it. Now the serious bargaining begins. How and when do we get paid? For the next two hours we sit and listen to every crazy story imaginable explaining why we can't get our money for two weeks. We don't buy it. At 8:00 p.m. an officer arrives who straightens everything out within an hour. A sergeant will accompany the driver to the bank in Srinagar tomorrow, where the driver will borrow the money to make the restitution.

The next morning we eat breakfast and wonder, will we get paid or won't we? Did we ask for too little, or too much? Does the driver really have a wife and two kids, or was that just a part of his bargaining tactics? We are running out of money ourselves. Even if we are paid, how can we possibly replace the bike with just $125?

The driver and the sergeant return in the afternoon. Still we argue and haggle about how we will be paid. The police write a totally fictitious tale of how Tass "was taking her tea beside the road when the truck drove by, and, through no fault of the driver, a stone was kicked up by the tire, which struck her bicycle and caused all the damage." Tass refuses to sign the document, and for two hours they refuse to pay us. Finally, when they realize Tass is not going to give in, they give her the money.

We catch a bus back over the Zoji La Pass, for the third time. On the way we discuss our options. We are so close to Ladakh we can't turn back now. We have little choice but to leave both bikes in the nearby village of Kargil, and hitchhike into Ladakh. Since there is only one road, we'll pick everything back up on the way out. Hopefully we'll find Tass another bike in New Delhi for the ride across Europe and the United States.

20

Mountains And Monasteries

The next morning we load our backpacks and catch a lift with two Sikhs. They are shocked at our desire to ride on top of the truck instead of inside the cramped cab. After repeated prodding they give in, and we scamper up the ladder and settle into a spot on the brightly painted wooden box over the cab. The truck, heavily laden with flour and sugar, roars slowly up the valley.

The hardest part about losing the bicycle is accepting our loss of freedom. This is a section of road we had been looking forward to riding since Kathmandu. Now we are unable to stop when we want to enjoy the view or take photos. We are removed from the activity along the highway. Before, we were participants; now we are spectators watching the scenery pass by. It is easy to get depressed when we think of how much more enjoyable it would be riding our bikes. Yet our spirits are lifted as we ride out in the sunshine. Everything we need is in our backpacks. Even though we can't stop at every overlook, we can still follow our original plan and camp on each pass.

As we travel into Ladakh the landscape becomes more barren. Mountains of rock are devoid of trees. The hills are so desolate they are hauntingly beautiful. The sun is incredibly bright; the air, crisp and dry.

Mountains far in the distance are so clear and sharply defined they seem touchable. Occasionally clouds darken the mountains near us, which explode with a dazzling intensity when the sun again strikes the rock. Oranges, purples, yellows and reds are painted across the landscape. Everything looks surreal.

As the sun sets behind a group of mountains just over the border in nearby Pakistan, we arrive at the top of 13,430-foot Fatu La Pass. The driver is aghast when we yell out to stop the truck and let us off. He insists we stay in the truck until we reach the monastery at Lamayuru. He cannot understand why we would want to sleep here. In fact, he can't understand why we would come to the region at all. Most Kashmiris consider Ladakh to be a barren and miserable place.

We unload our gear and hike up a ridge to a spot that will give a view of the sunrise, and we set up camp. The next morning is so pleasant we skip catching a ride. Instead, we walk to Lamayuru. The area is filled with eroded buttes and deep, twisting gullies. In the middle of the largest canyon is a huge, white Buddhist monastery perched on top of a ridge. Below the monastery lies a small town and an irrigated valley with fields of green barley.

We hike past rows of whitewashed *chortons*, each housing a sacred Buddhist relic, then pass long rows of *mani* walls, built of countless stones inscribed with sacred prayers and chants. The path switchbacks up the cliffs to the monastery. The position of the building could not be more precarious. The walls on three sides are built up from the very edge of the cliff. On top we stop in a tea house and join a monk for buttered tea. He is an enthusiastic character. Before long he and I are slapping each other on the back and having great laughs as we bargain over a few religious souvenirs he wants to sell.

After our tea we explore the monastery. The courtyard wall is covered with stunning paintings of Tibetan deities. The bright color, vivid expressions, and feeling of movement jumps out at us. The more we see of Tibetan art, the less busy the paintings look. Rather than appearing cluttered, the paintings flow together in a balance that is pleasing to the eye.

Inside the *gompa*, windows high above us send streaks of light filtering down to the floor. Brightly painted pillars fill the room. Every inch of the building is covered in reds, yellows, greens, blues and golds. Benevolent deities and beings of menacing power erupt out of the walls; fierce, grimacing faces lean out of the archways; painted dragons chase each other across door lintels.

The Ladakhis practice a branch of Mahayana Buddhism known as *Vajrayana*, The Diamond Vehicle. The knowledge gained from the teachings is said to cut the bonds of ignorance like a diamond cuts all other substances, yet cannot be marred itself. The religion has a strong emphasis on serving others. The highest goal is to be free of selfish desires, to be as pure and radiant as a diamond.

The Buddhists of Ladakh have built a number of large monasteries in the mountains along the Indus River Valley. We hitchhike and walk our way toward Leh, the capital of Ladakh, taking detours to visit a number of monasteries along the way. The side canyons we hike are desolate. No trees. No grass. Nothing but sun, wind and rock. We walk into another world, another reality. The stillness is overwhelming. The stark landscape acts like a giant mirror, forcing us to look back at ourselves.

On the last leg of our journey to Leh, we catch a ride in the most decrepit truck we have seen in all of India. Three miles down the road it overheats and pulls over to stop. A young boy is sent off with a bucket in search of water. Good luck. Twenty minutes later an absolutely packed bus chugs up the hill. We abandon the truck, flag down the bus, and squeeze on board. Six miles later the bus has a flat tire, which takes an hour to change. As the tire is being fixed, the decrepit truck that had overheated passes us without stopping. After the tire is changed, we ride only three miles and find the truck broken down in the middle of the road, with no place to pass. It takes an hour and a half to get the truck out of the way. It is a typical Ladakhi journey--seven hours to go less than 40 miles.

Leh, the capital of Ladakh, is located at 11,554 feet in a wide section of the Indus River Valley. The region was once a popular caravan route into Tibet, but when the Chinese invaded Tibet in the 1950's, the border closed. India paid little attention to Ladakh until 1962, when they discovered the Chinese had built a road into eastern Ladakh and were claiming ownership of the territory. India responded by building a road into western Ladakh, establishing a number of military bases, and closing the entire area to travel. In 1974 the Indian government lifted most of the travel restrictions. Now, with loss of trade over the ancient passes, tourism has become Ladakhs' main source of revenue.

Leh is a fun city, with curio shops, restaurants and even a newly opened English used book store. It is summertime. The markets are full of giant vegetables, delicious apricots and bumper crops of apples. The soil seems too dusty and rocky to produce a crop, yet irrigation results in phenomenal growth. The mountain air, low in oxygen but high in nitrogen, combined with intense ultraviolet rays, creates greenhouse conditions.

We check into a two-story Tibetan-style hotel surrounded by vegetable and flower gardens. The next day is the start of a week-long celebration of traditional Ladakhi music and dance. Everyone at the opening parade is dressed in beautiful clothing. The most striking are wealthier women who wear *peraks*, headdresses with large black, elephant-like ears, and material

A Ladakhi woman selling vegetables in the market, northern India.

covered with turquoise stones running from the top of the head half-way down the back. Elaborate rows of silver jewelry and Tibetan coral are stitched along the sides. Necklaces of turquoise, coral, and amber are draped over layers of clothing made from dyed wool, silk brocades, embroidered shawls, and combed goat skins.

The rest of the women, and many of the men, wear *chibis*, a colorful stove pipe hat with little wings that stick out on each side. Men and women wear large hoop earrings, often with big chunks of turquoise and coral that are so heavy a string is often looped over the top of the ear to support the weight. Others wear strands of fresh-water pearls.

The big event of the second day is an archery contest. Being a former archery buff, I take a close look at the equipment. The bows have no notch on the string for fitting the arrow, nor is there a rest on the bow handle to place the arrow, it is simply laid on the hand. The arrows also look tricky to use. They have little fletching and the points are exceptionally heavy.

The contest starts with two officials from the Indian government attempting to shoot the first arrows. It is obvious neither has ever shot a bow. The combination of ancient equipment and inexperienced archers produces hilarious results. The first arrow flies ten feet and lands with a plop on the carpet the contestants are standing on. The second arrow lands next to the first. With a firmer grip on the bow and a more forceful pull of the string, each diplomat tries again. This time the arrows make it to the end of the carpet, twenty feet away, but still 30 feet from the target. More arrows are fit to the bow and sent on slow, arching projectories, falling far short of the goal. At last, after repeated coaching, the two men hit the pile of earth on which the targets sit. Close enough. The contest is officially open.

Immediately the local archers crowd in to shoot. Arrows fill the air. The Ladakhis have more strength, but no more control than the diplomats. Arrows fly high into the air. Others zing out of the bow, hit the earth, and skid at high speed all the way to the dirt pile. The mound of dirt soon looks like a pin cushion, but no one hits the target.

After the first round of shooting, *chang*, a locally made home brew, is brought out to fortify the participants. A group of men collects the arrows and heaps them in a pile in front of the archers. Round two begins. No one takes turns, instead men fire at random as quickly as they fit arrows to their bows. Finally, someone hits the target. But with so many shooting it is impossible to tell who it was. No one seems to care anyway. Everyone is busy notching bows. The wail of oboes and sound of drums fill the air, along with cries for more *chang*. The archers prepare for round three.

During the week long festival we take breaks to explore the area. We hear about an oracle, an old woman who makes prophecies and goes into a trance to heal people. One morning we catch an early bus to her village, and hike through barley fields to her house. Along with 10 villagers, we are ushered into a dimly lit kitchen with a small altar in the corner. A young woman bustles about the room stoking the stove and lighting butter lamps.

Lamu, the oracle, comes into the room and begins to chant. Like so many religious ceremonies we have seen in Asia, there is a lack of solemnness in the Western sense. The oracle chants and rings a bell while more people come in. Individuals in the audience shift about talking with each other and paying little attention to the ritual.

As the old oracle induces her trance, she puts on ceremonial clothing: an embroidered silk cape, a wide sash, two scarves and a headdress with a picture of Buddha. Accompanying her outward change in dress is an inner change. The oracle's voice deepens and her actions become jerky, like a puppet on a string. After half an hour of playing a small, one-handed drum and a bell, she faces the audience, grabs a stick, and whacks a man in the front row who is sitting too close.

By now, nearly 30 people are crowded into the small room. After a few moments, the first person in line, the man hit with the stick, moves forward to be healed. He explains his illness to the oracle and then opens his shirt to bare his chest and stomach. The oracle moves closer, blows gently on his body and then puts her mouth to his chest to suck out the

Leh gompa with lines of prayer flags, Ladakh, India.

243

illness. After sitting back up, she spits a dark substance into a silver bowl. The villagers believe the saliva contains the evil which caused the man's problems, and it is carefully examined by the oracle. One by one the audience kneels before her, Tibetan Buddhists, Hindu soldiers and even a few Muslim women in veils. Sometimes the oracle uses a small wooden tube to suck out the spirits, and once she spits a hard black substance into the bowl. The trance lasts two hours. When it is over the oracle chants and removes her ceremonial clothing while the audience talks and laughs as they head out the door.

One of our favorite hang-outs during our time in Leh is Spitok Monastery, where we watch the monks create a large *mandala* of colored sand. The work takes ten days. We always catch the early bus to the monastery and arrive in time to have buttered tea with the monks before they settle down to work.

A *mandala* is a complex geometric design with spiritual meaning. *Mandalas* are most often painted, but the *mandala* at Spitok is made of colored sand on a six-foot diameter circle of wood. Four monks work at a time, each with a long, thin silver tube full of colored sand. By rubbing a knife handle across little ridges on the tube, the vibration releases sand from the needle-like end in precise amounts to create crisp, distinct designs.

It is a work of devotion. The monks dote over the project, making sure everything is done just right. Though they work hard, they are a jovial bunch. One morning as we sit around the *mandala* watching the monks work, a monk sneezes violently. Tass, ever the jokester, exclaims, "Aye ya yai," in a low but easily heard tone. For a second no one says anything. Then the monk who sneezed looks up at Tass, smiles, and chuckles. Another monk looks up and chuckles. The first monk laughs again and soon everyone is laughing--not just little giggles, but side-splitting hysterics.

Most of the monasteries in Ladakh were founded by *rinpoches*. The Buddhists of Ladakh view the *rinpoches* as semi-divine beings, enlightened souls who, through repeated reincarnations, remain on earth to guide others to Buddhahood.

The Stakzong *rinpoche* is the incarnation of the founder of Hemis Monastery, Ladakh's most important monastery. When he was 17 he was sent to a monastery in Tibet for further studies. A year later, in 1959, the Chinese invaded. He was never heard of again.

Last year, 26 years after overrunning the Tibetan monastery where he was studying, the Chinese government announced the Stakzong *rinpoche* was still alive. Negotiations began immediately to bring him back to Ladakh. Now we find he is making his first return visit next week. We delay our own departure another week to be a part of the festivities.

On the morning of his arrival the streets of Leh are lined with brightly robed monks chanting, clashing cymbals, blowing horns and beating drums.

A woman of Ladakh, India, wearing a turquoise-covered perak.

The lay people, also dressed in their best clothes, crowd behind the monks, pressing in for a good view. Many people carry two-foot-long bundles of burning incense. The town smells wonderful. The crowd continues to build through the morning. It soon becomes obvious only the most aggressive will be able to squeeze to the front for a glimpse of the *rinpoche*.

A battalion of policemen with long sticks attempts to keep order around the vehicle. We don't even see his car. All we see are clubs swinging in the air. Tomorrow the *rinpoche* goes to Hemis Monastery. We'll try again.

At sunrise we try to get a bus to Hemis, but they are all reserved for monks. So we hitch a ride with a jeep and leave just ahead of the *rinpoche's* entourage. In each village along the way the streets are full of banners and crowds awaiting the *rinpoche's* car. Everything smells of incense. In places the road is painted with Buddhist symbols, in other spots the symbols are laid out with colored powders. Ribbons and hand-painted

245

signs hang everywhere. In one village a group of school children in neat blue uniforms waits in line. Little girls hold flowers, little boys stand at attention with their hair neatly combed. As we approach the mountainside leading to the monastery, monks line the road. When our vehicle can go no further, we hike up the hill and join the crowd near the monastery entrance.

When the *rinpoche* arrives everyone goes wild. The crowd surges toward the car. The driver responds by flooring the gas pedal and racing for the monastery gate. But the car loses its momentum as it unsuccessfully negotiates a tight switchback, which has been made even smaller by the mass of people on the road's edge. The car stalls. Monks jump to the rescue and begin pushing the car up the steep hill. Seconds later the engine restarts, and the car careens through the next two corners as the driver races the motor and the monks push from behind. Near the monastery the car is again halted in a sea of humanity. Everyone is shouting excitedly.

The monks whisk the *rinpoche* out and spirit him off to the main *gompa*. We follow the crowd into the monastery courtyard where everyone waits for a glimpse of the man when he moves from one building to another. *Rinpoche* groupies. After a long wait it becomes apparent nothing is going to happen the rest of the day. We set up camp in the courtyard of a restaurant outside the monastery wall.

At sunrise we stake out a small spot under a shaded balcony overlooking the central monastery courtyard. People from all the surrounding villages likewise come early for good seats. By 10:00 a.m., when the buses from Leh begin to arrive, the place is packed. With each jostle of the crowd we lose a portion of our turf. I am squeezed between a wall and a pole with a crowd of eager Ladakhis leaning over me so I am unable to stand up. Tass is pressed into the railing. Yet we have comfortable seats compared with the crowd below, which is twice as congested, and in the hot sun. The Indian police, who are here for crowd control, are recruits from outside Ladakh. Each carries a *lathi* stick, which they brandish over everyone's head in a threatening manner. Yet the Ladakhis take little notice. They press against the police and each other as they squirm their way to the front of the crowd.

Everything is in a controlled state of disorder until the police at one section of the crowd abandon their posts for 10 seconds to help other police control a different section of the crowd. It is a major tactical error. The unguarded crowd breaks forward en mass and rushes ahead 20 feet, taking up much of the room reserved for the ceremony. The police return and try to move the people back, but the crowd is unable to back up--even if they wanted to, which they don't--as the people behind continue to push forward. Everyone simply sits down. The police threaten the front row with violence, and finally they begin shuffling backwards. Since the rear of the crowd does not move, the center becomes even more squished.

Masked dancers at Hemis Monastery, Ladakh, India.

The big horns sound, and a procession of dancers emerges from the main *gompa* down the stairs to the courtyard. With slow, deliberate steps in time to the music, 12 monks begin the first ceremony, the Dance of the Black Hats. Each wears a large, black, fur-rimmed hat with tall center spires adorned with painted skulls. Their long-sleeved robes are made of bright silk brocade, topped with aprons embroidered with fiendish demons and skulls.

When the dance is finished, other monks come out escorting the *rinpoche* to a raised dais below us. The crowd presses forward. The police scamper about trying to restore order while everyone is being crushed. Pandemonium in the monastery.

More dancers emerge carrying a large image of Padmasambhava, the charismatic monk who brought Buddhism to Tibet after having sorceristic showdowns with the priests of the older, animistic, Bon religion. The dancers all wear masks, some gruesome, some benevolent. They move slowly to the drum beat, occasionally using hand-held *dammarus*, small two-sided drums made from the skulls of dead monks. The skull paintings and human bones are not meant to be gruesome, but merely a reminder of the transitory nature of life.

The dancing continues through the day. After watching from a cramped, squatting position since morning, we can barely stand up when the last ceremony is finished. We wobble to the monastery kitchen to drink buttered tea and then head back to our campsite.

The next morning starts with another dance, and then the crowd is told the *rinpoche* will personally bless everyone. The courtyard becomes a battleground as eager Ladakhis push against the police to be the first blessed. We watch the fray the remainder of the morning. We consider getting a blessing ourselves, but joining the frantic crowd is too intimidating. We leave for lunch. Later in the afternoon, when the crowd has mellowed, I work my way through the long line. The *rinpoche* looks tired and simply dips a small tasseled wand on my forehead as I walk past.

Reluctantly, we depart Ladakh, far behind schedule, pick up my bike and the remains of Tass's bike, and recross the Zoji La into Kashmir. After four days of buses and all-night trains, we arrive in New Delhi.

We quickly realize that New Delhi is not the place to buy a new bike for Tass. The locally made bikes are all heavy, one-speed clunkers, and imported bikes are out of our price range due to high import taxes. We also face the sad reality that Tass's Trek is totally beyond repair. We salvage the seat, handlebars, rear luggage rack and panniers. We give everything else away for scrap metal.

Our flight to Egypt leaves in the middle of the night. In the evening we flag down a three-wheeled taxi to take us to the airport. Since our panniers take up the back of the taxi, my bike sticks outside the vehicle. Just before the airport terminal the taxi driver asks me to ride my bike the last few hundred yards. He will have to pay *baksheesh*, a bribe/fine, if the airport police catch him carrying too much luggage.

I ride the last quarter mile and arrive to find the taxi already gone and Tass standing next to our pile of luggage. Suddenly my stomach sinks. I don't have our small day pack, which is one of my luggage responsibilities, and it is not in the pile next to Tass. I left it in the back seat of the taxi. Tass didn't see it when she unloaded the vehicle and assumed it was on my back. Worse yet, I committed the ultimate travel sin. In the rush of packing, I threw my money belt, which contains my passport and our airline tickets, into the backpack--which is now in a three-wheeled taxi that departed two minutes ago.

I run out and flag down a regular taxi. But when I get in, a policeman stops the car and refuses to let me leave. The taxi is authorized only to bring people **to** the airport. The taxi driver sees the panic in my eye and gives me a nod. I jump back out, run down the sidewalk and turn the first corner to find the taxi waiting for me, out of sight of the policeman. I jump in, and off we zoom, searching for one three-wheeled taxi in a city swarming with three-wheeled taxis.

My only chance is to go back to where the little taxi picked us up, in hopes it is the driver's home turf and he will return there. As we race down the highway, I stare at each three-wheeled taxi we pass, looking for any distinguishing features. Ten minutes later we come up behind a group of four of the taxis and from our headlights I spot a piece of familiar-looking fringe hanging from a tailgate. I point out the vehicle, and the driver of the car I am in nearly runs the smaller vehicle off the road as he forces it to stop. I jump out and, with tremendous relief, recognize the driver. A quick search reveals our small day pack, which had fallen behind the back seat. The driver tells me I am very lucky. He was not going back to where he picked us up. In fact, at the very next corner he was turning to a different part of the city, and we would never have found him.

I return to the airport. Tass is stunned to see me; she was certain I was on a hopeless chase and that we would miss our plane. We give each other a shaky hug and walk down the concourse to our flight to Egypt.

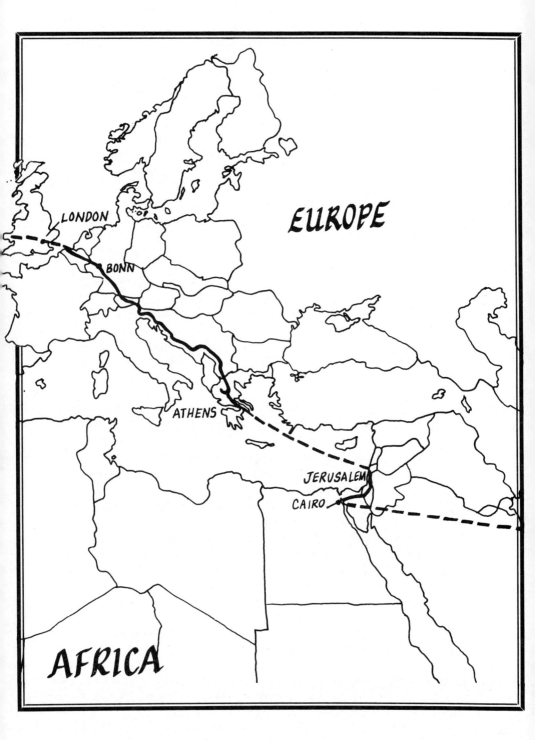

21

The Victor

At the Cairo airport we are told we must cash $300 U.S. to enter the country. Since we only have $300, the last thing we want to do is convert it all into Egyptian *rupiahs*. We put up a major argument and are taken to a supervisor, where we make a compromise. We cash $100 and get a three-day visa.

After India, the streets of the Egyptian capital appear full of private automobiles--some with women drivers!--and everyone drives on the right-hand side of the road. There are no rickshaws and, alas, no street vendors selling food. But the most noticeable difference is a lack of color. No bright saris, colorful turbans or flashy jewelry. One on one, the people greet us with a sincere, "Welcome! Welcome to Cairo!" Yet we see few smiling faces on the street. Everything is subdued; there is a lack of the vibrancy felt in India and southeast Asia.

High import tariffs also make Egypt a poor place to shop for a bicycle. Instead, we head straight to the National Archeology Museum. The next day we take a bus to Giza. The city goes right up to the eastern side of the pyramids. Within moments the tour guide operators descend on us. We bargain with a number of camel owners until we come to agreeable terms with a man named Iraham, who suggests we take two camels for the three of us, at a reduced rate. We climb aboard. With great gurgling snorts and growls, the camels rise off their haunches and lumber into the desert.

The sun beats down on us, and the heat and dust cause the air to shimmer. Due to the haze, visibility is very low. We stop occasionally to allow Iraham to change mounts, riding first with Tass and then me. He chatters incessantly.

"Very hot in desert. I am Bedouin. Some no live in desert. I live in desert. I Bedouin like desert. You no live in desert. Too hot. I live in desert with camel. Not horse. Not donkey. Camel. Camel live in desert. Horse no good. Donkey no good. Camel good. One week, two week, no water no problem. No food horse dead. No food camel no problem. Three week, four week, no problem. No food camel no problem. Five week no problem. Six week no water, camel good. Not dead. Horse drink water, dead. Camel drink, no problem. Hit with stick, camel drink little water, not dead. Much water, dead. Little water, not dead. Camel ship of desert. Camel good. Bedouin like camel."

Iraham takes us to other pyramids and burial grounds; we poke among the ruins, Tass shoots some pictures, and then we ride back to the Great Pyramid and the Sphinx. All too soon it is time to leave.

We get up at 4:30 a.m. the next morning, catch a bus that is supposed to take us across town, where we will get a bus to Israel. Instead, the first bus drops us off at the airport. We seem to have this reoccuring difficulty with airports.

Somewhere, in another part of the city, our bus is leaving for Israel in 20 minutes. We waste five minutes running around asking directions before we locate an English-speaking taxi driver who declares it will take 20 minutes to get to the correct bus terminal. We throw all our gear inside, and off we roar.

We have ridden with wild bus and taxi drivers throughout Asia but nothing compares with our ride through Cairo. Each time we think we will crash, a small space opens between traffic--just at the last second--and our driver, without any hesitation, keeps the pedal on the floor, avoiding crashes only because everyone else is quick to get out of his way. We screech into the station, at what we think is the last second, only to find the bus is running 30 minutes late. Typical high-stress-for-no-reason scenario.

In Jerusalem we call Caroline and Kadish Gabiel, whom we met at the monastery in Thailand and then again in Kathmandu. They returned to Israel five weeks ago and just got an apartment last week. We sit up late into the night catching up on news and then collapse on their foldout couch.

Back in Thailand we had dreamed of spending a few months in Israel, perhaps staying on a *kibbutz*. But now we are living on borrowed money and feel the need to get home sooner and resume working.

Our first priority is to find Tass a bike. We check the classified ads and visit a number of bicycle shops. Multi-speed bikes are not cheap in Israel either, but at least we have more of a selection. We spot a few potential used bikes but no great deals, so we go sight-seeing to think things over.

We walk to the old city and enter via the Jaffa Gate. The wall that presently stands around the old city was constructed in the 1500's by Suliman the Magnificent, a Muslim sultan of the Ottoman empire. Suliman built the wall as a gift to the city to help protect all the places that are venerated by Muslims, Christians, and Jews. His architects did not share his generosity and built the structure as it was in the second century A.D.--leaving the site historians believe to be the location of the Last Supper outside the wall. The engineers didn't see any reason to pay a much greater expense simply to include one small building. When Suliman found out one of the sacred sites had been left outside the wall, he had all his architects executed. Such is history in the Holy Land.

The old city is divided into Christian, Armenian, Jewish and Muslim quarters. We walk down the tightly packed David Street, where shop-keepers sell every type of religious item imaginable: olive wood carvings, rosaries, gold and silver medallions and Byzantine icons. Other shelves are filled with brass pots, Bedouin jewelry, authentic terra cotta lamps more

View of Jerusalem from inside a church on the Mount of Olives, Israel.

253

than 2,000 years old, and boxes of cheap imitations.

Our first stop is the Church of the Holy Sepulchre, built over the site where Christ is believed to have been buried. Six groups share the Church, and, because of this, the building is constructed with the lack of master planning found in a cliff dwelling: space for each new family member is found by tacking an addition onto the most convenient spot. Latin Catholics, Greek Orthodox, Armenian, Syrian, Coptic and the Ethiopian Christians all vie for space within the Church. Shrines and altars crowd together competing for position over the most sacred places. The majority of the building is run by the Greek Orthodox church, which controls the center basilica, the monument over the tomb and the main altar over Golgatha. The Catholics have a sanctuary off the dome room over the tomb and a smaller section of Golgatha, plus a few other nooks and crannies. Everyone else has side rooms, altars, naves and asps that "cling to the main shrines like barnacles," as one of our guide books states.

Since this is the Church of the Holy Sepulchre, our first question is, where is the tomb of Christ? Tass envisioned a rock tomb on a hillside with shrubs around it; my expectations were almost as romantic, but fade quickly as we walk through various shrines to a dark, crumbly, domed room, 70 feet in diameter, half-full of scaffolding for repairs. A large stone edifice covered with cheap, gaudy hanging lamps sits in the center of the room. Can this really be the tomb?

The tomb where fourth century Christians believed Jesus had been buried was located in an abandoned quarry and cut into a vertical slab of rock. When the emperor Constantine's engineers tried to build a large church over the site in 326 A.D., the workmen tore out the entire hill, leveling everything except a small portion of the original rock tomb. Likewise, there was massive excavating around the site believed to be Golgatha, where Christ was crucified, as the engineers leveled and flattened areas to support walls and to fit the whole area into a building.

Other than a few minor alterations, such as being set on fire by the Persians in 614 A.D., the building remained intact until 1009 A.D. when a fanatical Muslim caliph had everything leveled to the ground. In 1042 reconstruction began, and from then on the history of the building is a patchwork of construction, destruction, restoration, earthquake, and fire.

The stone monument now before us was built by the Greek Orthodox Church in the nineteenth century, to replace the eleventh century structure of wood that burned down in 1808, which was nothing but an edifice to represent the original rock shrine that was destroyed in 1009. Despite all this, the rock before us is called the Tomb, and pilgrims enter to find a marble coffin, the Sepulchre, heavily adorned with ornate lamps and other tacky paraphernalia.

It is hard to believe that what is before us has evolved out of the same roots as our own religious beliefs. It reminds us of the Burmese Buddhas covered with blinking lights. Bizarre shrines in southeast Asia didn't bother us because we had nothing at stake. In the shrines of Asia we didn't focus on the temples, but on the desire of people to uplift and make themselves better, morally and spiritually. We were touched by the feelings of people.

All we are able to focus on here are doctrinal and cultural distractions. The glitter, draped over symbols of our own beliefs, affronts our sense of what is holy, or even respectful.

We leave the tomb in a daze and walk through the hallways of shrines and altars. Luckily, we meet a Franciscan monk in a room below the summit of Golgatha. He encourages us back to the main sights.

"Don't look at all the distractions," he repeats tactfully. "Focus only on what is important."

We begin to envision the spot as it was 2,000 years ago. "And this," he says, pointing to empty space, "was a steep hillside. And just over there a ravine." Using our imagination, things slowly take shape.

It is hard to know how to react to many of the Christian pilgrimage sites of the city. Jerusalem has a sacredness that is greater than the total of its churches, mosques and synagogues, which is a good thing because many of the places we visit are run down. Yet each morning we want to go out and see more, to understand more.

The tragedy that led to the state of Israel is one more intense aspect of this land. It's a sobering experience to stand in a grocery store next to a gray-haired old woman with a tattooed number on her forearm, a memento from a concentration camp. An avalanche of horror stories and ghastly images comes to mind. I stare at the woman, wondering what atrocities she must have endured. How does she cope with the memory? Does she still have nightmares?

And what is it like living in Israel today? Occasional bombings, forced army duty each year for the men, threats of war, terrorism, and on top of all this low wages and an inflated economy. It is not a land of milk and honey despite any Old Testament claims.

On Friday we meet Caroline and Kadish for the pre-Sabbath rush at a large food market, a long, covered street crowded with shouting vendors. The Jewish Sabbath begins Friday evening. Since no work should be done on the Sabbath, everyone is stocking up on food for the day of rest.

That evening Kadish reads from the Old Testament, and they show us all the ceremonies to usher in the Sabbath.

To outsiders the idea of a lengthy Sabbath filled with rules and rituals might sound like a burden. But to orthodox Jews it is a part of the week savored to the fullest. Kadish describes the Sabbath as a guest you've been looking forward to entertaining: You work hard to get all your chores finished and out of the way so when your guest arrives you have all your time to enjoy his or her company. Many people, eager for the start of the Sabbath at sunset on Friday, do pre-Sabbath rituals an hour before the sun goes down, just to get in the mood. Likewise, others have post-Sabbath ceremonies to prolong the event, the way you might go to the door and then out into the street to say good-bye to your guest.

After supper, we go to a Hasidic section of town. We walk down the streets listening to the sounds of singing and praying inside. Each group of houses has one "open house" where people can come together to worship. We walk inside. Tass and Caroline go into a back room to join the women, while Kadish and I stay in a front room and join a group of men singing around a large table. The men smile and nod at us and continue their devotions. It is a loosely-structured time of worship. There are set rituals and prayers, but there is also a spontaneity that gives the evening a relaxed feeling. At the end of a song a seventeen-year-old boy continues to hum softly. He gently thumps his hand on the table in rhythm, eager to resume singing. Everyone else sits back, taking a short break.

A man next to me asks a few polite questions while the boy humming at the end of the table increases his volume. Soon the others join in, following his lead. An old man in the corner yawns occasionally. It isn't the yawn of a bored person, but the yawn of someone who is tired but doesn't want to go to bed because he might miss some of the fun.

Just before midnight we go to a large building, a prayer/meeting room. Kadish and I are allowed through the main door, but Tass and Caroline have to go upstairs. Like second class citizens, they join the other women to watch the activities from a screened-off balcony.

The large hall is full of tables stacked high with books. Hasidic men sit everywhere discussing religious topics. The men wear long black coats and black felt hats. Some wear black pants, others wear knee-length black stockings and bloomers. Most have beards, and all have two long dangly curls hanging from their temples. Oddly enough, their clothing is not from any Jewish tradition but is the attire of a seventeenth-century Polish nobleman. The curls are a remnant of a time when anti-Jewish laws were passed to ridicule Jews by making them look silly. Now they are worn by choice.

In the center of the room two raised bleachers, ten feet apart, face each other. Two hundred men stand packed on the bleachers. Between the bleachers, surrounded by a group of attendants, sits a gray-haired man at a small table. The man is a revered teacher, the crowd his disciples. They are here to watch him eat and get food from his table--it is said eating from the table of a righteous man can bring spiritual wisdom.

The crowd on the bleachers all *shukle* as they pray, bobbing their heads and torso forward from the waist in a constant rhythm. Hair curls swing wildly as they shout out prayers at an almost frantic pace. I am amazed their hats don't fly off, and that they can read their prayer books. Because each man prays his own prayers at his own pace, there is no group rhythm or unity. The sound is loud and discordant.

Occasionally the old man hands out bits of food, prompting a free-for-all as the most aggressive scramble for the food. The meal will last for hours, with each part broken into lengthy ceremonies, prayers, and rituals. The *shuklers* will go nearly all night long.

Up above the bleachers on the screened balcony where the women sit, I see fingers protruding through small openings. Someone is peeking through the latticed wall. I wonder if those are Tass's fingers. Knowing she is behind the screen bothers me. It seems so disrespectful to bar her from the service. I am baffled how a man could follow a religion that excludes his own mate.

During our time in Jerusalem we continue to shop for a bicycle. After much deliberation, Tass buys a used Japanese 10-speed, the Victor. With its steel frame and components it weighs 10 pounds more than her Trek. We buy a triple crank for more gears and install the few items salvaged from the Trek.

Finally, forty-two days after the accident on the Zoji La pass, we have two bicycles loaded and ready to ride. We say good-bye to Caroline and

A Hasidic Jew praying at the Western Wall, Jerusalem, Israel.

Kadish and head south for Masada, the famous fortress on the edge of the Dead Sea. We climb the mountain and then camp in the desert.

Since the Dead Sea is more than 1,200 feet below sea level, any direction we travel is uphill. We head north. A scorching headwind sucks the moisture from our bodies. The landscape is devoid of trees; there is nowhere to get out of the sun. We stop in Qumran, the site of the Dead Sea Scrolls, and then travel to Jericho. It is a hot, dusty town made even more forlorn by two abandoned Palestinian refugee camps on separate sides of the city. Jericho is the oldest and, at 838 feet below sea level, the lowest city on earth. The first walls were built around the city in 7000 B.C. In 1200 B.C. Joshua came through the area and knocked the walls down. We visit a few archeological sights and load up with dates and figs before riding onward.

The West Bank is a hot, desolate, sandy waste. It is hard to believe so many people have died fighting over this land.

We visit a number of archeological sights and stop at a *kibbutz*, where we talk with an old man working on a fleet of thirty, community-owned bicycles. He moved here from the States 15 years ago and hopes to stay here, fixing bicycles, until the day he dies. The old man is keeping productive, bringing dignity to a simple task in a community that values his work. The thought is comforting to me, an alternative to condos and golf carts.

We ride through steep rolling hills as we work our way toward Mount Tabor, the traditional sight of the transfiguration, where Christians believe Christ was lifted into heaven. To the west on the top of a neighboring range of hills, we see the houses of Nazareth. To the east, the valley drops into the Sea of Galilee.

A steep road leads to the summit of Mt. Tabor. At the top we rest in the shade of some trees, letting the sweat dry from our bodies before putting on different clothes to go inside the basilica. After spending so much time in ornately painted Buddhist *gompas* in Nepal and India, I have a much better appreciation of religious art. The bright mosaics of angels in the church are stunning. Definitely an inspired work. We join a group of pilgrims singing hymns, and then reluctantly leave the mountain to sprint over the hills to the Sea of Galilee. We must get to Tiberias to buy supplies before the shops close on the Sabbath.

That night we camp on the shore of the Sea of Galilee. The lake is beautiful, but the coastline is a mess of litter and broken bottles. A number of people picnic along the beach, a few windsurf.

Our last day in Israel is spent riding to the port city of Haifa, where we will catch a ferry to Greece. The customs officials won't let us take our bikes through with the automobiles. Instead, we are sent to the passenger line, which winds through a series of railings to keep the slow-moving queue in order. Everyone else has normal size luggage while we struggle at each switchback with our loaded bicycles. After customs we arrive at the top of a long escalator. We push our bikes onto the escalator and slam on the brakes to keep from tumbling down the stairs.   At the bottom we release the brakes, shoot out onto the floor, across the dock, and up the ramp into the ship.

22

Riding On VISA

We use our VISA card to buy the ferry tickets from Israel to Greece. We travel fourth class, along with 40 other people, and camp for three days on the rear of the upper deck. We lay down our groundcloth next to three people from New Zealand, set up our stove, eat, read and lay in the sun.

On September 17th we dock at Piraives, a suburb of Athens. We spend two days looking at "crumblies," as we jokingly call our archeological explorations, then pack up for the ride across Europe. Our plan is to ride to Zubrugnee, Denmark, where we will catch a ferry to England. We can't afford to dally. It is September 20th, and we have Europe and half the States to cross before winter. Still we plot a scenic route, along the Adriatic coast of Yugoslavia, through the Italian Dolomites, over the Austrian and Swiss Alps, through Germany's Black Forest to Belgium and the coast.

The sky is dark gray, and we battle headwinds as we leave Athens. London seems far away. Can we ride across Europe in 30 days without bicycle burnout? It seems we are crawling up the hills. In the evening we camp in a windy canyon between pine trees and piles of litter. The sky is tornado cloud-black.

After two days the weather clears, and we cycle at a moderate pace through the Greek countryside. Roadside shrines line the highways: birdhouse-shaped metal boxes with slanted roofs and glass fronts built on three-foot-high poles. Inside are bottles of oil, flowers, candles, and pictures of the Madonna and child, or various saints. The worship of Mary is popular in the Greek Orthodox religion, and many churches are devoted to her.

The countryside is more barren than we expected. We ride past small farms where old men and women stoop laboriously hand-picking cotton. The huge cottonwood trees beside the road are dropping their yellow leaves. Despite the falling leaves, nature's warning that we are running late, we take a detour at the Plains of Thessolony and ride westward to Meteora.

Meteora is a stone forest. The word means rocks in the air, and the landscape is covered with enormous rock monoliths sticking up like smoothed-over skyscrapers. In the sixteenth century, Greek Orthodox monks built 24 monasteries in the region, each perched on top of a rock pinnacle. The monks often searched for the most precarious site to construct the monasteries. By the eighteenth century the monastery population began to decline. Today only six of the buildings remain, five

Dates and figs for sale at roadside markets, Greece.

THE ROAD OF DREAMS

of which can be visited by tourists.

That evening, while studying our new maps of Europe, we discover our route is 375 miles further than we estimated from maps purchased in India. We decide to keep our itinerary anyway. If we are going to ride across Europe we might as well see something along the way, even if it means further delaying our arrival in the United States.

The next day we pedal back to the main highway running north. We also reconnect with Ian, a bicyclist from England we met on the road a few days ago. We camp together on the shaded bank of a slow moving river. It's amusing to be with a cyclist just starting his trip. We realize how efficient we have become. While Tass unloads the bikes I get out our stove and start cooking rice. The tent goes up, and we take turns taking a sponge bath and changing into clean clothes while the other chops vegetables and finishes preparing the meal. Meanwhile, Ian doesn't even have his stove out, his gear is spread throughout the campsite, and he is still struggling to put up his tent.

But Ian is a strong rider, and he stays with us for two days. We ride up the flat coastland, chatting and drafting off each other. The sea is on our right and the Olympus mountains on our left. We part company near Thessaloniki, where Ian turns east toward Turkey. We wave good-bye and watch him ride down the highway. We can't help feel envious. He has his whole trip ahead of him. We wish we could turn east ourselves, back to Asia.

Instead, we pedal into southern Yugoslavia. Suddenly, there are no road signs on the highway, or markers to identify villages. Each town rises out of the gray plains, lumps of dilapidated apartment buildings, gray crumbling houses with broken shutters and broken windows, yards full of rusted tin and iron, garbage and trash strewn about. Tass nominates one dreary village for "The Ugliest Town of the Trip" award. No signs advertise food stores, so we have to peer through the windows and doors of every building to figure out which is the food market. In many villages there are no services. We ride through towns of 300 people without a single store.

When we do find stores there is little for sale. The shelves are stocked full, but with only one or two items. Liquor dominates, with half of each store devoted to alcohol. Jam is also in good supply. Biscuits and chocolate sweets fill another quarter of the shelf space. The last 10% of the store is a pathetic supply of bread (if you get there before noon), cheese and sometimes eggs. The only vegetables are onions and peppers, apples the only fruit.

Vehicle traffic is mostly foreign cars. The locals use horse carts. Stocky, ruddy-faced peasants, hard-working people with big, thick hands and ankles, fill the fields. Most are slow to smile, but a few burst into grins when we wave. At a rest stop a group of farmers wave for us to follow them into their field where they load us up with all the grapes we can carry. The grapes are sweet and melt in our mouths. We have such a stockpile that it takes two days of non-stop grape eating to lighten our panniers back to a reasonable level!

At a vegetable market selling only red peppers, a man asks if we are from Russia. He is stunned when we reply the United States. Our Serbo-Croation is not good enough to catch all of his remarks, other than his surprise that "capitalists" would ride bicycles. He asks if we own a BMW. When we tell him all we have are bicycles, he laughs and shakes his head in disbelief.

After two days we leave the lowlands of southern Yugoslavia and begin the climb into the mountainous state of Montenegro. We ride up a twisty mountain road that passes through 27 tunnels. None of the tunnels has lights, and all are curved. In the longer ones we ride in total darkness--a few times we slow and peer into the void before deciding which way to go.

In the mountains people are preparing for winter. Workers gather the last of the crops. Bushels of apples are loaded onto carts and wagons. My instinct for survival is awakened as I ride past. I feel like a squirrel who has just realized everyone else's tree has a big stash of nuts while I have no nest and no food reserves. We are not going to make it home before winter, and once we are home we will have no money, no home, no car, and no jobs.

Two days later we leave the mountains and descend the breathtaking Tara Gorge down to the Adriatic coast of the Mediterranean. The coast, full of foreign tourists, is like a different country. The towns are clean and, at last, the markets have food. Large hotels line the coastal highway.

We crank out the miles. The days are sunny and warm; the water along the coast is a crystal-clear turquoise blue. The only break we allow ourselves is a daily stop to eat lunch on the beach, read for an hour, and take a dip in the ocean. We average 75 miles per day, and it is not long before we arrive in Italy.

We take a circuitous route through the Italian Alps. In early October we begin climbing into the Dolomites. The houses along the road are immaculate. Flower boxes at each window burst with color. Even though we ride into a rugged mountain range, we start from such a low elevation that much of the area has a long growing season and pleasant climate. The trees have just begun to turn color.

The canyons and the road get steeper. We soon see our first ski area. Before long we are passing chair lifts in almost every valley. In the resort town of Cortina we wake up to find camp covered in frost. We quickly warm up as we resume climbing even higher, winding between ski trails as the road twists up to Falzarego Pass. After dropping into another valley, we

Tass riding over the Austrian Alps.

ride over Brenner Pass into Austria.

After the breathtaking scenery in the Dolomites, we take another sidetrip and turn south to follow the picturesque Silvretta highway through the Verwall region. At the top of the pass we drop down nine miles of 14% grade on a wonderfully smooth road, dropping over 3,000 feet. There is little traffic. We take each corner at heart-pounding speeds. At the bottom we vote it one of the finest downhills of the trip.

We spend only three days in Austria, riding through the southwest corner of the country before crossing into tiny Lichtenstein, six miles wide and 16 miles long. Mist and clouds cover the mountains. We see little scenery. A few hours later we enter Switzerland. The wind we hoped would blow the clouds away instead brings nasty weather. Visibility drops to zero. The road climbs through the Swiss Alps, but we are unable to see anything.

In Zurich we stop at a bank to borrow more money on our VISA card and then stop at an optical store to get a part for my glasses. Sitting in the room full of mirrors, I take the first real look at myself in months, perhaps in two years. I look rather crusty and weathered. My clothes are old and worn. Suddenly, I feel self-conscious about my appearance.

We spend our first night in Germany camped in the Black Forest. During the night a major rainstorm moves in. In the morning we decide to leave the mountains and try to drop below the storm by taking the lowland route up the Rhine Valley. As we ride down into the valley, the rain and mist hush everything. The chains on our bicycles whirl softly, the only sound we hear. We keep our heads down as we crank out the miles, each of us in our own silent world.

In the town of Mullheim we stay with Renate Lehmann, a woman we met in the monastery in Thailand. It is the first night since Athens, 28 days ago, that we have a hot shower and sleep in a bed. The next morning we sit in the kitchen, drink coffee, and stare out the window at the cold, pouring rain. How nice it would be to sit and relax instead of having to jump on the bikes and ride 70 miles. Yet Renate looks at us with envy. She is having difficulties giving up her traveling lifestyle and settling back into her old environment. Will we be having similar problems in a few months?

We ride off in the storm. By mid-afternoon we are soaked and miserable. I watch the rain drip off my nose and stare at the spray from the front tire splashing onto my feet. At lunch we take refuge at a roadside bus shelter and try to squeeze all our gear under the roof. Tass makes sandwiches while I start up the stove. Bundled pedestrians with overcoats and umbrellas scurry past.

More rain the next day. It's hard to look up while riding in the rain. We constantly find ourselves hunched over. Again I spend the day watching the water splash from my front tire onto my feet. I feel I am in a dream. The road passes by at a slow but steady pace. My legs pump involuntarily. I feel like a spectator watching someone else riding. Are those wet feet truly mine?

The wind changes, the afternoon rain blows into our faces. I have to constantly wipe my glasses to see anything at all. We camp in a muddy field and wake up to more rain. In Rudeshiem we stop for lunch and spend half an hour riding up and down the streets trying to find a spot to eat out of the wind and drizzle. Finally we go to the train station, which is full of people commuting into nearby Bonn. We take off our rain gear and make lunch in a corner.

Occasionally we get up to check the weather. More heavy rain. Neither of us makes a move to leave. Instead, I splurge and buy a _Time_ magazine. Tass reads a newspaper someone left behind. Halfway through the magazine I get up to see it is still pouring. Suddenly we both look at one another, the same thought occurring to each of us. This is a train station! We don't **have** to ride out of here in the pouring rain. We pull out our VISA card and buy two train tickets into the city.

In Bonn we stay at the home of a man we met bicycling in Yugoslavia. The next morning we get up at dawn, fully intending to hit the road early. Instead, one cup of coffee leads to another, one good laugh leads to more. Before long our early morning start has slipped away. George tries to persuade us to relax, spend another day in Bonn, and he will give us a lift out of the city the following day. The sky is full of storm clouds. A fierce wind blows from the west, our direction of travel. It's been 34 days since our last rest day in Athens. George's roommate offers to run to a local bakery to get fresh croissants for a second breakfast. That is an offer we can't refuse! We stay.

Thirty minutes into our second breakfast a strange thing happens. We both begin to feel tired and achy. We feel like going back to bed, but we resist the urge. When everyone goes to work we head out to see the city. We make a half-hearted attempt to explore downtown, but we quickly lose momentum. We return to the house for a nap. It seems the effort of riding across Europe has suddenly caught up with us.

The next day the weather is still miserable. George insists on giving us a lift all the way to the ferry at Zeebrugge, Belgium, saving us three days of riding. Our desire to ride further in Europe has disappeared. We happily accept his offer.

Our time on the ferry is spent sleeping in a quiet corner of the passenger lounge. We wake up at the white cliffs of Dover and are soon riding off the boat onto English soil. Scattered clouds fill the sky, but no rain. We ride through scenic rolling hills past old barns and farmhouses. Half-way to London we camp in a quiet spot nestled under a group of trees. The next day dawns clear and beautiful, and we continue our ride through the farm country.

The front fender on my bike, which has required constant mending the last six months, comes loose again. I stop and do a temporary repair, figuring I'll take everything apart and fix it properly in London.

Later in the morning, as we ride down a hill, I don't see a large hole in the road. I hit the pothole, and the impact knocks the fender completely loose. The fender catches the tire, buckles, and is pulled into the front fork, instantly locking my front wheel. My bicycle and I both flip straight into the air. Time stops. It seems that I hang in the air for an eternity, yet I don't have time to get my hands up to catch myself before coming back down, head first, and planting my face in the asphalt. My bicycle catches up with me a second later and lands, all 100 pounds, on my back. Tass, who is directly behind me, tries to swerve out of the way, but my bicycle bounces off me and flies into her front wheel. Down she goes, too.

I lay unmoving, my face in a pool of blood on the pavement. I open my eyes to see a pair of shoes run up to me, but I can't move my body or my head to look up. I hear Tass's voice, twenty feet away, asking if I am okay. Another voice asks Tass if she can move. I hear her say she doesn't think she can get up. I am also unable to move, or even talk.

Finally, I hear Tass struggle to get up. More shoes come up to me. Hands help me up. Voices say we have to get out of the middle of the road. Our gear is spread up and down the highway. I hobble to the ditch to join Tass while a group of people collect our stuff. Tass's back seizes up, she can barely move. My head is spinning. I wonder if my jaw is broken.

We sit beside the road in a daze, asking each other if we are all right. An ambulance arrives, and the attendants ask us the same question. I am not sure we are qualified to answer, but after moving around a bit we feel we have no life-threatening injuries. Rather than leaving the bikes and going off in the ambulance to a hospital 20 miles away, we decide to stay with the bikes and let the ambulance go back empty. The attendants, who do nothing to stop the bleeding on my chin, get in their vehicle to leave. As an afterthought, one runs back and hands me a stack of Band-Aids.

A man from a nearby pub invites us in to clean up. While we wash out our wounds, he lights the fireplace to get rid of our chills. A woman in the kitchen makes us a hot toddy. We take up residence in front of the roaring fire.

After a few hours we thank our hosts and head outside intending to ride, but only go a quarter mile before abandoning the effort due to my delirium and sharp pains in Tass's clavicle. We stick out our thumbs, and in five minutes a van stops. The couple is going to London, straight past the farm along the way that is our next destination.

In Srinagar, India, we had met Rory Barratt, who gave us the address of his family's home, Capers Farm. We sent a card in Italy, announcing we might be coming through. Then this morning, before our accident, I called to say we would be arriving today. So the Barratts are expecting two fit world cyclists to pedal up to their door. Instead, we pull up in a van and climb out dazed, poorly bandaged and badly bruised.

Sheila and John, Rory's parents, take one look at us and whisk us away to a local clinic. Tass has dislocated her clavicle and wrenched her back. She is given an arm sling. I cracked some ribs and am given a stitch in the chin. The next three days are spent recuperating with the family, who treat us wonderfully. On October 29th Sheila gives us a ride to Heathrow Airport.

We are held up in traffic and arrive a bit late. We seem destined for confusion whenever we get near an airport. We hastily check our bikes and luggage and then race to the gate. We are excited, but also apprehensive. Are we ready for the United States?

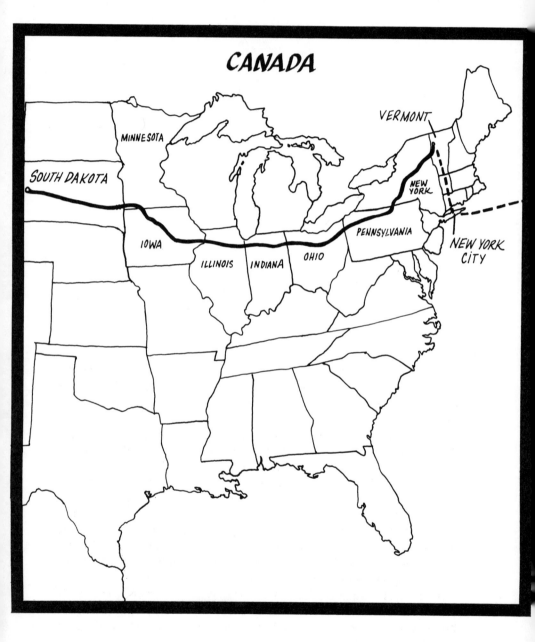

CANADA

SOUTH DAKOTA

MINNESOTA

IOWA

ILLINOIS   INDIANA   OHIO

PENNSYLVANIA

VERMONT

NEW YORK

NEW YORK CITY

23

Riding On Goodwill

In the New York airport we are stunned to hear a voice call our names. In front of us is Doug Beaver, whom we met in Greece a month ago. Doug took the initiative to contact my folks, find out when we would be arriving, and then came to pick us up. We load our gear into the back of his Blazer and ride to his home, where we spend three more days recuperating from our crash. I still have a hard time chewing, so I have a chiropractor re-align my jaw. Tass's clavicle slowly returns to normal.

Our good friend, Suzanne Martell, lives in Vermont. We haven't seen her in six years, so she offers to fly us up to Vermont for a visit. Tass and Suzanne traveled together through South America in 1975-76. Then in 1978 all three of us spent a few months together in Mexico and Guatemala. Suz meets us with roses at the airport and introduces us to her husband, Michael, and her two children. We spend three days together, and all too soon it is time to get back on the bikes.

We are both sad as we leave Vermont. We are tired of saying good-bye, tired of the whirlwind tour we have been on since Athens. Being out of money and leaving on November 4th is of little help. But we are too close to quit. In fact, we don't even consider it.

We pass through New York's Adirondack Mountains three weeks late for the fall colors. All the leaves are on the ground. Bare trees silhouette the skyline. On the second day an icy wind picks up near nightfall. It feels like it is going to storm. Back to our old tricks, we stop at a laundromat to warm up, then head out and pitch our tent next to a warehouse. In the morning we wake up to two inches of snow. After breakfast I do the dishes in the snow next to the tent, and two men from the warehouse invite us inside to warm up. But by the time we get our stiff and frozen tent packed up, they have left. They leave a note asking us to please lock the door when we leave.

Two days later we hit more bad weather near Casanovia. This time Ralph Stowell, a short, burly fellow in a pickup, stops to invite us in. We stay in his home during a two-day rain storm and then move on. Two days later we are stopped by another snowstorm in Elmira and are invited into the home of Penny and Chuck Smolos.

We hit still another snowstorm before leaving New York, and the weather doesn't get any better in Pennsylvania. We cross Denton Pass in a snowstorm and pedal by a number of cars stuck in the ditch. We feel like icicles on bicycles.

Snowstorms give way to drizzling cold rains in Ohio. We stop at a United Methodist Camp run by an old acquaintance, while another friend

Snowstorms and icy roads plague us on our ride across the U.S.

we worked with in South Dakota, drives up to meet us.

It is raining on the day of our departure. Rather than bicycling in the storm, our host, Bruce Baldwin, gives us a tour of Amish country, and drops us off at a guest room he arranged for us at Northern Ohio University.

We hopscotch from house to house, and are passed along from friend to friend. The hospitality of everyone we meet constantly keeps up our spirits. Tass's dad picks us up and takes us to his home in Michigan. After our stay he gives us a lift back to our route across Indiana. We next stay with Kathy Trotter, a friend and former boss who now works for the United Methodist Church in Indiana. Kathy lines us up with still more places to stay further west. The few nights we end up in a town where we don't know anyone, we are lucky enough to meet people and be invited into their homes.

In DeWit, Iowa, we spend an evening reading and drinking coffee at the Variety Cafe. When it closes at 9:00 p.m. we head out to camp. As we are getting on our bikes, a woman pulls up in a car and asks where we are going. When we tell her she shrieks, "It's too cold to camp! You can stay at my house!" Then she adds, "I hope you don't mind being alone at the house. I have a bowling match tonight."

She drives off, and we follow her on our bikes. At her house she introduces herself as Char Nothdorf, and we sit down to chat for a moment. When she finds we have bicycled around the world, she cancels her game to spend the evening with us. In the morning she cooks us a big breakfast and sends us on our way.

We arrive in Sioux Falls, South Dakota, on November 28th. Our friend, John Knecht, and his family have prepared a wonderful post-Thanksgiving celebration for us. We leave a few days later, only 400 miles to go.

Crossing the States has been the hardest part of our entire trip. The weather has been cold and unrelenting. The flu we caught in Ohio is still plaguing us. Tass is racked by coughing bouts. My sinuses run continually and my throat is raw.

I think of the people who have been so kind to us this last month of riding. I really wonder if we could have made it without their support. Much of our energy has come from everyone's goodwill.

Actually, we have been riding on goodwill much longer than just the last month! I think back to over two years of hospitality. People from all walks of life have reached out to us. Some shared our language and customs, many did not. Yet they have all touched our lives and contributed to our goal, to our dreams.

What we have experienced the last 26 months has far surpassed our wildest expectations. Yet our journey was never started with a desire for an end reward. Even though we did have destinations, the real goal was not any specific spot on the map. The journey itself was the goal. Each day was its own reward. Because of that, no matter where the path took us, we were always on the trail. It wasn't always easy, but it was always interesting.

The third day crossing South Dakota is the coldest. The strong, icy headwind goes through our clothes. I cram two pairs of wool socks down my pants to prevent crotch frostbite. Riding down the highway, the wind chill is 31 degrees below zero.

At mid-morning on our fourth day crossing South Dakota the wind suddenly dies. We pedal at a relaxed rate and make great time. We talk of how close we are to the finish. It is hard to believe. Even though we are ready for a break, we are uneasy about ending our journey.

The last two days are a dream. The weather warms, the sky clears. We further slow our pace to savor the ride. At mid-morning we come over a ridge and catch our first glimpse of the Black Hills in the distance. Home is in sight.

Friends and relatives drive out to meet us on the road; others ride out on bikes to escort us into Rapid City. The local TV and radio stations spread the word. It seems nearly everyone is honking and waving as they pass. It is a tremendous morale booster. We stop at Black Hills Bicycles, where we bought our Trek bikes three years ago, and are greeted by another group of friends. We go out for Mexican food, go to bed early, and get up to a huge breakfast before climbing on the bikes one more time. The last day, just 50 miles to go.

We leave Rapid City with a strong **tailwind** blowing out of the east! A perfect last day. We dally along the highway, stopping at every store, truck stop and mini-mart, any excuse to get a cup of coffee or hot chocolate and just enjoy the moment. My folks drive out to meet us with champagne. In Whitewood we stop at Tass's sister's house for a reunion. Only 14 miles to go.

At the exit into Spearfish a group of people stands by the road and cheers. We slow even more as we pedal through town. A crowd lines the driveway to my parents' home. We ride, holding hands, under a Welcome Home sign, breaking a red ribbon at the spot where we started our trip, 26 months ago.

Back home in South Dakota after 26 months, 22 countries and 14,000 miles.

Epilogue:
Lap Two

Our first winter home is spent living with Fred and Jo Richey, who kindly offer us not only a spare bedroom but their basement, where we begin to inventory and sort the 8,000 pictures from our trip. Fred hires us to give slide programs at an In-service for school teachers. The response is so enthusiastic we create **Images of the World**, a series of slide programs about our trip, and other travels. We also start our own publishing company. It is not long before we are traveling full time giving presentations.

Still, we just can't stay off our bikes, or stop traveling. We spend a winter cycling through Central America and Mexico. We will soon publish another book, <u>The Andes to the Amazon</u>, about a mountain bike and boat trip in South America.

We spend our summers on the mountain bike racing circuit. Tass makes the United States Mountain Biking Team and gets ninth in the Veteran World Championships in 1993.

When the subject of future plans comes up we think of travel and look at the world map pinned to our wall. Who knows? We may go around the world again. Lap Two.

Acknowledgments

The seeds for this journey were planted over a lifetime. I would like to thank my parents, who taught me a love of travel during frequent family vacations. They instilled in me an independence, which sometimes caused them anxiety, yet they always encouraged me to follow my own dreams.

My sister, Bobbi, helped open my eyes to the adventures of foreign travel when she invited me, her 19-year-old younger brother, to go on a trip across Africa.

And everyone in my family--Mark, Bobbi, Betty and Jerry--loaned me the funds to continue onward when my dreams were bigger than my pocketbook.

Countless people helped and encouraged Tass and I along our route. We are unable to list everyone by name, but your kindness has not been forgotten. We would especially like to thank:

Western United States--John & Darlene Thacker (WY), Taylor Ranch (WY), Mark Junek (WY), Marge Stower (UT), Rodney & JoLynn Stevenson (UT), Keith & Linda Nielson (UT), Rim Cyclery (UT), Janet Summers & Reed Smith (AZ), Dee Lucas & Kim Beson (AZ), Paul & Rose Sharman (AZ), Paul & Suzie Lidbeck (AZ), Todd & Gwen Ehrenborg (CA), Gary & Sharon Vaplon (CA), Barbara Churchill (CA), Mark Shostrom (CA), Roger Derrico (CA), Shena Sandler (HI), Pat Zukemora (HI), Carolyn Conrad (HI), Randy

& Sarah Stoddard (HI)

Fiji--Rachel Luidiak, Ram Kishore & family, Rakesh Kumar, Johnny Abdul, Persami Gouder (Mac)

New Zealand--Sue Elliot & Mark Blazey, Tom & Gail Elliot, Peter Sales & Kathy Farhi, Chuck Auchterlonie, Terry & Rick at Dalrachney sheep station

Australia--Steve Lyons & Jono Brown, Barbara Rogers, Sue & Lou Doherty, John & Betty Holmes, Jenny Bowley & Gavin Ginn, Eric & Edie Barnard, Carol Keliher, Patrick Maloney, Russell Morrow, Kevin Jay, Tom Kiy, Tony & Marie Tucker, Trinity Cycle Works, Dennis & Francis Bonner, Tony & Margo Wood, Tim Wood, John McKeon

Indonesia--Ananton & Katrina, Mud Jeni, Anari Pakem, U. Simanjuntak, Butar Sinaga

Singapore--Hock Swee Leong Bicycle Shop

Malaysia--M. Genepathy, M. Nalliah

Thailand--Dave & Janice Rika, Djama (Dang), Luang Poh, Veerasak (Yod) & Oy Yodrabum, Benjamin, Suwanee (Mu) Siroros, Bagjune Sagwona

Nepal--Jeff Lowe, Tom & Dorene Frost, Nancy Craft, Bruce and Debbi Roghaar, Mark Twight, Ellis Tobin, Phu Tsering Sherpa

India--Suna, Chimet Wangchan, Maharaj Ramesh Panchpuri, the monks of Spitok and Hemis Monasteries

Israel--Caroline & Kadish Gaibel

Germany--Renate Lehmann, Georg Müller

England--John & Sheila Barratt, Rory Barratt

Eastern United States--Doug Beaver (NY), Suzanne & Michael Wilson (VT), Frank & Colleen Miccoli (NY), Ralph Stowell (NY), Chuck & Penny Smolos (NY), Perly & Suzan Richar Bowen (PA), Olmstead Manor (PA), Chuck Morritz (OH), Bruce & Gail Baldwin (OH), Fred & Barb Thacker (MI), Kathy & Dick Trotter (IN), Don & Charlotte Nothdorf (IA), John, Paul and Lou Knecht (SD), Kent & Minnietta Millard (SD), Bob & Melba Brown (SD), Bill Harlan & Chris Rovere (SD), Philip & Laurie Sloat (SD), Tony Jedrykowski (SD), Bob H. Miller (SD), Jan O'Berry and Juliana Quinn at Black Hills Bicycles (SD), Jeanette Thacker (SD), Beaner Thacker & Rock Reman (SD).

Once our journey was over, then came the enormous task of integrating what we had learned and experienced into our lives at home. For support and encouragement with our slide programs we would like to thank Fred and Jo Richey, Curt Ireland and Cynthia Strom.

Special thanks to Larry Kaplan and Donna Zaino for their hospitality and enthusiasm in booking our slide programs into California schools.

For help in turning our story into a book, I want to thank my parents, Betty and Jerry, for their encouragement of my journal writing during our trip. Dugan helped start me on the five-year project of condensing the journal into The Road of Dreams. Susan Braunstein, Curt Ireland, Cynthia Strom, Jo Richey, Bill Harlan and Bobbi Looney all provided assistance in editing. Susan Scheirbeck helped with design. Debbie Hummel drew the maps. Ralph Kopp gave me the key to his house and extensive access to his computer for the last month of editing and typesetting. Ken Martin at Johnson Publishing was always patient and helpful during the printing.

And last of all, I want to thank my wife and partner, Tass Thacker. Tass was the one who first suggested we travel to Asia on bicycles, and she was an ideal companion throughout the journey. Tass helped me to see the world with humor and compassion. I can't imagine a better friend.

Equipment List

Preparing for a cycling journey requires countless decisions regarding equipment and gear. Traveling style also affects equipment choices. We prefer to carry more gear, which means more weight and more work, but that enables us to do more things off the bicycles. However, we didn't carry all the gear all the time. For example, we often shipped snorkeling gear to ourselves care of General Delivery at a Post Office in an area where we would need it again. The same was true of cold weather gear.

Bicycling Gear

bicycles - 18-speed TREK sport/touring bikes (we now tour on a 21-speed TREK model 520s)

panniers - 2 large rear bags, 2 fronts, and I handlebar bag

rain covers - for all panniers, plus a cover for gear strapped to top of rear rack (sleeping bags, pads, tent, backpacks)

plastic bags - to line inside each pannier during rainy weather

bungie cords - to strap on extra gear on top of rear rack

luggage racks - Blackburn rear and front lowrider

bottle cages - Tass 3, Bruce 4 (extra to hold fuel bottle)

spare water container - 2 qt. foldable plastic container to fill each evening before camping

reflective marker - strapped to outside of rear luggage

mirror - mounted on brake hood

kickstand

fenders - must have plenty of clearance or will clogg on muddy roads

bell - a handy item on crowded third-world roads

cable/padlock - to lock the bikes outside the tent at night

small padlocks - put on pannier zippers when storing bikes

helmets - we had hot and uncomfortable helmets which we abandoned in Australia (After 4 years of mountain bike racing we now use Matrix ultra-light helmets that are cool, comfortable and safe)

bike repair kit-- We sometimes carried no spare tires (crossing the U.S. and Europe) and other times up to four tires (leaving Singapore and Kathmandu). We didn't carry heavy tools, like headset and bottom bracket wrenches, and never regretted the decision. Here's what we had: spare tires, 2 tubes, patch kit and tire levers, chain tool, screwdriver, pliers, adjustable wrench, cone wrenches, 2-3-4-5-6 mm allen wrenches, extra spokes and nipples, spoke wrench, chain lube and waterproof bearing grease

Camping Gear

tent - Walrus Orbit, 2-person, 4-season tent large enough to put all bike panniers inside and still be comfortable

nylon ground cloth - to lay under tent and protect floor

nylon tarp - cover bikes while camping

sleeping bags - down bags which zip together, rated to 25 degrees

ensolite pads - cut to fit from knee to shoulder and 20 inches wide

straps - to hold sleeping pads side by side

pillows - 8"x 5"x l"

cotton sleeping sheets - for hot tropical nights, doubles as a sarong

mosquito net - used in *losmans* throughout Asia

daypack - handy for shopping or day hikes

backpacks - Dana Design packs with a removable internal frame

stove - kerosene stove (new choice- MSR International)

fuel bottle - 1 qt.

water purifier - our biggest mistake was **not** carrying one (we used iodine drops, new choice - MSR WaterWorks)

cook kit - 2 pots and one lid

wind screen - made of collapsable foil

pot gripper - for handling hot pots

fry pan - 8" teflon with folding handle

Misc. kitchen equipment - plastic plates, cups (also used as bowls), 2 spoons (double as forks), 1 knife (which we shared), Opinel folding knife, spatula, mini whisk, can opener, pot scrubber, bandana (use as hot pad, dish towel, wash cloth), lighter and matches, spices

Miscellaneous Gear

flashlights - with a headlamp attachment.

candles - to read and write during long evenings in the tent

jar lids - placed on plate as a candle holder

light bulb - 100 watt, Asian hotels have 40 watt bulbs (bad for reading)

clothsline cord - for boot repair, tie down straps, and drying clothes

sewing kit - nylon patches, elastic, safety pins, needles and thread

hacky sack - share with kids everywhere

snorkel gear - Bruce's mask is prescription for his eyeglasses

nylon stuff sacks - color coded to organize clothes and gear in panniers

postcards - the big hit in Asia was a picture of a traditionally dressed South Dakota Sioux Indian

watch - with alarm, essential for early flights or adventures

Camera Gear

camera - Pentax ME SLR with 28mm, 50mm and 200mm lenses
camera extras - pannier lined for protection, lens brush, cleaning cloth
film - 220 rolls Kodachrome 25 and 64, 10 rolls Tri-X black and white
(bought film along the way, exposed film airmailed home from large cities and developed in the United States)
batteries - 1-2 sets of spares
notebook - Tass wrote down every picture she took
binoculars - Minolta pocket models weighing 8 oz. each

Clothes

rain gear - coat & pants
jacket - polar fleece
light sweater - wool or polar fleece
sweat pants - great lounging in the tent
cotton pants - when we wanted to look presentable
cycling tights - wool
cycling shorts - 2 pair, lycra
cotton shorts - lightweight with pockets
skirt - Tass wore in areas where shorts are not appropriate
T-shirts - 2 pair
Tank top - light cotton
long-sleeve shirt - lightweight cotton, to protect from bugs and sun
polypropelene top and bottoms - for cold weather
cotton underwear - 5 pair each
anklet socks - 3 pair each
wool socks - 1 pair
swimsuit
cycling gloves - fingerless
mittens - wool or polar fleece
overmitts - unlined, nylon
overboots - windproof and waterproof
hat - wool with ear flaps
visor
boots - lightweight for hiking
shoes - we cycled in tennis shoes
rubber thongs - great to have in scummy showers

Personal Items

towel - thin and cheap (dries quick)
toothbrush, toothpaste and floss
sun lotion and lip sunblock
soap and shampoo - biodegradable
contact lens solution - for Tass
insect repellent
sunglasses
hairbrush - handle cut off to save weight
ear plugs - handy in noisy hotels
first-aid kit - small mirror, tweezers, foldable scissors, moleskin, band-aids, antibiotic creme, aspirin, Tylenol, aloe vera gel, gauze pads, tape, hydrogen peroxide, multi-vitamins, vitamin C, acidophilus, malaria tablets, Tinaba for giardia, talcum powder to prevent chaffing

Paperwork

passports
visas - obtain from embassies 2 or 3 countries ahead
immunization card
travelers checks - can never have enough, our trip cost $18,000
money pouch - small nylon pouch worn under clothes
journal - to help write this book
notebook - section for each country, to note information learned from reading and talking with other travelers
address book - keep track of friends
pens - ballpoint will not smear if pages get wet
maps - because of discrepencies we sometimes carried 3 maps of an area
books - guide books, language books and dictionaries for each country, plus field guides for birds, animals and fish when snorkeling (we also carried novels about life in each country, contemplative books, and plenty of books to read just for fun)
star charts - learn the constellations

Glossary

baht - Thai currency

bagus - Indonesian meaning good

balaclavite - people wearing balaclavas in tropical climates!

baksheesh - tip, bribe or a donation to a beggar

becak - Indonesian bicycle taxi

bemo - Indonesian motorized three-wheeled taxi

bula - Fijian greeting meaning hello

chai - spiced milk tea from Nepal or India

chang - Tibetan homemade rice beer

chorten - Tibetan Buddhist religious structures

colt - small Indonesian shuttle bus

dahl - lentil sauce

dahl baht - lentil sauce poured over rice; the staple diet of many people in Nepal and India

dharmsala - a guest house for religous pilgrims, also a city in India

dhoti - a wrap-around loincloth with some of the cloth pulled up between the legs, very comfortable in hot climates

dokar - a large wooden cart, usually pulled by an ox

dzopchuck - cross between a yak and a cow

gado-gado - fresh vegetables covered with spicy peanut sauce

gamelan - Indonesian musical instrument similar to a xylophone

gangs - narrow alleys in Indonesian cities

ghee - rancid yak butter

giardia - water-borne disease of the upper intestine causing diarrhea and vomiting

gompa - Tibetan Buddhist monastery

homestay - cheap hotels in Singapore

kava - Fijian drink made from the root of a pepper plant

kibbutz - co-operative or collective farm in Israel

kraton - umbrella carried by Buddhist monks in Thailand

lapilli - small pebbles created during a volcanic eruption

lassie - a yogurt drink

lathi - bamboo police stick

losmen - small inexpensive hotel

Mahabarata - a holy book of India from which many doctrines of the Hindu religion take their source

mandala - Tibetan geometrical design with religious meanings

mandi - Indonesian bath, taken by standing next to a basin of water, dipping a cup in the water and pouring it over oneself

mani wall - built of stones carved with Buddhist prayers and chants; when passing a mani wall, always walk by with the wall on your right

mantra - a repetitive prayer or chant

metal roads - New Zealand slang for gravel roads

Om Mani Padme Hum - Tibetan Buddhist chant ("Hail to the Jewel in the Lotus") which affirms that a part of God resides in every person

perak - Ladakhi women's headdress, covered with turquoise stones

pitji - small cap worn by Muslim men

prahu - small dug-out canoe

Pruscita Bhumi - Balinese celebration to purify the earth

puja - religious ritual

rinpoche - enlightened Buddhists who, through repeated reincarnation, remain on earth to help others

roti or *roti chani* - light, flaky tortilla

rupiah - unit of money used in numerous countries

sadhu - Hindu holy men who have given up everything to seek religious salvation

sari - long cloth wrapped around the body to make a dress; worn by many Hindu women

sarong - long piece of cloth wrapped around the waist to make a skirt

selmat malam - Indonesian meaning good night

sepeda - Indonesian for bicycle

shaman - traditional healer, or a witch doctor

shikara - gondola like boat used on Dahl Lake, India

shukle - a Jewish prayer where a person bends forward at the waist in a constant bobbing motion

sing-sing - Papua New Guinea dance festival

sirdar - leader/organizer of a group of porters, Nepal

suva-suva - Fijian welcoming ceremony using kava

Tamangs - an ethnic people of Nepal

terai - flat, lowlands of southern Nepal

Therevada Buddhism - ("the teaching of the elders") a sect that follows the original Buddhist teachings, but excludes ideas of later Buddhists

trambulan - Indonesian pancakes, folded and filled with nuts and jam

tramp - a hike in New Zealand

tsampa - barley-flour porridge or paste, eaten in Nepal

Vajrayana - ("the Diamond Vehicle") a branch of Tibetan Buddhism with an emphasis on compassion

warung - small Balinese restaurant

wat - Buddhist temple in Thailand

Wat Suan Moke - ("The Garden of Liberation") where we take a 10-day vow of silence

Wat Tham Krabok - the drug re-hab monastery

Wat Tha Khae Nauk - the temple under the fat Buddha

wayang kulit - Javanese shadow puppet play

yak - Nepali beast of burden found above 9,000 feet in elevation

Images of the World
Slide Presentations and Assembly Programs

Multi-Cultural assembly programs are available for elementary and middle schools, high schools and colleges. We also have adult presentations for workshops, seminars, teacher in-service training, civic and community events.

World Bicycle Tour   The story of The Road of Dreams told in dramatic color! Appropriately edited for public schools. Audiences are also encouraged to pursue their own dreams and goals.

Volcanoes of the World   Smoking volcanoes, lava, eruptions--this program is updated yearly with new travels. From the Ring of Fire to the Sahara Desert, see how volcanic activity has shaped the earth.

Rainforests and Mayan Ruins   Bicycling through Central America to see cloud forests, rain forests, nesting sea turtles and the winter migration of Monarch butterflies. We visit magnificent Mayan pyramids, colorful highland markets and stay with descendants of Aztecs in Mexico.

The Andes to the Amazon   Mountain bike over the South American Andes and travel by bicycle and boat into the Amazon Basin. We climb to 19,324 feet before dropping into the worlds largest and most diverse rainforest. We also visit the Galapagos Islands.

Africa   Join Bruce as he travels by truck and jeep from north Africa through the Sahara, into the jungles of Zaire, and on to the vast game parks of Tanzania and Kenya.

For information, please contact:

Images of the World

PO Box 2103

Rapid City, SD 57709-2103

THE ROAD
OF DREAMS

Copies of this book may be ordered from the publisher. Standard library and wholesale discounts are available.

The Road of Dreams	$12.95
Shipping and handling	$2.50

(S.D. residents add 6% sales tax = $.78)

Please send check or money order to:

Images of the World

PO Box 2103

Rapid City, SD 57709-2103